Building Blocks

Buckeye CableSystem's Communications Revolution, from Printer's Ink to Cable to Fiber

Tom Dawson

Hamilton Books

An Imprint of
Rowman & Littlefield
Lanham • Boulder • New York • Toronto • Plymouth, UK

Copyright © 2015 by Hamilton Books
4501 Forbes Boulevard, Suite 200, Lanham, Maryland 20706
Hamilton Books Acquisitions Department (301) 459-3366

Unit A, Whitacre Mews, 26-34 Stannary Street,
London SE11 4AB, United Kingdom

Library of Congress Control Number: 2015942883
ISBN: 978-0-7618-6624-4 (pbk : alk. paper)—ISBN: 978-0-7618-6625-1 (electronic)

∞™ The paper used in this publication meets the minimum requirements of American National Standard for Information Sciences Permanence of Paper for Printed Library Materials, ANSI/NISO Z39.48-1992.

This book is dedicated to the late Ellen Jackson,
who retired as Buckeye's Marketing and Programming Director
on July 1, 2002,
and who had the foresight to save records,
pictures, histories, and other material
that proved so important in researching this book.
She was a true friend and untiring colleague,
and is missed by all who knew her.

Contents

Foreword

When business scholars look back at the first 20 years of the 21st Century, they will see it was dominated by company names that forever changed the way we communicate and function. Apple. Google. Twitter. Facebook. Big companies that represent a *brand*. Somewhat faceless, these companies function and expand like the 1's and 0's they represent, ever intertwining themselves into our lives, our homes and our businesses.

It's no wonder then how often I hear of those who yearn for the "good old days" when things all around us seemed simpler and more straight-forward. A time when we didn't have to be so "connected."

The truth of the matter is that technology might have been less complicated "back then," but solving problems, particularly from a business perspective, was not.

No matter when, success in business always comes down to assessing the situation, evaluating the risk, taking decisive action, and then maximizing the opportunity. Those fundamentals never change.

What *has* changed over time, if you ask me, is that we see fewer family *names* today that stand behind their business, their product, and their service to their customers and to their communities.

In the 20th Century the name of the family defined the business and the product it sold or service it provided—Ford, Heinz, Boeing, Marriott, (JP) Morgan, Wrigley, Turner, Dell, and Hewlett, just to name a few.

And, one more . . . Block.

In my work with the American Cable Association, I have had the privilege of working with smaller and medium-sized businesses all around the country that are delivering to their customers the very best in broadband, video and phone service—connecting their customers to the possibilities of tomorrow.

And no company has exemplified the very best in service, dedication and loyalty to their customers than Block Communications and Buckeye CableSystem.

These traits didn't happen overnight, however. No, they were refined through more than a century of business, but, more importantly, through a commitment to public service, primarily in the newspaper business.

As a lifelong resident of the Pittsburgh area, I grew up, in a sense, with the Block family and its newspaper, the Pittsburgh Post-Gazette. To me, the PG was always a cut above in integrity, honesty and service. Back before the 24/7 media cycle we now live in, the PG was the trusted source for news and information, and the PG connected us to the world we lived in.

It never came about for me to work for the Block family at the PG after I graduated from journalism school, but the PG was then and still is to me "One of America's Great Newspapers" that set a higher standard. And that standard traces back to one word and one family—Block.

My personal introduction to the Block family and our working relationship came in a new industry—the wired and connected world of broadband, cable and phone and Buckeye CableSystem.

After graduating from law school and finding a career in the cable television industry, I first met Allan Block in the mid-1990s. I immediately saw this was a man, a family and a company that was building upon its newspaper roots and experience to take communications to the next level for their customers, co-workers and communities. In Buckeye CableSystem, they have done it, and they continue to do it every day.

Today, Buckeye CableSystem is the only independent company serving a major metropolitan area with broadband, video and phone service. The company is one of our country's leading and most successful independent companies, exemplifying the very best not only in service, but also in leadership. And the company has built the most technologically advanced broadband network to fully meet the needs of their customers today and beyond.

Buckeye CableSystem and the Block family have connected their customers to the future. This accomplishment of time, service and success is noteworthy in so many ways in today's business world amidst its frenetic pace. But what is most interesting and noteworthy to me is how Buckeye and all who serve and have served there have achieved this stellar accomplishment by connecting the foundations of its past to the exciting possibilities of tomorrow.

It starts with one name that stands for *something* important and represents much, much more than a brand . . . *Block*.

Matthew M. Polka, President and CEO
The American Cable Association, Pittsburgh, PA
May 2015

Acknowledgments

Many people helped me with the preparation of this book. Most important, Allan Block gave me total access to corporate records and people involved with Buckeye and with Block Communications, and was very generous with his time as I interviewed him numerous times and pestered him with questions, especially about his father, grandfather, and other family members. His help was invaluable, and his memory of decades-old incidents is truly amazing.

Of specific note are Penny Perrine and Candace Tubbs, who served as my administrative assistants while I was working and generously helped me after my retirement with various tasks in the preparation of this book. Then there are Sandy Chavez, Debbie McNulty, Sheena Smith and Wendy Assally, who kept Block Communications' headquarters on an even keel despite my frequent disruptions during the preparation of this book. They were most helpful in digging through corporate records, making copies, searching for obscure books and other documents, and putting up with me in general.

Keith Wilkowski, an able attorney who also is vice president, business & legal affairs for Buckeye, provided valuable input and advice throughout the production of this work. Jason Rademacher, a Washington attorney with Cooley LLP, also provided valuable input and advice.

And while research for this book took me to the newspaper files of *The Blade*, the *Sandusky Register*, and the *Monroe News*, *The Blade's* library was used most frequently, and Jordi Henry, librarian, put up with my frequent requests for 50 years' worth of files, pictures, and notes. She probably tired early of taking my calls.

A special thanks to Ron Schulz, who spent valuable time going through photo archives to find some of the historical pictures and ads, and to Charley Linden, for his efforts in editing and preparing the photos and ads for publication. He also is responsible for the cover design.

A hearty note of thanks goes to Nicolette Amstutz, assistant acquisitions editor at University Press of America/Hamilton Books, who was a tremendous help in the final editing and the mechanics of preparing this document.

Many others, in addition to those quoted or named in the book, have provided indispensable assistance in providing records, researching topics, checking facts, reading copy, and in general have been keys to the completion of this tome.

They are, in alphabetical order:

Dan Anderson, Patti Ankney, Mary Arquette, Lisa Babington, Harry Beam, Mike Bilik, Mark Boden, Donna Christian, Marge Cousino, Mike Dockins, Mimi Dornack, Sara Edinger, Rachel Ernst, Mary Fedderke, Kurt Franck, Kristi Frederick, Tom Gearhart, John Gibney, Susan Gibney, Tim Greenwood, Donna Gregg, Amanda Hargreaves, Fred Harrington, Lori Hauser, Ted Hearn, Chris Helberg, John Hoover, Joshua Horneck, Jim Jeffrey, Jackson Jones, Maryann Kafer, Brian Kenny, Dave Kielmeyer, Marlon Kiser, Stacy Kohler, Pam Koontz, Kathy Limpf, Rick Martin, Karen Masters, Linda Mayberry, Marge McBee, Jodi Miehls, Kim Nagle, Jim Nowak, Sally Oberski, Jane Overholser, Denton Parson, Jim Partridge, Lonnie Peppler-Moyer, Enrique Pinaya, Jackie Porter, William Schachner, Luann Sharp, Jackie Springer, Steve Staffan, Dina Sutton, Diane Vogelpohl, Linda Waldman, Doug Ward, Sandra Warfield, Matt Westerhold, Brian Woodrow, Chuck Worthy, and Brian Young.

For assisting me along the way and formulating my career, I give special thanks to two mentors, Joe O'Conor at *The Blade*, and Dave Huey, at Buckeye, for helping me develop into the writer and person I am today.

Special thanks to my daughter, Michelle, who insisted I use her lakeside summer home in Maine for a month in the fall to do some uninterrupted writing, and to my son, Brian, an accomplished magazine and book editor, for doing a superb copy editing job to make this missive much more readable than I had written it.

And finally, though not last, to my wife, Donna, who proofread copy, asked pointed questions about wording, facts, and interpretations I had made, and offered suggestions. My thanks, as well, for her putting up with me throughout my career, including my travels on assignment (in one 18-month period while at *The Blade*, I was out of town and missed her birthday, our son's birthday, our daughter's birthday, and our wedding anniversary).

She also put up with the obsession this book had become as I got into the research and writing.

In all, she deserves a medal for putting up with me for more than 50 years. Thank you all.

Introduction

This project was a labor of love, admiration and respect.

I retired at the end of 2009 after 40 years with Block Communications, Inc. (BCI), having spent the first 17 years at *The Blade*, the daily newspaper Block owns in Toledo, OH, before being transferred to Buckeye Cablevision, Inc., the firm's cable-TV operation in Northwest Ohio and Southeast Michigan.

I was asked to return to Buckeye early in 2010 as a consultant, continuing the compliance and regulatory work I had done for several years. I love work and love the company, so I readily agreed (My wife, Donna, told me I had flunked retirement).

The Block family, which owns the 115-year-old company, has been a pillar of the Toledo community since 1926, when Paul Block Sr., the firm's founder, purchased *The Blade*. I have long admired the family's integrity, honesty and fair dealings, and have been proud to be associated with them.

I've worked closely with two generations, and tangentially with the third, of the family and feel I know them and the companies well. I have the utmost respect for the Blocks' commitment to the community, to the businesses, to their customers, and finally to their employees.

In mid-2012, I was contemplating permanent retirement at the end of the year but had not completely come to grips with such an alien concept. I landed my first full-time job in 1963 and had worked without interruption every day since (vacations and weekends notwithstanding), so not having something productive and mind-expanding to do was something of a frightening concept.

Thus, I didn't have to think too long when, in late 2012, Allan Block, current chairman of BCI and grandson of the founder, asked me to write a history of Buckeye, which turned 50 years old on February 3, 2015. Thinking

1

about writing a book took me back to my newspaper days (and, in a happy coincidence, enabled me to avoid having to make a decision about full retirement).

The history of Buckeye is a fascinating tale that begins with an immigrant rag-picker's son in upstate New York in the late 1880s, who set off at age 20 to establish his own business in New York City. Along with the media empire he built over the course of his lifetime, he passed down his business acumen and integrity to succeeding generations. In addition, I'm certain, he passed along a family gene for strategic thinking—a sometimes unorthodox yet uncanny ability to gauge the current marketplace, assess business trends and even envision the future of the industry. The results of this gift are the insights, innovations and companies that are the subject of this book.

Members of the Block family have never been afraid to cut against others' supposed conventional wisdom when it came to issues or actions about which they felt they were right.

Most of the time they were.

It's an engrossing, almost picaresque tale—and as a former reporter and editor not only for *The Blade* but for newspapers in Dayton and Findlay, Ohio, prior to that, I couldn't turn down Block's request to write this history. I hope you enjoy reading it as much as I did writing it.

I

The Early Years

Chapter One

"She Wanted Pictures with Her Radio"

Cable's Earliest Days, from Concept to Reality

Residents of Toledo, OH, had cable television some 20 years before inhabitants of Detroit and Cleveland, a surprising fact that can be traced to a family gene for inventiveness, entrepreneurship and strategic thinking—a gene whose roots date to the late 1800s and the son of a then-recent immigrant rag picker in upstate New York.

Buckeye Cablevision, Inc., known today as Buckeye CableSystem, was incorporated in 1965 and enrolled its first customer in West Toledo in March 1966. Yet nobody thought of providing cable television to the larger nearby cities of Detroit and Cleveland, or to many other large metropolitan areas in the United States, until the 1980s.

Why?

Although some big cities had cable television, for the most part many people figured there wasn't a viable business model in providing such a service in large cities where residents already could receive decent off-air broadcast signals—a philosophy grounded in the very foundations of the cable industry.

Development of cable television is generally credited to John Walson, an appliance dealer in Mahanoy City, Pennsylvania, about 50 miles northwest of Reading, in the late 1940s. Mahanoy City sits about 1,300 feet above sea level, and Brown Mountain, to the southeast, is another 500 feet higher. Television itself was relatively new at the time. Walson wanted to sell TV sets to consumers, but because broadcast signals travel in straight lines, Brown Mountain prevented him from getting good reception from Philadelphia stations on the electronic marvels in which he envisioned a great future.

Walson got the idea to build an antenna on top of the mountain, where it could receive line-of-sight television signals. At first, he took potential customers up the mountain, where he had built a small structure to house and demonstrate his TV sets. That soon became impractical and time-consuming, so he ran a wire from the tower to his appliance store.

People watched the sets in his store, but when they got their purchase home, they found that the picture was either nonexistent or of poor quality at best. They'd go back to Walson's store, discover why it was able to receive a better picture and ask if they could run a wire from his store to their house.

In 1974, in one of a series of interviews of early cable leaders conducted for the industry's Cable Center in Denver, Walson said he began his system in June 1948. However, his records from the time were destroyed in a fire, so verification of the exact date relies on verbal statements made in the 1970s by various parties.

Another version of cable's origins gives credit to an Astoria, Oregon, man named Ed Parsons, whose wife "wanted pictures with her radio," according to Matt Stump and Harry Jessell, in *"Cable, The First Forty Years,"* in the Nov. 21, 1988 issue of *Broadcasting* magazine (subsequently renamed *Broadcasting & Cable*). He visualized a means of spanning the more than 100 miles and three mountain ranges between Astoria and Seattle, where the first broadcast television station was about to launch in late 1948.

When the station went live on Thanksgiving Day, Parsons was able to receive a somewhat distorted signal via a rooftop antenna on a hotel and send it across the street to his apartment.

Whichever version is correct, that, in a nutshell, is the genesis of the cable-television industry.

So what, exactly, does that have to do with Toledo getting cable 20 years before its big sisters nearby?

Conventional wisdom at the time held that cable TV would be useful only to serve rural audiences that could not receive a good signal from distant television broadcast towers. Who in Toledo would pay for cable when they could get a good picture off the nearby broadcast towers in the Toledo suburb of Oregon, near Lake Erie?

There also was no interest in building the capital-intensive systems in larger cities where residents could get good reception from nearby towers. How intensive were those capital requirements? Some wags have claimed, only half in jest, that to build a cable system costs $10 million to hook up the first customer, but just $10 for the second one. After all, everything needed to operate a full-scale cable system must be in place before the first customer can be connected; there's no scalability at that stage.

The late Paul Block Jr.—who in the mid-1960s was chairman of the board of the Toledo Blade Co., publisher of Toledo's daily newspaper, *The Blade*, Buckeye's parent at its founding—said later that he got into cable for one reason and one reason only: He didn't want to err the same way his father had decades earlier.

Paul Block Sr., who in 1900 founded the company that was the forerunner of *The Blade,* had the opportunity to obtain radio-station licenses when the Federal Communications Commission offered them to what at the time was a fledgling industry.

The elder Block, who owned more than a dozen newspapers by that time, was not enamored with radio. He thought the new technology would never amount to much and offered no business prospects, so he didn't pursue it with his customary interest in new businesses. However, he did acquire a low-power AM radio license in Pittsburgh in 1931.

As William Block Sr., Paul's second son, recalls in *Memoirs of William Block,* edited and published by William Block Jr. in 1990, the station, WWSW, was a 250-watt station, but it wasn't until 1949 that the FCC approved increasing its power and allocating it the 970 MHz frequency on the radio dial.

"I didn't know where cable was going, but I didn't want to make the same mistake my father made," Paul Block Jr. told a colleague in the mid-1970s.

However, those close to the Block family believe there was more to it than that. Starting with Paul Block Sr.'s innovations as a pre-teen paper carrier in Elmira, New York, the family has long shown an aptitude for strategic thinking and being able to see ahead of the curve.

In 1885, Paul Block and his family emigrated from Konigsberg, East Prussia, to the United States, settling near Elmira, where his father, Jonas Bloch, became a rag merchant. Dr. Frank Brady, in his 2001 biography of Paul Block Sr., (*The Publisher Paul Block: A Life of Friendship, Power & Politics*, University Press of America, Inc.) points out that when he arrived in America to begin his new life, Bloch anglicized his name to John Block. That name would be bestowed upon his grandson, John Robinson Block, now publisher and editor in chief of the family's two daily newspapers, *The Blade* and the *Pittsburgh Post-Gazette.*

In an era when young children were expected to do productive work, 10-year-old Paul Block got a paper route delivering the *Elmira Telegram.* The youngster quickly became a local celebrity of sorts after he was assigned to shepherd a large St. Bernard, Colonel, which was the paper's mascot. He and Colonel became familiar sights on the streets of Elmira as he peddled his papers.

After making a number of suggestions to the publisher of the Elmira paper about improving sales, Paul began to receive promotions. He proved his worth as an advertising salesman, and in 1895 when he was not quite 20, left his family's sparse home and moved to New York City to start his own national advertising-representative business.

How many other 20-year-old recent immigrants would have had the dream, entrepreneurship, initiative, business plan and sheer chutzpah to leave the comforts of rural family life and move to the country's largest city to engage in a relatively new industry, national newspaper advertising?

New York City at the time was still in the throes of the Gay '90s, and Block, filled with ambition and eager to build his future, found life there to his liking. Before leaving Elmira, he had arranged a job as a publishers' representative with the Richardson Company, a national advertising firm.

His experience with that firm led him to seek greater ideas, bigger ambitions and broader horizons. By December 1900, he had left Richardson Company and formed his own firm, Paul Block, Inc. A consummate businessman, he later set up headquarters at 175 5th Avenue, in the Flatiron Building—the iconic triangular structure that was one of Manhattan's first skyscrapers—for the aura of success it lent to his new firm.

That company was the forerunner of today's Block Communications, Inc., owner of Buckeye Cablevision, Inc., as well as the two newspapers, a telephone company, a fiber-optic and coaxial-cable construction firm and another Ohio cablevision outfit, Erie County Cablevision, Inc. (The two cable companies together operate under the trademarked name of Buckeye CableSystem).

Block Communications—whose current chairman of the board is Allan Block, grandson of the founder and twin brother of John Robinson Block—also owns or manages seven TV stations in Ohio, Kentucky, Indiana and Idaho; in late 2014, it purchased MetroCast Mississippi, a provider of cable, telephone and Internet services in 16 counties in the Magnolia State, and Line Systems, Inc., a Philadelphia broadband telecom firm.

During his time in New York City, Paul Block Sr. quickly proved himself adept—at Richardson Company, at making friends, and at getting acquainted with the kinds of people who could help further his career. He followed the same instincts that led him to promote the *Elmira Telegram* and was able to catapult himself into the company of such luminaries as New York Mayor "Gentleman Jimmy" Walker, Admiral Richard Byrd, publisher William Randolph Hearst, Joseph P. Kennedy and President Calvin Coolidge.

On May 1, 1927, after Paul Sr. had opened the new *Blade* building on Superior Street in Toledo, President Coolidge interrupted a cabinet meeting to press a gold key in the White House that symbolically started the facility's presses for the first time. Admiral Byrd named Paul Block Bay. a long ice-filled bay east of Guest Peninsula in Antarctica, after Mr. Block, who helped finance his 1928 expedition. And the explorer named two mountains in Antarctica Mount William Block and Mount Paul Block Jr., after Mr. Block's sons. The name of the bay later was shortened to just Block Bay.

As Paul Sr.'s business grew and his wealth increased, he began acquiring newspapers, ultimately building a chain of 14 dailies in Cleveland, Brooklyn,

Memphis, Pittsburgh, Detroit and Newark, among others. He purchased the *Toledo Blade* in 1926, becoming only the second owner of the newspaper since 1865 (The paper was founded in 1835, just two years after its home city was born when Vistula and Port Lawrence, two pioneer communities hard along the western shore of the Maumee River, consolidated).

Paul Sr.'s inventiveness and foresight was passed from father to sons to grandchildren to great-grandchildren and would resurface regularly as ensuing generations came of age and began to run the family enterprises. "I was in awe of my father," William Block Sr. said in *Memoirs of William Block*. "I admired him for his quick mind, his energy and hard work, his sense of humor and his accomplishments."

After Paul Sr. died in 1941, his sons took over operation of the newspapers, with William Sr. overseeing operations in Pittsburgh and Paul Jr. moving to Toledo permanently. (He had worked on *The Blade* in 1935 following receipt of his undergraduate degree in 1933 from Yale University. He stayed in his *Blade* internship until 1938, when he went to Columbia University, where he earned a doctorate in research chemistry. He also spent a year at Harvard University.)

To Toledo, Paul Jr. brought his innate integrity, honesty, business acumen and sterling intellect. He was author or coauthor of some 20 scientific papers published in *Medicinal Chemistry* and *Endocrinology,* as well as in the journals of the American Chemical Society, according to Mr. Block's obituary written by Pat Green in the March 16, 1987 edition of *The Blade*.

Executives who worked with him later believed that had he not inherited a newspaper business, he would have been a successful and happy chemist, both as a teacher and researcher.

For years he maintained a chemistry laboratory at his riverside home in South Toledo. He held a patent on a compound he developed that was the world's only potential treatment for a thyroid condition which, when seen in fetuses, caused lung disorders in one in seven newborns and resulted in some 10,000 infant deaths annually.

His research and development of the compound were noted in a lead article and editorial in the *New England Journal of Medicine*. As *Blade* science editor Michael Woods wrote in an article accompanying Mr. Block's obituary in the paper, Dr. Hans J. Cahnmann, an organic chemist with the National Institutes of Health, noted that "if you wanted samples of these thyroid analogs for your own research, there was only one place in the world to go. Why, it was Dr. Block in Toledo."

He also served for many years as an adjunct professor of chemistry at the University of Toledo, and among his lifelong friends were countless leaders in scientific fields. In 1977, President Jimmy Carter appointed him an at-large member of the U.S. Metric Board, a creation of Congress to coordinate and plan a process of voluntary metric conversion throughout the country.

Paul Jr. also played a part in the formation of the Center for Photochemical Sciences at Bowling Green State University, some 20 miles south of
Toledo, and its subsequent Ph.D. program in photochemical sciences. In the
Fall 2012 issue of the university's *BGSU Magazine,* Dr. Douglas Neckers, a
retired chemistry professor, founder of the Center for Photochemical Sciences and key force behind the Ph.D. program, said that Block had made
"critical contributions to the BGSU program."

Bonnie Blankinship, the author of that piece, wrote of Dr. Neckers: "He
has enjoyed the friendship and professional support of other visionaries such
as Harold McMaster, the Toledo chemist and inventor who founded the
automotive supplier Glasstech . . . and Paul Block, publisher of the *Blade* and
chemist who developed synthetic thyroid hormones and a lung treatment for
premature infants."

Paul Jr. showcased his gift for innovative thinking in, among many other
instances, the novel way he helped stave off television's invasion of the
lucrative advertising territory dominated by newspapers. As the story has it,
he convinced Toledo's utility department to provide him with residents'
minute-by-minute water use. Comparing these figures with programming
schedules showed him that water use spiked during TV commercials and
station breaks.

He gave this information to his advertising team, instructing them to point
out to potential advertisers that people took bathroom breaks when TV commercials came on—and thus the smarter ad buy was in the pages of *The
Blade*.

Under Paul Jr.'s leadership, the family enterprise continued to prosper,
revolving mainly around newspaper publishing for many years but venturing,
under both his stewardship and that of the next generation, into such diver-
sions as radio and television stations.

Today it encompasses not only the two newspapers but also TV stations, a
communications-system construction firm and the two cable-television operations, as well as a modern telephone system taking on—and successfully
competing with—the likes of AT&T, Verizon and Frontiervision.

Discussions in 1964 over the sale of the Block family's half-interest in
TV station WIIC, an NBC affiliate in Pittsburgh, led to the formation of
Buckeye Cablevision. The FCC granted the license for WIIC (since renamed
WPXI) on September 1, 1957, to the *Pittsburgh Post-Gazette* and Pittsburgh
Radio Supply House. Both firms also owned radio stations in Pittsburgh at
the time.

The owner of the other half of WIIC offered to sell the Blocks that
interest, but "my father and uncle thought the price was too high, so (they)
investigated selling our half to someone else," Allan Block said later. Cox
Enterprises had put in a bid for the entire station.

The deal was struck not in the business offices of either the Blocks or Cox, but in a most unlikely venue: the 1964 Democratic National Convention in Atlantic City.

"I went over to see Leonard Reinsch (Cox's chairman and a prominent Democrat)," William Block said in his memoirs. He was very busy running the convention in Atlantic City for Lyndon Johnson. But we had a meeting in his office at the convention center, talked about the sale and agreed on the price. So after the convention was over and he had free time again, the deal was consummated, and the station was sold to the Cox people."

During discussions of the sale, involving Reinsch and Paul Jr. and William Block Sr., among others, Reinsch broached a new idea. "Cox asked if the Blocks would be interested in a cable system, which Paul and Bill had never heard of," said John Willey in a 2002 interview conducted by Jim Keller for The Cable Center in Denver as part of its Hauser Oral and Video History of Cable project. At the time, Willey was associate publisher of *The Blade*; later he was president of the Toledo Blade Co., as well as the inaugural vice president and a director of Buckeye Cablevision.

Paul Block Jr. was as interested in promoting the Toledo area as he was in building the family holdings. He was instrumental in getting state laws passed to create the Toledo–Lucas County Port Authority and the Medical College of Ohio, now part of the University of Toledo. This new development therefore piqued his interest, in part for what it could bring to Toledoans—and, of course, he didn't want to make the "same mistake" his father had made in radio.

In his memoirs, William Block recalled the discussion at the Democratic Convention: "Reinsch said to me, 'You know, there's a new thing coming along, cable, and this is something you ought to get into.'"

Cox, headquartered at the time in Atlanta but with strong ties to Dayton, Ohio, the location of its flagship newspaper, the *Dayton Daily News,* had some experience in the relatively new cable business, and Reinsch thought starting operations in both Toledo and Pittsburgh was a good idea.

"'What we ought to do is to organize some companies to get franchises for cable. I'd like to tie in the *Post-Gazette* and *The Blade* in Toledo,'" William Block remembered him saying.

"Toledo was able to get some action from their City Council, and it wasn't too long after that a franchise was granted," he added. "In Pittsburgh, there was no movement, and we couldn't seem to get any action from City Council. . . . It just dragged on and on." Ultimately, the Blocks lost interest in cable in Pittsburgh.

Paul Block Jr. and other *Blade* executives, including Willey, general manager Wayne Current and treasurer Hal Davis, met with Cox representatives over several months as the two sides discussed a possible deal. A third party,

Ohio Bell Telephone Co., a forerunner to today's AT&T, was later brought into the talks.

The three companies ultimately decided to proceed, with *The Blade* and Cox forming Buckeye Cablevision, Inc., which was incorporated February 3, 1965. *The Blade* would provide the local political and market knowledge, Cox would supply the cablevision managerial expertise and Ohio Bell, which was prohibited by law from offering video services, would construct the communications lines and provide the technical expertise on the distribution plant, which it was permitted to do.

The original agreement called for the Blocks to have controlling interest, 60 percent, according to Allan Block. In 1969, the agreement was modified to reduce Cox's share from 40 percent to 20 percent with an option for the Blocks to acquire that portion also, which they did in 1974, becoming sole owners.

The Blade's Willey and Current were tasked with developing Buckeye; Current was named the firm's first president. In consultation with Cox executives, the two set out to find an executive to run the day-to-day operations of the new venture.

One candidate seemed an unlikely prospect; his varied career experience included stints in the tractor business and as manager of the Chambers of Commerce in Daytona Beach, Florida, and Virginia Beach. However, Baltimore native Leo Hoarty had left the Virginia Beach Chamber and started the city's first AM radio station, and that background, plus a lack of knowledge of the field and a chance answer in an interview, carried the day.

Hoarty and a few partners had started the Virginia Beach radio operation, he told Jim Keller in 2002, in another of the series of interviews of early cable leaders by Mr. Keller for the Cable Center's Hauser project. "We applied for a license, WBOF, and went into business," he said. "Later we picked up a defunct FM station in Norfolk and a radio station in Newburn, and we sold those very successfully. I found myself in the tractor business by mistake and I got out of that."

Hoarty had studied radionics (the science of broadcast communications) in college and learned to operate radio and radar equipment while in the U.S. Navy during World War II—hardly a standard background for the tractor business.

"I read in the paper that Cox Broadcasting and Henry Kaiser were going to come together and build a cable-TV amplification factory. I didn't know much about cable."

Not one to let a little thing like lack of knowledge be a deterrent, Hoarty was intrigued. "I thought I was very qualified for the job as president of that company, so I went down to Atlanta and applied and spoke to Leonard Reinsch," he told Keller. "'Leo,' Hoarty said Reinsch told him, 'I have good news for you. You're not going to get that job. We've already hired a president who probably won't last a year. You know how big corporations in partnerships fight, but I've got just the man you want to see.'"

Hoarty said Reinsch told him to go down the hall and see John Campbell, who was vice president of business development: "He's heading up our new cable-TV department, and if you pass the test we've got a major project for you. Go see John and come back."

"After going to lunch with Campbell and their treasurer," Hoarty continued, "I went back down the hall to see Mr. Reinsch, and he said, 'We're going to build a great . . . ' and then started telling me about this magnificent cable system they're going to build in Toledo, Ohio. I didn't know where Toledo was at the time. Finally, I got the job to go to Toledo and start the system."

He moved his family to the Toledo suburb of Maumee in the fall of 1965 and became general manager of the new business. He was assigned a desk in a building across the street from *The Blade* that earlier had housed the *Toledo Times*, the now-defunct morning paper owned by the Block family.

Hoarty worked out of the makeshift office in the *Times* Building for about nine months before the company acquired a building at 1122 North Byrne Road, at Secor Road in West Toledo. He worked for Cox but reported to Current and, in turn, to Willey. When the shares of ownership in Buckeye changed in 1974, Hoarty said in a 2014 interview, "I was given the choice of staying with Cox and moving to another of their operations, or to stay with Buckeye.

"I liked the Blocks and Mr. Willey and Mr. Current, and my family was settled in the Toledo area, so I decided to stay," he said. "I was very impressed with Buckeye and *The Blade*. John and Wayne met with me for lunch once a week, which was how I kept them up to date with my problems.

"We had severe opposition from all sides," he said, recalling various lawsuits filed against the firms in the early days. "John kept Buckeye publicity locally to a minimum because of the legal battles we had going on," he told Mr. Keller in the 2002 interview.

Curious about how he had come to find himself in the cable business, Hoarty later asked Campbell why he got the job in the first place. "'You said the right thing,'" he said Campbell told him. "In answer to a question, I told him that I thought cable TV, which I knew nothing about, looked like a big threat to the networks, and he said, 'You're right. It is a big threat to the networks.' And it turned out that way."

At the time, the major broadcast networks were the National Broadcasting Company (NBC), the Columbia Broadcasting System (CBS) and the American Broadcasting Company (ABC).

The networks would produce programming in their studios on the two coasts and transmit via wire and microwave to the television stations cropping up in cities around the country. The networks generally paid the local stations to carry the programming, recouping the cost by selling advertising nationally.

Though local and state franchising today has become the norm in the cable industry, at the outset no one—not the FCC, state Public Utilities Commissions nor local governments—knew exactly if or how to regulate this upstart industry.

Willey, the associate publisher of *The Blade,* noted the problems Buckeye experienced early on as it worked through this quandary. "We talked to the city council and city officials about a permit to use city streets for our cable," he said in the 2002 Cable Center interview.

He added that Joe Nathanson, of the law firm Spengler, Nathanson, Heyman, McCarthy and Durfee (now Spengler Nathanson P.L.L.), who had been retained by Buckeye in consultation with Cox, "decided, even though it was not legally required, (that) a city permit would be a good thing to have for public relations, if nothing else. So we decided to go for a city permit." There followed a series of meetings with city officials and hearings before the city council, which was undecided on the question of whether it had either the need or the right to regulate cablevision.

Various entities lodged a number of objections at the hearings. A group called the Committee for Free TV wanted the city council to delay action until the FCC made a decision about its role; the Independent Theater Owners of Ohio argued for a delay while a possible regulatory role for the Public Utilities Commission of Ohio (PUCO) was debated.

In March 1965, Tennyson Guyer, a Findlay minister and Ohio State Senator, introduced a bill giving the PUCO jurisdiction over cable operations in the state. During hearings on that measure, the Washington-based National Community Television Association (now the National Cable Telecommunications Association, or NCTA) testified against the bill, while the Cox-Blade plan was brought up by a proponent.

Ken Pritchard, representing the Independent Theater Owners of Ohio, made no secret of his desire for regulation. He claimed that cable TV in general threatened the future of free television and that the Toledo proposal specifically would put the subsequent operator in a position to form a separate network and bid on television rights to Cleveland Browns football games, removing them from free TV, according to a March 24, 1965 article in *The Blade.*

The Guyer bill never became law, however, and the PUCO was not involved in cable regulation until the Ohio Legislature began crafting a statewide cable-franchise law in the mid-2000s—and even then the agency's involvement was only tangential. Oversight of statewide cablevision franchises was ultimately assigned to the Ohio Department of Commerce.

In Toledo, meanwhile, the city was not the only entity uncertain about possible cable regulation. The FCC in 1959 had announced it could find no justification for itself to oversee the industry, but in 1962 decided it would regulate cablevision fed by microwave.

But Toledo in 1965 was dealing with a local situation and company in addition to two other hometown firms: Lamb Enterprises, Inc., along with two of its subsidiaries, which also sought permission to operate cable systems; and Overmyer Telecasting, Inc., which objected because of competitive concerns. (Both companies will be discussed in greater detail later.)

After many hearings over more than half a year, Willey said, "We wound up getting . . . a unanimous vote in favor of the Buckeye permit."

Added Leo Hoarty in his 2002 Cable Center interview: "They (*The Blade*) wanted to protect their newspaper, which was a very valuable property and a very respected property, and also wanted to get into this new line of communications. They were awarded the franchise, and we were instructed to get it built and underway as soon as possible." This was 1965, in a major market "where you didn't really need cable. You had good off-the-air signals, reasonably.

"At that time," Hoarty recalled, "San Diego (owned by Cox) was thriving as a cable system, probably the first really successful [urban] one in America, but it was pumping in seven or eight channels from the L.A. area. Cox had the idea that we could improve the Toledo reception with microwave signals, and they had a plan to put a microwave chain across America." (Today, the San Diego system is the oldest continuously owned large-city cable system in the country, and Buckeye is the second oldest.)

"They called it a T-bone," Hoarty said. "It would go down the central United States and across the northern part," passing through Toledo. "At that time we thought we could bring in a lot of distant signals, but later the FCC said you can only bring in two."

The new cable operators thought they could bring in all the Detroit signals and one from Lansing, MI., but the nascent industry was in a state of considerable flux nationwide, with broadcasters casting a wary eye on—and filing many lawsuits against—this upstart industry, including against Buckeye locally.

Meanwhile, as the cable greenhorn, Hoarty began planning his stint as general manager of the Toledo system: "I was trying to figure out what to do." He asked Cox's John Campbell for an operational book of some sort, telling him, "You know I don't have any background in cable."

"That's OK," Mr. Campbell replied. "We don't have (an operational book) either. You're going to write one." Campbell gave Hoarty a short list of contacts with some experience in cable, even if scant, with whom to get in touch. "Jump in your car and go visit them," Campbell said. "Take pictures, make notes, pick up some things. There are some smart guys in this business. You'll learn about cable."

"But the truth is, the industry was very small," Hoarty said in 2002. "Cox had (fewer) than 30,000 subscribers in all of their systems."

Learn he did, though, becoming something of an industry pioneer and, later, the first non–cable owner or head of a big company to be elected to the NCTA Board of Directors.

After arriving in Toledo, he finalized arrangements with Ohio Bell to use its poles and easements under a leaseback arrangement, whereby the telephone company supplied the transport of the signal that Buckeye, the new cable company, would furnish. "We were probably the first major market leaseback," Hoarty said.

The original leaseback was 430 miles, he recalled. "John Campbell insisted I walk that 430 miles with the telephone company, because 'If you leave it to them, we'll have more poles leased than we need.'"

Because it is such a capital-intensive industry, for cable television to hope for even a reasonable return on investment, the cable system has to pass as many homes as possible per mile of cable. The original idea was to provide service to the Old Orchard and West Toledo residential areas first, for reasons of housing density and demographics: The upscale residents of those neighborhoods were most likely to subscribe.

Cox engineers suggested building a tower on King Road, just south of Central Avenue in Sylvania Township, and the company's management decided to use it as a head-end site. (In cable lexicon, a "head end" is the assemblage of reception antennae, electronics, amplifiers and other equipment where TV signals are received, processed and routed along wires to customers' television sets.)

The township zoning commission delayed the plans slightly in October 1965, when it refused to grant a conditional use permit filed by Buckeye for the tower. Speaking at length in opposition to the tower was Dean Bailey, a prominent developer who owned land in the area and feared the tower would detract from his plans for residences there.

Ultimately, though, the township permitted the tower construction on King Road to proceed, according to an Oct. 14, 1965 article in *The Blade* (Interestingly, the same Dean Bailey developed the former Southwyck Shopping Center and surrounding office buildings in South Toledo, where Buckeye would relocate its headquarters in 1986).

"Our head end was seven miles from our system," Hoarty told Keller in 2002. "So the leaseback portion was at least seven miles before we had the first customer, and we found that wasn't very good."

Regardless, the red-brick North Byrne Road office, near the University of Toledo campus was up and running. This was, as it happened, just a few days after the FCC reversed its 1959 no-jurisdiction-over-cable finding and decided that it did, indeed, have jurisdiction over *all* cable systems, not just those fed by microwave, and issued the first of many regulations that would make a substantial impact on the industry over the next half-century.

The Calumet Avenue home of Buckeye's first customer, the Rev. John Roberts, pastor of Indiana Avenue Missionary Baptist Church, was put into service March 16, 1966, little more than a year after the fledgling Buckeye was incorporated. Thus, this wondrous new technology—television delivered by cable instead of over the air—became a Toledo reality. The service cost $5 per month, with hookups to additional sets $1.50 each per month, up to three sets. The programming consisted of 10 channels, mainly the broadcast stations in Toledo and Detroit.

However, Willey said in his 2002 Cable Center interview, the newly issued FCC rules created some stress. In order to be in operation, "The FCC said in effect we had 30 days from a certain date to hook up 50 customers in order to continue wiring the city." The loyalty of several *Blade* employees who lived in the area was summarily tested—they felt some arm-twisting to encourage them to become customers, and quickly.

The pressure was effective. "Leo worked hard and got at least 50 customers hooked up within a day or two before the deadline," Willey said.

"If we hadn't got the 50 customers by November 1, 1966," Hoarty said in 2014, "we would have had to start the entire application process over and disconnect the customers."

Meanwhile, various problems—lawsuits and complaints to the FCC, notably—continued to be thorns in the side of Buckeye's management.

When Buckeye began operations on March 16, 1966, it carried WJIM-TV on channel 6 from Lansing, but the FCC on May 27 ordered the firm to discontinue carrying the Lansing broadcaster. The agency had issued an order, effective Feb. 15, 1966, which prohibited cable firms in the top 100 markets (which included Toledo) from carrying signals of distant stations if such carriage extended the signals beyond their "Grade B Contour."

The agency defines a Grade B contour as an area "in which a good picture is available 90 percent of the time at 50 percent of the receiver locations," which excluded the Lansing station while allowing the Detroit stations in most of Buckeye's service area. The order was published in the Federal Register March 17, the day after Buckeye began operations, but was effective a month earlier.

Buckeye appealed to the agency, claiming among other issues that the order constituted an invalid retroactive regulation. The company claimed that the order did not follow the Administrative Procedures Act, which sets up public comment periods and stipulates such orders may not be effective until 30 days after publication in the Federal register. The agency disagreed claiming that the "cut-off date—February 15——is the date of the Commission's first and widely circulated public announcement that it had adopted the distant signal rules and that they would be applicable to operations thereafter commenced."

Despite Buckeye's arguments about the Administrative Procedures Act, the FCC in 1968 upheld its May, 1966 cease-and-desist order, and Buckeye was forced to take WJIM off its system. The ruling had widespread impact throughout the cable industry.

In 1966, Lamb Enterprises, Inc., and two of its subsidiaries, Wonderland Ventures, Inc., and CATV, Inc., all of Toledo, brought suit in U.S. District Court in Cleveland, claiming that Buckeye and Ohio Bell were conspiring to monopolize the cable-television market in Toledo and its suburbs. The suit sought $68,639,825 in triple damages, *The Blade* reported on March 23, 1966.

The suit claimed that in 1965, the three Lamb firms had contracted with Ohio Bell to provide cable service and granted them priority. Lamb alleged that Buckeye and Bell entered into a similar contract later in 1965, conspiring to block any other cable service in the city.

In 1971, the case finally came to court and after a five-week trial, the federal-court jury ruled in June in favor of Buckeye and Bell, finding that there was no "contract, combination or conspiracy" among the defendants, nor any attempt to create a monopoly in cable service.

In 1968, Overmyer Telecasting Inc., which operated WDHO-TV (the predecessor of WNWO, today an NBC affiliate) and was owned by national warehouse magnate Daniel Overmyer, filed a complaint with the FCC claiming that cable television would harm the broadcast station by carrying out-of-market TV signals.

Overmyer filed its complaint under the auspices of an FCC provision that allowed any broadcast-television station in the country's top 100 markets to seek special relief if it felt it was being harmed economically by a cable service.

In December 1968, the FCC ordered Buckeye to halt installation to customers over lines already installed in four areas of Toledo and not to proceed with plans to extend its plant into Perrysburg, pending outcome of the Overmyer objection. At the time, Buckeye had 20,300 customers in Toledo, but growth had to stop until the FCC issued a ruling.

Four years later, in December 1972, the FCC dismissed the Overmyer objection, approved Buckeye's request for special relief in the four Toledo areas and granted it certificates of compliance to allow it to serve the rest of Toledo and expand into Perrysburg.

In January 1969, meanwhile, Lamb Enterprises had sued the City of Toledo, claiming that the ordinance granting Buckeye's non-exclusive franchise in 1965 was unconstitutional—in part because it levied a gross-receipts tax on a company doing interstate business, in violation of the U.S. Constitution's Commerce Clause, and because the operating regulations in the 1965 franchise ordinance did not contain definite standards. It further claimed that Toledo's City Council erred in denying Lamb subsidiary Woodruff, Inc., a franchise in 1965, *The Blade* reported on Feb. 4, 1966.

U.S. District Judge Don J. Young ruled in July 1970 in favor of Lamb, but the U.S. Sixth Circuit Court of Appeals in Cincinnati overturned that ruling in January 1971.

Nettlesome lawsuits aside, Buckeye continued to expand thanks to Hoarty's cagey marketing talent. For example, he showcased the operation in its early days, when it had only a small handful of customers, by commissioning a trailer in which to show programming. In August 1966, he parked it at a strip shopping center at Dorr Street and Secor Road, now the site of the University of Toledo's Gateway project.

The trailer had a dozen TV sets, one for each of the 10 channels the system carried, one for color and one for closed-circuit use. The trailer, Hoarty said, was a first for cable-industry marketing. Buckeye personnel were on hand, including Bill Aubry, who was transferred to Buckeye from the circulation department of *The Blade*.

They were there to answer any questions on all topics: descriptions of the antennae atop the King Road tower, how the signals were handled in the head end, how the coaxial cable that carried the signal to the battery-sized adapter attached to the back of the television set in the customer's home worked.

Visitors also were given the opportunity to see themselves on videotape on the TV set reserved for closed-circuit display of this breakthrough technology.

BUCKEYE BITS

Don't Tell the Boss You're Going to Get Bigger than He Is

Leo Hoarty, the first general manager of Buckeye Cablevision, came to town in 1965 and reported to two executives of *The Blade:* general manager Wayne Current and, in turn, to associate publisher John Willey. However, he had never met the big boss, Paul Block Jr., publisher of *The Blade*.

"I was at some dinner meeting shortly after I got to town," Hoarty said. "I knew very few people."

He introduced himself to the man sitting across the table from him.

"Hi, I'm Leo Hoarty," he said, offering his hand. "He said, 'I'm Paul Block,'" Mr. Hoarty remembered.

"Then I said, 'Oh, I work for you; I run Buckeye Cablevision. And you know something—Buckeye is going to be bigger than *The Blade* someday.'

"He wasn't very pleased with that remark."

Hoarty acknowledged that in 1965, he had no clear foresight into the fantastic growth of telecommunications or the demise of the newspaper industry. "John Willey opened my eyes to the potential of cable," he said. "But I had no idea then that Buckeye would grow as it has."

Chapter Two

"We Were Doing It the Hard Way"

Twice the Channels, but Twice the Problems:
Buckeye Begins to Grow

In 1966, Buckeye's service was limited to an area bounded by West Central Avenue on the north, Nebraska Avenue on the south, Secor Road on the west and Detroit Avenue on the east. Ambitious expansion plans were running through Leo Hoarty's imaginative mind.

Operational trouble was brewing, however. Those early months saw increasing customer complaints about signal quality and service response time, and Ohio Bell and Buckeye blamed each other for the problems. Buckeye would eventually sever ties with Ohio Bell in late 1974 and begin preparations to build its own plant.

"We had to find a new head end within the system and transfer everything, and try not to interrupt service and forsake or give up the old head end," Hoarty recalled in his 2002 Cable Center interview. "This was not *The Blade's* fault; this was a Cox problem. They picked the first head end.

"I'd say we (built) maybe 100 miles of leaseback before the Blade Company bought out the leaseback and decided to build their own and run their own cable system, which was a very wise idea," he added. "Nobody at the Bell Company knew about cable, and oftentimes our little office-manager lady would figure out from the telephone calls where the troubles were and call Bell and tell them to go fix it."

Buckeye had a few customers and a fledgling managerial and technological organization, but faced significant problems with its physical plant—the electronics and wires that gave residents a picture on their television sets.

Bell workers would fix the problems when they got around to it. "That was part of the problem," Hoarty told the Cable Center. "They had a heavy union problem in addition to not knowing much about the industry, and they wanted to learn.

"They wanted it to be right, but the performance was rather slow, and it was not an important thing (to Ohio Bell). Their whole cable-TV operations (were) so small, so tiny compared to the overall Bell operation that it was hard to get attention."

Also during this time, the Internal Revenue Service, doing regular audits of the Toledo Blade Co., decided the local newspaper publisher had too much retained earnings, much of it from the sale of the Pittsburgh television station to Cox. To allay further action by the IRS, the Blade used the money to purchase daily newspapers in Red Bank, New Jersey, and Monterey, California; funds also were earmarked to start the cable system.

Buckeye first engaged Cable Dynamics, Inc. (CDI), to do preliminary design work as well as conduct the walk-out to see what poles would be needed and what work would have to be done on them to allow attachment of coaxial cable, which would carry the television signals. CDI was also to contract with construction firms to build Buckeye's plant, and for its efforts was to be paid 1 percent of construction costs.

About this time a young native of St. Louis was being discharged from the military on the West Coast. James Dryden had learned the rudiments of communications over wired and microwave transmission systems while serving with the U.S. Air Force at Vandenberg Air Force Base in Lompoc, California, and on Johnson Island in the Pacific Ocean.

Discharged in San Diego, he was hired by a friend, John Dolan. Dolan (not part of the prominent Dolan family that started and still operates Cablevision Systems, Inc., of Bethpage, New York, on Long Island, one of today's top 10 cable firms) was an engineer and part-owner of TeleVue Systems, a small cable operator with outposts in several small California communities.

The entire video-entertainment industry was in flux, with broadcast networks and some local TV stations fearing that independent and network-owned television stations, and now this upstart cable industry, were a looming threat to their viability.

To hedge their bets, networks and broadcasters cast an eye toward getting into the cable business, and CBS bought TeleVue Systems. Shortly thereafter the FCC, which was trying to determine its role as regulator of the nascent cable industry, grew concerned that ownership of cable systems by networks would lead to market dominance and forced CBS to sell its cable operations.

A CBS executive formed a new company, Viacom, and bought the network's cable operations. Dryden and Dolan became consultants to Viacom, testing systems and advising the firm on electronics and other operational aspects. Dolan subsequently joined CDI, and Dryden was hired by Viacom and sent to Northern California to run one of its systems.

Dryden later was hired by Hughes-Datacom, one of the business interests of the late Howard Hughes, which was building cable systems and had some operations in Southern California. It was therefore back to Southern California for Mr. Dryden. Hughes-Datacom was expanding its operations, though, and offered to send him to either Bloomington, Minnesota, or Columbus, Ohio.

"I didn't know anything about either city but figured Columbus is bound to be warmer than Minnesota, so I went there," Dryden said in interviews for this book. Hughes-Datacom was building a cable system in Ohio's capital city for Warner Cable, a forerunner of Time Warner Cable, which operates nationwide and today competes with Buckeye in several Northwest Ohio communities.

After a short stint in Columbus, Dryden looked for a way out. "I was getting tired of traveling between Columbus and Southern California every 10 days or so," he said.

Once again, he looked to his friend John Dolan, who by then was vice president of CDI. Dryden met with Dolan and Joe Hale, CDI's president, and was hired and sent to Toledo. CDI garnered the Buckeye business in Toledo several years earlier when Hale and an acquaintance of his, Wayne Current (general manager of *The Blade* and Buckeye's first president), met in California to discuss Buckeye's troublesome situation with Ohio Bell.

With an eye toward a future without Ohio Bell, Buckeye bought eight acres of land at 4818 Angola Road, between Reynolds and Wenz Roads, and in 1967 constructed a 355-foot tower, a head-end building and a warehouse of some 30,000 square feet.

At the same time, Buckeye was forming a cable construction firm to build the system that CDI was designing to replace the soon-to-be-departed Ohio Bell.

The name of the new firm, Rockwell Construction Co., was chosen by the late Bernard J. Baker, a prominent Toledo attorney who was chief counsel and corporate secretary to the Toledo Blade Co. As *Blade,* Buckeye and CDI executives discussed at length various names for the company, an exasperated Baker offered Rockwell, after the popular fishing club near Castalia, Ohio, to which he belonged. The group was hooked, and the name stuck. Dryden became a foreman with the new firm.

The Ohio Bell leaseback was a single coaxial-cable system, the standard at the time construction was initiated. Capable of carrying only 12 video channels, it had fallen into disrepair. Rockwell's first task was to rebuild, starting in 1978, most of the 430 miles of the Ohio Bell leaseback system (excluding only those parts that went from the King Road tower site to the Old Orchard area), again as a single-cable system. Once that was complete Rockwell became inactive, laying off workers and mothballing its trucks and construction equipment in a warehouse near Toledo Express Airport, Dryden said.

In the ensuing years, as more programming became available and more capacity was needed, cable firms were moving toward building dual-cable systems. The technology and electronics were improving, but not to the extent that a single cable could carry more than 12 channels. A second cable and accompanying electronics could double capacity.

"We started out with one cable, but then our consultant recommended a dual cable," Hoarty said in the 2002 Cable Center Interview. "Personally, I hated dual cable, because I realized the problems we had with one—we'd have more with two. People would be confused with the switches; the lady of the house wouldn't like two black cables coming into her room. So we switched to white and tan cable color for the inside and did our best to hide it so it wasn't . . . ugly,"

The two cables weren't both filled with channels at first, Hoarty said, though "we did originate our own channel. We had a camera crew and staff that went out and made films at the zoo, the churches, the school activities.

"We did it on film and later it switched to tape, but we were doing it the hard way," he added. "We also rented some films directly from Hollywood and ran all-night movies. In the early days they were very poor films. They were expensive and poor because Hollywood wouldn't release anything that was good."

Cable firms in other parts of the country were doing similar programming, but none to the 24-hour extent that Toledoans could experience. In addition to the programming, Buckeye under Hoarty offered 24-hour technical service in case of major outages.

"We knew we were in an industrial city that had a second shift," he said. "We knew that because we had such a wonderful response to our all-night movie channel; people liked it.

"Sometime about then I had the idea that we should have a 24-hour service crew. The union fought it tooth and nail," he continued. "We had the Communications Workers of America (CWA). They voted in union when we started. We only had three installers, but they voted union. I did my best to talk them out of it, but I didn't succeed. I said, 'Why don't you try me out? See if I'm going to be a terrible manager before you resort to union, start paying dues,' and they didn't see the logic of that.

"I thought they had a wonderful chance to test me for six months or a year and see how we treated them. I knew we would treat them well. But the union objected to the 24-hour thing." (Members later decertified the CWA and came to be represented by the Teamsters.)

"They also didn't like that we put on women as techs and installers," Hoarty said. "We were probably the first in the industry, because I remember we had some magazine write us up, had a picture of one of our girls climbing a pole."

In 1974, a young receptionist at Buckeye, Mary Ann Carroll, expressed interest in becoming a technician and installer—unheard of at the time. A graduate of the now-closed McAuley High School in Toledo, a Catholic all-girls academy, she had attended Ohio University. She found the outdoors intriguing—her hobbies included mountain climbing, sailing and tending horses—and she wanted out of what she regarded as the humdrum indoor activities of a receptionist.

After pestering management for a few weeks, she got the job—climbing poles in all kinds of weather with 40 pounds of gear strapped to her small frame, crawling over ceilings in attics and through crawl spaces beneath floors.

"Everybody told me I would find rats, snakes and all kinds of things, but I've only found cobwebs," Carroll told staff writer Melda Lynn in a February 12, 1974 article in *The Blade*.

A woman's entry into what was traditionally a male bastion created no problems, coworkers remember. "It was more of a novelty to have her in the field," Ron Frankforther, another field technician at the time, said. "I don't remember any incidents. She was dating another technician, so maybe that made a difference to the guys," he said in a 2014 interview.

Hoarty departed the company on September 15, 1974, over disagreements with Paul Block Jr., about various operational issues. While profits looked good on paper, that was not exactly the case. The combination of complaints to *The Blade* that vendors weren't being paid, and a lengthy absence by Buckeye's treasurer due to illness, soon revealed a reason for the robust paper profits. *The Blade* sent one of its accountants, Danny Dansack, to Buckeye to fill in for the ill treasurer. He soon found the bad news that was the source of the supposedly handsome profits Buckeye was reporting: drawers full of unpaid bills.

In 1975, Paul Jr. hired John Karl, a young industrial engineer, as Buckeye's president. Karl at the time was with Booz, Allen & Hamilton, a national business-consulting firm.

A native of Litchfield, Connecticut, and a graduate of Bates College in Lewiston, Maine, Karl had been a consultant to Cable Satellite Access Entity, an organization set up by cablevision firms to investigate the feasibility of using satellites in their operations; to the United Church of Christ for its cable activities; and to the Congressionally appointed Sloan Commission on Cable Communications (The Sloan Commission likened the development of cable television to the first use of moveable type and the invention of the telephone). Karl joined Booz, Allen in 1963 after a stint with MacMillan Publishing as systems director.

Shortly after his arrival, Karl and Frank Reinemeyer, who replaced the ill treasurer who left behind the drawer of unpaid bills, decided to cut ties with CDI and save the 1 percent of construction costs it was paying the firm for design and oversight services, Dryden recounted.

They hired Ricky Watson from CDI, who became a one-woman design department, and decided to reactivate Rockwell Construction, which had been put on ice when the initial portions of the dual cable system were completed. Dryden, hired to head it, began to search for as many former Rockwell employees as he could.

He found Ron Durham in Kalamazoo, Michigan, and brought several others back, including Don Marvin, Rich Hurd, Tom Ryan, Jay Hoot and Don Johns—all of whom are current employees of Buckeye or recent retirees. In the late '70s, Dryden said, he was moved over to Buckeye's engineering department, and Durham was put in charge of Rockwell. (Rockwell was later disbanded entirely; employees were offered jobs at Buckeye.)

Buckeye later got back into the construction business with Metro Fiber and Cable Co., which was incorporated April 5, 1994, to build the hybrid fiber and coaxial-cable system that would bring Buckeye customers many new entertainment and Internet services. That system upgrade also paved the way for Buckeye to get into the telephone business through Toledo Area Telecommunications Services (TATS), which later became Buckeye Tele-System (See Chapter 7).

To build the customer base to be served by that expanding physical plant, Karl turned to Toledo's largest and most prominent advertising agency Wiederschein-Strandberg and later to Tailford Associates (later Cooper-Tailford Associates). Ed Gibbs and Tony Barone, two creative types with Wiederschein, would develop in 1975 the iconic stylized eye that has been part of Buckeye's logo ever since.

The logo has been a tremendous marketing advantage. Research done in 2000 by Stan Odesky Associates, a local market research firm, found that the Buckeye logo was the most recognized logo in use among local firms. Doing so-called "mall intercepts," where shoppers are shown a number of logos alone without any wording or other identification, 73.2 per cent of those queried identified the stylized eye as belonging to Buckeye. The second most recognizable logo was recognized by 59.2 per cent of those queried.

A young advertising copywriter, a soccer injury, and an apology over a chance glass of wine resulted in many of the promotional efforts over the next several years—efforts that helped feed the rapid growth the company saw during the 1980s.

"I was a soccer coach in the late 1970s," said Jim Cooper, the young copywriter working on his own. "I was coaching one of the young kids by the name of Frank Bloomquist. I grabbed his jersey and he fell down and broke his collarbone." Cooper went to the youth's home to apologize and check on his recovery. "His mother, Karen, offered me a glass of wine and we got to talking," Cooper said later. Ms. Bloomquist just happened to work at Widerschein-Strandberg.

Because of the commonality of backgrounds and mutual interest in advertising, the discussion turned down that avenue and Cooper later was offered a position as an account executive with Widerschein.

"My first account was Buckeye in 1980," Cooper said. Among the highlights he remembers from his Buckeye involvement were the launches of such networks as ESPN, MTV, WTBS superstation, the Nashville Network; a nationally produced commercial for Buckeye, and what he believes was the first direct-response ad, at least locally.

At the time, cable was thought of as an improved antenna system, able to provide better broadcast signals than the traditional roof-top antennae or the so-called "rabbits ears" found on set tops. For example, a 1977 advertisement in *The Blade* said simply: "The Cablesystem Tower is as tall as a 35-story building. Can your tower top that?"

But with the advent of satellite programs (See Chapter 12) cable was transitioning to a supplier of all kinds of content, rather than just a conduit to deliver better broadcast signals.

"The first one was ESPN, and ironically in those days they called it E-SPAN." he said. "That period was really active with the launching of channels," which became big events locally. They were "highly significant events, with large crowds invited.

"Every time we launched a network we wanted to do something significant with the stakeholders, the public or public-opinion thought leaders" and usually, though not always, press-worthy events were held in large meeting halls, he said.

An example of one not held in a large venue was for WTBS, the Atlanta superstation, which was launched with a luncheon at the former Frank Unkle's Restaurant on the Maumee River near Walbridge Park, now the Lighthouse Cafe.

Among those on hand was WTBS' owner, Ted Turner, the entrepreneur who inherited an outdoor advertising firm when his father died and built it into an empire including at various times Cable News Network, now CNN, Turner Network Television (TNT), Turner Broadcasting System (TBS), the Cartoon Network, the Atlanta Braves baseball team, and who would become the largest landowner in the United States with the acquisition of large ranches in Montana.

Turner was an avid boater whose yacht, Courageous, had won the prestigious America's Cup race in 1977. Knowing of his boating fascination, Buckeye made arrangements to have a local boater dock his Chris Craft cruiser at the restaurant dock and after the luncheon several Buckeye executives and Cooper accompanied Turner on a boating tour of the Toledo riverfront.

Cooper also was instrumental in one of the early direct response ads, at least locally. In direct-response advertising, a product or service is described briefly and the viewer is urged to telephone for additional information or to place an order.

He also was a part of producing a commercial in Hollywood for Buckeye. He and Allan Block, who had just become marketing director at Buckeye, traveled to Miami, Kansas City, and Hollywood interviewing producers for the commercial, finally choosing a Hollywood man. The ad featured aluminum foil wrapped around a "rabbit ears" antenna and warned of the difficulties of obtaining a good broadcast signal with the set-top contraption, and even hinted that the viewer could suffer an electric shock.

"That era was the beginning of the launch of the satellite networks," said Cooper, now president and chief executive officer of the CooperSmith agency. "It was really exciting to be in an emerging industry such as cable."

Meanwhile, earlier in the decade the FCC had lifted the freeze it imposed halting cable firms from expanding in urban areas, and Buckeye continued expanding beyond its initial small coverage area in Toledo, a prospect not undertaken lightly, Allan Block would say later. "The financial plan to build out the entire city was $18 million," he said, noting that was a sizable outlay in the early 1970s for a firm whose EBITA (earnings before interest, taxes, and amortization) was in the low $2 million range. "We stuck it out and went ahead," he said of his family's decision to proceed.

The service area was expanded to West Toledo and East Toledo, as well as to Perrysburg and Rossford (both in Wood County), in 1973; Maumee and Sylvania in 1974; Northeast Toledo in 1975; Washington Township, Sylvania Township, Springfield Township and Oregon, plus Perrysburg Township in Wood County, in 1977; Ottawa Hills in 1978; Harbor View in 1983; Holland in 1982, and parts of Central Toledo in 1983.

The extension into the central city area became a bone of contention when a group of local individuals went to Toledo City Council early in 1982 and asked for a franchise to enable them to build a cable television system to serve the area, bounded roughly by Western Avenue, Detroit Avenue, Manhattan Boulevard, Suder Avenue, and the Maumee River.

One of the men, Sylvester Gould, Jr., claimed that the unserved area, containing an estimated 70,000 residents, had been subjected to "electronic redlining" by Buckeye, according to a March 14, 1982, article in *The Blade*.

Gould had been an employee of Toledo's labor relations department but in 1978 became coordinator of human resources at the former Medical College of Ohio. In 1980, he was elected president of the board of Trustees of the Economic Opportunity Planning Association of Greater Toledo.

Others involved in the effort included Wayman Palmer, Calvin Lawshe, and Waymon Usher. Palmer at the time was executive director of the city's economic development department, while Lawshe and Usher operated a market research firm, Lawshe and Usher Associates, that did economic development and marketing studies mainly in inner city neighborhoods.

Lawshe was a standout athlete at Macomber High School and the University of Toledo, and later would join the UT faculty. Usher later joined the city of Toledo as commissioner of the economic development department.

The group organized Toledo Central City Cable Television, Inc. (CCTV), with Gould as president. In February, 1982, CCTV officials told City Council that they intended to invest $4 million to $6 million and make the service available six to nine months after the franchise was granted.

But at a March 3, 1982 meeting of council's services committee, Mr. Gould said that the company had no solid commitments for financing or utility easements, but would have if a franchise is granted.

Council member Donna Owens (who later would become Toledo mayor) said that she was concerned about Mr. Gould's "electronic redlining" statement and that Council shouldn't move ahead until Buckeye was given a chance to respond. She also cautioned council against proceeding without the same "exhausting examination of its financing and plans that Buckeye went through when it was granted a city franchise in 1965," according to a March 10 *Blade* article.

Karl submitted a letter to council saying that Buckeye did not oppose CCTV's franchise, and said Buckeye was committed to continued expansion of its system to serve all areas in the city. He said the company had been adding to its service area steadily since its inception.

Council granted the franchise on March 16, 1982.

In July of that year, the group brought in Don Barden, of Barden Communications of Inkster, MI., as an investor, majority partner, and president of the company. Barden, a former Lorain, OH city councilman and TV personality, operated a small cable system in Inkster and had franchises in several other Detroit suburbs, as well as part interest in a Lorain cable firm.

He referred to himself as "The Black King of Cable TV," according to a July 9, 1983 *Blade* article which pointed out that despite the promise to council in March, 1982 that service would be available in six to nine months, CCTV still was not providing cable service some 16 months after the franchise was granted.

Robert Church, CCTV general manager, told *The Blade* then that although no tower had been built and no wiring had been done "we're still hoping for late this year or possibly early in 1984." He said the delay was caused by a decision to "switch to a different technically superior system," but added that the firm still hadn't decided what system to use.

Interested residents had been asked to sign up in advance and pay a $25 deposit. Mr. Barden told *The Blade* that some 4,000 potential customers had signed up; only a few days earlier Mr. Church said fewer than 2,000 had registered.

By a year later, however, the CCTV prospect was dead. Barden had withdrawn his involvement, Gould charged that Barden was in the venture only to bolster his chances of winning the cable franchise in the city of Detroit, for which he had applied earlier, according to a May 1, 1984 article in *The Blade*. Barden, in the same article, said the local investors had "misled him into thinking the Toledo franchise was economically viable" but when he discovered that Buckeye had started serving the area in February, 1983, "it was not viable" and he withdrew from the firm.

He said the $25-per-potential-customer deposits were being held in escrow and would be refunded to anyone who asked for it. The firm's local office on Monroe Street had been closed earlier in 1984, he added.

Buckeye by that time had built the area as part of its overall expansion plans, and CCTV was a non-issue in the city.

Buckeye's continued expansion throughout the 1970s and early 1980s piqued the interest of TV viewers anxious to take advantage of the expanding programming line-up, and the company saw its subscribers growing at the rate of 1,000 every month or so. In fact, by its 10th anniversary in 1975, Buckeye boasted of being the second largest independent cable television system in the country.

But the growth was not without its own problems, notably the general lack of competent subcontractors and another being the ability to deliver a good signal to areas farther from the Angola Road head end.

Paul Szymanowski, who later would become treasurer, said that despite the robust growth of cable throughout the country, getting materials for the expansion was not a problem, "but good contractors were a problem," he remembers. "Our installations were going fast and we had trouble hiring enough contractors to keep up with the work."

Buckeye at the time had about 80 employees, and a majority of them were office personnel—accounting, marketing, and customer service representatives (CSRs), plus a fairly large outside sales staff. Construction and installations were handled by subcontractors with Buckeye's field technicians devoted to maintaining the system.

As to getting signals to the far ends of the expanding system, television signals degrade as they are pushed through coaxial cable, so amplifiers must be installed approximately every quarter-mile to boost them. In industry parlance, these strings of amplifiers are known as cascades. The signal coming out of each amplifier is slightly degraded, so after about 30 to 35 amplifiers, or 10 to 12 miles, the signal is not watchable.

That means that the signal emanating from Angola Road could not be sent to homes roughly beyond the West Toledo area, or beyond the nearby south and west suburbs. To solve this problem, Buckeye established three hub sites—one at Flower Hospital in Sylvania, one at St. Charles Hospital in

Oregon and one at a tower the company built on land it bought on Creekside Avenue in North Toledo, near Sylvania Avenue and Lagrange Street.

Microwave links fed the signals from the Angola Road head end to each of the three hub sites, where coaxial cable spread out to subscribers' homes. This arrangement enabled Buckeye to send good signals much farther than with the long amplifier cascades needed if every area were wired directly from Angola Road.

BUCKEYE BITS

Buckeye General Manager Takes on President Nixon

Leo Hoarty became known for many things while serving as Buckeye's first general manager, but one that probably escaped the notice of Toledoans was his reputation in the Nixon White House.

While serving on the board of directors of the National Cable Television Association (NCTA), Hoarty mounted a battle to liberate pay TV from regulations that President Richard Nixon had imposed, preventing the concept from being shown on TV, especially cable TV.

He raised about $25,000 for a newspaper ad campaign in a few key papers, and started a national petition drive signed by some of the biggest names in broadcast and cable television.

"I was mad at [Nixon] for his war, so I didn't send him the signed petition [on which] we spent so much time and effort," said Mr. Hoarty, at the time a vocal critic of the conflict in Vietnam.

"I personally didn't think it mattered, as our efforts [regarding pay TV] were known to Nixon and the White House. I thought it might help stop the Vietnam War if they were scouting about looking for my by-now famous petition.

"Some time passed, and I was in D.C. for one of the [NCTA] board meetings and found myself at a table with one of the White House aides. He asked me 'What happened to your Pay TV petition?' I said I forgot to mail it. He said, 'We figured differently and told the president you probably didn't mail it hoping to slow down our war efforts.' He was right on!

"Nixon just wanted to see in detail who signed the darned much-talked-about paper."

Hoarty's notoriety in the White House probably wasn't common knowledge in Toledo, though. "John [Willey] gave me permission to pursue my antiwar, anti-gun stuff as long as I kept Buckeye's name out of it," Hoarty said.

II

Building for the Future

Chapter Three

"Our Localness and Service Will Set Us Apart"

At Buckeye, the Customer Has Always Been Right

Nationwide, the cable industry in its early days, operating as a virtual monopoly, was not noted for friendly customer service—and in many ways Buckeye was no different. It was in this area that Allan Block made his first significant operational change and in which he began his ascent in the corporate hierarchy.

Allan, grandson of the founder and twin of John Robinson Block, graduated from the University of Pennsylvania and worked as a management intern for the *Gainesville Sun,* a New York Times property in the Florida city, then at *Newsday* on Long Island as a market researcher before returning to Toledo and the family enterprises.

He could see that his twin was destined to take over the editorial operations of the newspapers, and that his cousin, William Block Jr., was certain to take over the business operations of the family's newspaper's holdings.

"I was excited by cable," he said in a 2014 interview. "My father thought electronics was a threat to the newspaper business." Allan was named coordinator of electronic technology planning for the company, and soon attended several seminars on electronic transmission of data.

"Starting in 1979 we were buying more broadcast," he said, with WLFI-TV in Lafayette, IN, joining the fold that year and television stations WDRB in Louisville, KY, in 1984 and KTRV in Boise, ID, in 1985.

He became fascinated with the electronic side of the business. "The others (John Robinson and William Jr.) chose not to be, but I found it exciting," he said.

As Allan started to move up the management chain in the mid-1980s, he learned more about day-to-day operations and began to feel uneasy about the way Buckeye was mirroring others in the industry. For example, he found that when his father had complained about his inability to get through on the phone to Buckeye management, instead of fixing the problem, those in charge simply had another phone line installed and gave the unlisted phone number only to his father.

As he became more involved with the business, he felt that customer service was an area which needed some attention. Customer phone calls to the company often went unanswered, office hours were basically standard business hours and installation and repair hours were limited—in short, many in the industry failed to recognize that customers needed service when they were home from work, not when it was convenient for the vendor companies.

Allan travels frequently, logging dozens of airline trips each year, and had a certain disdain for the way airlines treated their passengers. He didn't want Buckeye to fall into the same rut. "Our service was never bad; I just felt it could be better," Block would say later.

He decided to do something about it, mounting a crusade to make Buckeye's customer service second to none.

"When competition comes," he said at the time, "they will have the same technology, the same programming and the same equipment. The only things that will set us apart will be our localness and our customer service."

To tackle the monumental challenge of changing the company culture and putting the customer first, he enlisted Dave Huey, who had recently joined Buckeye as executive vice president. A native of Ashtabula, OH, in the extreme northeast corner of the state, Huey came to Toledo in the mid-1960s when he was recruited to play quarterback for the University of Toledo Rockets football team—excellent training for the daunting duties that lay ahead, especially at Buckeye.

After receiving a bachelor of business administration degree from UT in 1970, Huey joined the Big Eight accounting firm of Ernst & Ernst (now Ernst & Young). A certified public accountant, he was with Nicholson Industries from 1972 until 1984, first as controller and later as vice president of administration, before joining Buckeye in 1985.

Coach Block and quarterback Huey put together a game plan to alter the company's two-decade ingrained culture, intending to transform its customer-service operations into a championship team, an accomplishment that later would draw national accolades.

With the coach calling most of the plays and the quarterback calling the occasional audible to change the play, if only slightly, the effort gained ground, and it became a company-wide—not just departmental—effort. Allan Block and Huey made a good team, and the "football"—the change in corporate culture—began advancing down the field.

Huey turned to Linda Mayberry, manager of business operations, and to get her buy-in and to instill in her the importance of filtering the message down to all the employees, "I told her if we weren't successful, she'd be the first one fired, and I'd follow her right out the door," he said later.

The firm moved from its somewhat small original headquarters, at 1122 North Byrne Road near Secor Road in West Toledo, to a larger, more attractive two-story brick building in an upscale office park surrounding the stylish Southwyck Shopping Center in South Toledo.

With the move—and acknowledgment of the reality that competition was indeed coming, perhaps sooner than later—Block and Huey put together a plan that included a new phone system that would permit call monitoring, precise recordkeeping that would allow for proper staffing when it was most needed and other features to help serve customers better. To speed up the change in corporate culture, the two also planned for more staff and better training, as customer care was to be *the* core concept at Buckeye from that moment forward.

Even with the move into the new building in the summer of 1986, a staff of 12 customer-service representatives (CSRs) still answered the phones only from 9 a.m. to 6 p.m. on weekdays and a half-day on Saturdays. The rest of the time, an answering service would handle the phones and pass along messages the next day.

Bonita Davis, who started that summer as an executive secretary, was transferred to the new position of customer-service supervisor to aid in the culture-change effort.

Gradually, phone hours were extended and more staff members were added, she said. Now known as Bonita Ash, she was named vice president of business operations in 2011. Soon the phones were answered at Buckeye until 9 p.m., then midnight, then throughout the weekend. In the early 1990s, the company implemented the practice, almost unknown in the cable industry at the time, of answering the phones 24 hours a day, 7 days a week.

At first, all calls were answered by the next available CSR, all of whom were familiar with the video products, prices and equipment. But after Buckeye in 1999 introduced Buckeye Express, its high-speed Internet service, it became necessary to divide the staff and have specific training for the different product areas. That became even more important when Buckeye Phone, the company's residential phone service, debuted in 2005. (Mr. and Mrs. Timothy Tscherne, of Oregon, were its first customers.)

Today, Buckeye's customer-care department has grown to 195 employees divided into technical support, sales, billing and general-information calls. Some 90 people are in technical support, 30 in sales, 70 in billing and general information, and five in support services. Of the 70 in billing and general information, 18 are assigned to staff the lobbies, with another 20 trained as backup when needed. Among the departments, 20 are managers or supervisors. In late 2014, a department was added to provide hands-on help with the customers' own equipment which is connected to Buckeye Express. (See Chapter 7.)

Though Allan Block fought the use of an automated answering system for a long time because he felt it was too impersonal for the customer-service standards he wanted to maintain, he finally relented when it became evident that customers had to be transferred to one of the specialized help areas: technical support, sales or billing and general information. Even so, he insisted that only a single-level system be used and that the customer would encounter a menu with no more than four choices before talking to a human being.

Today, the CSRs handle some 1.5 million incoming calls each year, 95 to 98 percent of which are answered in less than 30 seconds. Of those not answered in that period, the average wait time is no longer than about a minute. (Those numbers, understandably, are not sustainable during major outages such as those caused by severe weather bringing down cable lines or other unusual conditions.)

Because Buckeye has developed such a strong reputation for customer service, customers have in turn developed a culture of calling Buckeye for non-business-related information. "We've had mothers call in the evening to ask how they should dress their children for the school bus the next day," Ash said.

In the past, the vast majority of calls during primetime hours involved customers asking what channel a certain program was on or what time it would come on. Since Buckeye introduced its program guide with the late-1990s upgrade to digital service, those calls have waned, though some still come in.

Today, about half of all technical calls have nothing to do with Buckeye's video, Internet or phone service, Ash said. "They're questions about the customer's own equipment or general questions about how to use their own equipment. However, we still get calls asking how to dress the kids in the morning, if the roads are slippery, if we know about construction and so forth."

In addition to phone calls and lobby visits, customers pose approximately 5,000 questions each year to the company's Web site; some 3,500 take part each month in online chats through which they can receive live feedback from a CSR.

As part of the overall program to improve customer care, Buckeye also added lobby locations and extended hours. The three Toledo-area lobbies are scattered throughout the service area, again as a convenience to the customers who visit them some 270,000 times each year. About two-thirds of those visits involve bill payments, and a large majority of those are made by people without checking accounts or credit cards, while the rest involve equipment—picking up or exchanging a converter or remote.

The lobbies—at the Southwyck office, in the DeVeaux Village Shopping Center in West Toledo and on Navarre Avenue in Oregon—maintain the same hours, and each has a lockbox for after-hours payments. Those offices in the Toledo portion of the system are open from 8 a.m. to 7 p.m. Monday through Saturday and from noon to 5 p.m. Sunday. A separate lobby in Sandusky serves the Erie and Huron County portions of the system and is open from 8 a.m. to 6 p.m. Monday through Saturday, though closed Sunday.

In reality, Ash said, staffers open the lobbies 10 minutes earlier than the stated time and close them 10 minutes later as a convenience to customers who may arrive a few minutes early in the morning or just after closing time.

In addition, Buckeye has made arrangements with businesses such as convenience stores, drugstores, a credit union and carry-outs scattered throughout the area to accept payments and get them recorded in Buckeye's accounting system in a timely manner.

Starting in the late 1980s, the company began intensive training programs, which continue today. These started as one-hour monthly sessions, then 90 minutes; they now entail two hours of mandatory training every month for each of the 195 employees who deal with customer care.

When the company formalized this training program, supervisors impressed upon the CSRs the mission of the company . . .

Our mission is to be the preferred, innovative, community-leading provider of high-quality voice, video and data services. We will deliver services to our customers on time and on spec with consistent value.

. . . and the value of obtaining and retaining customers in the face of coming competition. Products, pricing and scheduling were all a part of the customer-care regimen.

At the same time, Buckeye put incentives in place to reward CSRs based on performance metrics such as sales, volume of calls handled and first-call resolution (in which a call is not transferred to a supervisor and the customer does not call back with the same problem within 30 days).

Incentives include cash bonuses, entertainment tickets, coupons for merchandise, days off with pay, having a limousine pick up honored employees to take them to lunch—all the way up to a three-day cruise for two.

When Bill Taborn became the winner of the first cruise in 1989, he wanted to take his fiancée. Times were different then, however, and it was generally not considered proper for two unmarried people to travel together. Taborn and his fiancée had a wedding date set for later that year but couldn't postpone the cruise, so they got married by a justice of the peace the night before it departed. (The two are still married; Taborn is now an installation supervisor for Metro Fiber and Cable Construction, a Buckeye subsidiary.)

Another part of the cultural change involved authorizing all CSRs to "do what it takes to satisfy the customer" without transferring the call to a supervisor. In addition, a grab bag with money, coupons and other prizes is part of the daily office routine, and any CSR who draws praise from a customer gets to take something from the grab bag as a quick reward.

The emphasis remains squarely on customer care. For example, each CSR is required to write a short, friendly note to a customer every day; some 800 such letters go in the mail each week. The CSR picks a memorable caller and, in the note, mentions something discussed on the phone or inquires about something the customer said—asking about an upcoming hospital visit mentioned in passing, say, or an activity involving the customer's children. "Often customers tell us how much they loved receiving a handwritten note from one of our agents," Ash said.

The CSRs are located on the ground floor in all four lobbies, and if they notice a customer in the parking lot having difficulty—unloading a lot of equipment from a car, for example—one will go outside and help. Once, back in the dual-cable days, a CSR determined that a customer would need a new A/B switch to solve his problem, and because the customer's house was on the way home for the CSR, she took a switch, went there and installed it for the customer.

The customer was happy, but the gesture backfired when the Teamsters Union, which represents some of the field crews, filed a grievance, as that work should have been performed by a union member. The company, unfortunately, had to put a halt to such extracurricular customer care.

Supervisors and managers initially handled the training, but in 2006, Buckeye established a training department within its human-resources department, headed by Lorrie Grup, who joined the company in 1975 as a receptionist.

The department was the outgrowth of the employment of Juanita Kesler, who had experience in human resources and training, among other strengths. She was hired in December 2004 in the marketing department as marketing manager for the residential telephone service Buckeye was planning to introduce early in 2005.

As such, she trained all customer-contact employees in the various aspects of selling phone service, the first widespread new product since the introduction of Buckeye Express, the high-speed Internet service, on June 28, 1999.

Following a six-month intensive company-wide staff assessment and reorganization called VIVA (Video, Internet, Voice Alignment), facilitated by an outside consultant, Buckeye established a learning-and-development department. This was put under the aegis of human resources and Grup, who by that time was vice president of HR. Kesler was named the new department's manager. Today, a staff of three conducts periodic training of all employees.

Kesler and her staff also implemented an online training program offered by Jones/NCTI, developed by Glenn R. Jones, whose connection to the cable industry dates to 1961, when he represented cable companies across the country in their acquisition efforts, Kesler said. He later went on to found Jones Intercable, formerly one of the 10 largest cable firms in the U.S., and now part of Comcast

The Jones/NCTI program provides online training for installers, digital technicians and customer-service employees, among others. So far, one employee has earned Master Installer Certification, nine have earned Master Technician Certification, eight have received Master Technician/Customer Premises Certification, eight have earned Master Technician/HFC (Hybrid-Fiber-Coax) Networks Certification and eight have received Senior Master Technician Certification.

In addition, Kesler and Jim Wolsiffer, Buckeye's director of technical operations, worked with Owens Community College and the Ohio Department of Education to develop a program in cooperation with Jones/NCTI through which Buckeye employees can earn an associate's degree from OCC in technical field operations. Because Jones/NCTI's training is online, staffers can study mostly at their convenience and earn their degree by spending only about half the time in classes on campus typically required.

The learning-and-development department also launched Power Hour, a series of online training sessions that Kesler says develop both technical and "soft" skills. Topics include training in software programs, implementing a social-media strategy, business writing, developing delegation skills and leadership attributes, managing priorities and time, and handling confrontational customers.

"It sounds trite," Kesler said, "but it's a development aspect to help each person be all he or she can be."

From its modest beginnings, training at Buckeye has grown to the point where employees completed 8,529 hours of instruction in 407 separate sessions in 2013, up from 5,641 hours in 301 sessions in 2007. The numbers for 2014 were off somewhat because in April, upon Grup's retirement, Kesler was promoted to vice president of human resources and her training position remained unfilled for three months. Nevertheless, employees still received 7,590 hours of instruction in 341 separate sessions that year.

The staff also conducts two- and three-day new-employee orientation sessions several times a year to acquaint new hires with Buckeye's history, culture and mission.

Customer care by the CSRs—the first people Buckeye subscribers encounter when calling the company—is only part of the story, though. Buckeye also pays a great deal of attention to how its employees behave while in customers' homes.

The first step was improving and reorganizing the company's moribund technical operations, a task for which W.H. "Chip" Carstensen was hired as field operations manager in April 1990.

Carstensen, a native Toledoan who was working in Delaware, holds a bachelor's degree in mechanical engineering and a master's in industrial engineering from the University of Toledo. He had served in executive positions with the Timken Co., in Canton, Ohio; Clairson International, of Ocala, Florida; and Metal Masters, of Dover, Delaware. He brought with him a wealth of experience in operations, labor relations and construction-project management.

What he found was personnel inefficiency and a general operational malaise. "(Employees) weren't being led appropriately—we needed to change some supervision, and mostly just motivate them in the right direction," he said in a 2014 interview. "They had drifted into very inefficient processes, and there was a fear of the union"—the Teamsters, which had replaced the Communications Workers of America some years earlier—which was "basically telling us how to run the show."

Carstensen was not welcomed by the field crews. "Even before I showed up for my first day I had gotten word from some supervisors and others that the union was going to show me who's boss around here," he said.

First, he found the side of his car keyed while it was parked at the Angola Road warehouse. Later, someone poured paint that matched the color of his office over his car in his driveway at home. "That was my baptism," he said. "I called the stewards in and said, 'Look, you can pull all these shenanigans you want. They aren't going to work. The way I run the show, this is a team.'"

He had dealt with union environments in the past, and although he had witnessed union decertification in an earlier job, "We felt it would be better to work with the union and have improved labor relations.

"So I pulled the two stewards together along with a couple of the supervisors early on and just had a couple of chats," Carstensen said. He asked for their perspective, and "I shared my vision as to what the operation could be. The most important thing is that we had people who were just putting in a half-day."

He told those employees that it didn't matter whether they were represented by a union or not. "You've got a job to do, and it's not getting done."

He instituted a more rigid system of recordkeeping on production and work quality, reorganized the maintenance of the general plant, power supplies and amplifiers, and started holding the technicians accountable.

"The first three or four years were spent gaining their trust," he said. The workers, he learned, felt management didn't provide proper equipment or training, especially regarding safety. "They were right. I agreed with them. I was always very big on safety and training in earlier jobs.

"That's how I won them over," he continued. "I promised I would get them the equipment, supplies, tools, everything you need to do your job. 'What you've got to promise me is that you'll use them and use them in the proper way, and give me the production I need.'" Carstensen lived up to his end of the bargain, and gradually attitudes began to shift. In addition to better equipment and training, more modest actions—such as being on-site before the technicians went to work and sharing coffee and family stories with them—helped foment positive change.

At the same time, he forced supervisors to take a more active supervisory role and made some changes where necessary.

He instituted incentives for meeting certain goals, and "disincentives" for not measuring up. The technician who had the lowest production in a month, for example, was henceforth required to have his supervisor ride along with him for three days the next month.

Overall, Buckeye has enjoyed relatively calm labor relations in its first 50 years. Only one dispute spilled over into a strike: on October 7, 1979, when 32 members of the Teamsters walked off their jobs when contract talks broke down. There were reports of scattered plant damage, especially in the Maumee area near where John Karl, Buckeye's president at the time, lived.

Paul Szymanowski, who was treasurer at the time, recalls an incident of exterior door locks on the Byrne Road building being disabled after someone squirted Super Glue into the mechanisms, and nails strewn about the parking lot. "We had the office employees park elsewhere and used company vehicles to ferry them to the office so they wouldn't chance ruining the tires on their cars, he remembers.

A Federal Mediation and Conciliation Service mediator scheduled a session with the two sides, which worked out their differences—and on October 27, a Saturday, the union ratified the contract. Workers returned to their jobs the following Monday.

After Carstensen's arrival and successes, the company revamped additional operations to make them more customer-friendly, lengthening installation appointment hours to 8 a.m. to 8 p.m. Monday through Saturday, the schedule that remains today. (Buckeye tried Sunday installation appointments as well but discovered that many customers didn't want someone coming to their home for installations on Sunday.)

Service calls, however, do happen on Sundays and are welcomed by customers. Emergencies, such as when the company's outside plant is damaged by a storm or traffic accident, are handled as quickly as a crew can be dispatched, 24 hours a day. Supervisors are regularly assigned stand-by duties in order to be able to take care of such problems.

Service and installation appointments are scheduled in two-hour windows (e.g., 10 a.m. to noon, 2 to 4 p.m., etc.), and if the technician does not arrive within that window, the customer is given a $20 credit. In the beginning, it was difficult to get the technicians to grant the $20 credit because they feared it would reflect badly on them.

However, Buckeye management recognizes that technicians sometimes encounter unforeseen problems, and in order to give customers proper attention and not force them to schedule a second appointment, a technician might have to be late to the next customer's house. Gradually, the crews came around, and today, they dispense some 100 credits in an average month.

For a small fee, too, exact-time appointments are available. Thus, if a customer has to rush home from work at lunch time to admit the technician, he or she can be certain that the technician will, indeed, be there at the appointed time.

Gradually, Buckeye updated its scheduling software and gave technicians direct contact from customer homes to the company's scheduling-and-billing computers to close out orders and obtain a new assignment. These changes have added precision to appointment scheduling, giving customers better, faster service overall.

Even earlier, however, at the start of the 1990s, Buckeye invested heavily in an automatic vehicle locator (AVL) system, which could tell a dispatcher where each truck was at any given moment and how long it had been at a customer's home. Prior to that, the next available technician had been sent to the next available job, even if that meant driving 20 or more miles from one end of the system to the other.

With the AVL, by contrast, the dispatcher could look at a computer-generated map of the area and see that a technician was nearby and had been on the scene almost long enough to finish his current job—and thus direct him to handle the job close by.

Introduction of the AVL and the attendant reduction in time spent driving led to a roughly 30 percent increase in productivity, Carstensen said; a side benefit was money saved on lower gasoline consumption.

While the AVL quickly proved its worth in fuel savings and better customer service, employees at first were wary of "Big Brother watching." Shortly after the system was fully operational, however, one technician was sitting in his service truck in a South Toledo strip shopping center completing some paperwork when a man who had just robbed a nearby credit union jumped in, pushed the technician out of the driver's seat and took off in the Buckeye truck with the technician trapped on the floor between the engine housing and the side of the vehicle in front of the right seat.

A witness called police, who notified Buckeye. The dispatcher called up the truck information on her computer screen and told police where it was and which direction it was headed. An unmarked police car was in the vicinity, and quickly apprehended the robber. Grousing about Big Brother summarily died down.

In 1991, shortly after the first wave of reorganization of the customer-care operations was completed, Allan Block devised another move to showcase the company's commitment to customer service: He and Dave Huey, who by this time was president and general manager, would send an annual letter to every customer pledging that good service was tantamount to Buckeye's business.

In the initial letter, sent November 25, 1991, they vowed, "As the managing executives of The CableSystem (as it was known at the time), we accept responsibility for ensuring the quality of service offered to our customers. If you experience any problems with The CableSystem which are not resolved through the normal channels or our customer relations department . . . please write or call us."

They then listed their *home* telephone numbers. The letters have been sent every year since, urging any customer who felt his problem went unresolved to call either executive any time, day or night.

This idea was so foreign to the cable industry that many executives derided Block and Huey for what they believed to be folly. "Are you crazy?" was a common refrain Huey heard. Yet he fielded perhaps a hundred calls that first year, most of which concerned industry problems such as why Buckeye was prohibited from carrying certain network programs on Detroit television stations. Since, the calls to the executives have declined each year.

The concept has been effective because Buckeye subscribers know that the company genuinely stands behind its customer-service claims, and employees want to do what's right by the customer so they aren't the cause of an irate call to the boss at his home.

Buckeye executives and employees frequently get favorable comments about the company's customer service, and word has gradually spread through the industry. As the Cable Television Consumer Protection and Competition Act of 1992 (commonly called the 1992 Cable Act) was wending its way through Congress in 1990, the National Cable Telecommunications Association (NCTA) engaged Peter D. Hart Research Associates, a Washington, D.C., public-opinion polling firm, to conduct a national survey of customer attitudes toward their cable operators. The findings were not good, and the 1992 Cable Act became law.

Some years later, a Buckeye executive was a panelist on a forum at the annual meeting of the Ohio Cable Telecommunications Association (OCTA) in Columbus. The topic was customer service. The moderator: Peter Hart himself.

As Hart introduced the panel, he paused when he came to the Buckeye executive to relate a story of that research. The results from Toledo were so much more favorable than Hart's findings in other parts of the country, "we thought our research was faulty—so we went back and restudied the Toledo area," he said. "I don't know what Buckeye does, but their customers love them. If they could package that and sell it around the country, we wouldn't have the 1992 Cable Act."

In the darkened auditorium, one could almost see a bright glow emanating from the area where Block and Huey were seated.

Good customer service wins subscriber loyalty and can be measured in real dollar value. Consider: When small satellite dishes first became prevalent in the late 1990s, the Federal Communications Commission required their operators, DirecTV and Dish Network, to report quarterly the number of customers each had in each Zip code. Buckeye regularly analyzed the numbers and found that dish penetration (the number of active satellite-dish customers) in the Zip codes serviced by Buckeye was half of both the state and national average.

If dish penetration in the Buckeye Zip codes had been equal to the state and national numbers, and assuming that those extra satellite-service customers all disconnected Buckeye to go to the dish, the value of those lost customers would have meant Buckeye was worth some $78 million less than it was at then-current subscriber numbers. Allan Block had once again drawn on the family gene for superb strategic insight.

However, in late 2013 and early 2014, a series of outages tarnished Buckeye's sterling reputation for customer care, and some customers chose to take their business elsewhere.

As R.J. Walker, Buckeye's vice president of engineering and information technology and services, noted, the problems began in the fourth quarter of 2013 with an increasing number of smaller, brief outages that typically affected only a small number of homes.

These weren't attributable to any one factor: Circuit boards failed, power supplies caused problems and software glitches emerged—"things you just can't prevent in the field," Walker said.

In October 2013, a power-supply failure caused a video outage—an unavoidable problem but one that caused great consternation and an omen of further blackouts. Over the Christmas holiday, troubles began to snowball. The Christmas season is typically a time of considerable Internet use (Buckeye introduced high-speed Internet in mid-1999; see Chapter 7), as children are home from school, computer games given as presents get their initial workout and severe weather keeps people indoors.

On Friday, January 3, 2014, during the overnight routine-maintenance window, an engineer was adding Internet Protocol (IP) addresses to a cable-modem termination system (CMTS), a device used to provide high-speed data services. "It didn't work out so well," Walker said, "and while it didn't cause major customer problems, it caused intermittent problems with scattered customers."

The next day, the engineer "took it upon himself to reboot that device," Walker said. "He did it in such a way that he thought it wouldn't take customers out of service, but he didn't have the knowledge he needed to (realize) that it would turn all the customers off."

Incoming calls to customer-service representatives, which had averaged about 4,300 each day throughout 2013, spiked to 8,018 that Friday and 7,418 the next day. On Friday, almost 1,700 calls were abandoned before the harried CSRs could answer. The figures for the next day were even worse when 2,569 callers gave up before they were able to talk to someone. Unknown is how many customers got busy signals when they tried to call, and simply gave up.

Approximately 16,000 customers fed from the hub in question lost Buckeye Express service for a time that day. The engineer was counseled and warned sternly.

On Tuesday, January 28, again performing routine maintenance, the same engineer hooked up some equipment improperly but didn't know he had done it wrong, Walker said, nor did he document what he had done.

The phones began ringing; incoming call volume jumped from 4,604 on January 27 to 7,796 the next day, with 1,500 abandoned.

Other engineers were unable to pinpoint the problem immediately. The engineer was asked if he had done anything he hadn't documented. "At first, he denied it," Walker said, "but by midmorning on January 28, he admitted what he had done." By that time, *every* Buckeye subscriber had lost data service; it was not restored until 2 a.m. January 29. Even though service was restored at 2 a.m., incoming calls tallied 5,246 that day, with 511 abandoned before a CSR could talk to the customers.

The errant engineer was fired immediately, but the series of problems caused several thousand customers to cancel their service. During that period, Buckeye lost a significant number of video customers, substantially more than the expected erosion the company, as well as the entire industry, was facing at the time due to additional competition from wired services as well as programming available over the Internet.

The devastation to the company's customer-service reputation hit Allan Block particularly hard.

"That was a shock to us," Block later said of the outage. "We were beginning to think we were 'entitled' to give better service, just because we always had and that's what we want to do. Our performance on that occasion wasn't as good as our self image, and that's something I regret.

"We were overconfident. There's no other way of looking at it. We got burned like anybody else who is overconfident," he said.

He ordered an immediate reorganization of the network-engineering department. "We began to re-engineer everything we had," Walker said.

An engineering consultant was brought in and the entire network recon-
figured. It had been built in the late 1990s and had seen periodic upgrades
and expansions as needed given that customers were increasing their Internet
use about 50 percent each year.

As had been planned earlier, the company replaced lasers and other electronic components through most of the system—and for the next nine
months, up to the point when Walker was interviewed for this book, Buckeye
experienced no outages. The marketing and customer-relations departments
immediately began the task of rebuilding customer confidence.

"We remain committed to our service being better than anyone else's,"
Mr. Block said.

BUCKEYE BITS

If You're a Supervisor, Why Are You Stealing That TV?

Where's a cop when you need one? It's a common refrain when something
goes wrong and you need a policeman quickly.

However, for Allan Gilmore, a Buckeye customer-service supervisor, in
1998 the question instead was "Why are those cops pointing a gun at me and
ordering me to drop the TV set I'm carrying?"

At the time, Buckeye was enlarging its lobby to better serve its growing
customer base. The Southwyck building has an outer lobby from which
customers can either go upstairs to offices or pass through a door into the
customer-service lobby to see a Buckeye representative.

For the duration of the remodeling, temporary quarters were being set up
in the outer lobby, and employees were moving equipment there. One employee accidentally pushed the "panic button," a hidden button that sends a
silent alarm to Toledo police in the event of a robbery or other emergency.

The cops answered the alarm rapidly; two policemen, guns drawn,
charged into the outer lobby just as Gilmore arrived carrying a television
from the customer-service area.

"They thought I was stealing it and ordered me to drop the TV and put my
hands up," he recalled. He and other employees quickly explained that he
was a staffer and not a television thief.

"I had to show my Buckeye ID and have a couple other people vouch for
me," Gilmore said. "It seemed like 15 minutes, but it probably was only three
minutes before they were satisfied and put their guns away."

Oh, A-Camping We Will Go

Although Buckeye goes out of its way to provide outstanding customer service, sometimes even that is not enough.

Allan Gilmore, a customer-service supervisor, recalls the time a customer paid the monthly service charge, but the check was returned by the bank for insufficient funds. Subsequent collection efforts were unsuccessful, the balance due on the account kept rising and, after several months, Buckeye cut off the customer's cable service.

The lady of the house called Gilmore that Sunday.

"She screamed at me for about an hour," he said. "She was complaining that because the service had been discontinued, her husband could not watch the NFL playoffs that afternoon.

"Finally, we hung up. I thought no more about it until I got a call from the lobby sometime later that they needed my attention," he said. "I went up there, and this woman, her husband and four children showed up and said they were going to watch our TV since we cut off their service at their home."

They brought along a cooler of beer, having apparently decided to camp out. After a period of disruption, Buckeye staff called the cops. "The police asked me what I wanted them to do, and I told them to please remove them," Gilmore said. The family was escorted out, and "the policeman said he would stay a while to see that they didn't return. Then he sat down and watched the playoffs."

Chapter Four

"He Who Owns Production Owns the Client Relationship"

Expanding into Advertising Sales and Production

As the company's subscriber base grew, Buckeye management began look-ing for new sources to continue expanding. In the early 1980s, the company's marketing manager, Gary Brubaker, had encountered at a national cable meeting some representatives from a cable firm in Tulsa, Oklahoma, and learned they had a modicum of success selling advertising, which they in-serted in "local avails."

Local avails are a part of programming contracts. Programmers such as ESPN, USA and others generate revenue from selling their services to cable firms for a set amount per subscriber, and through selling national advertis-ing in their programs. They also make a certain number of commercial breaks, or local avails, available in which the cable operator can insert locally sold advertising.

Brubaker came back from that meeting and suggested to Buckeye presi-dent John Karl that the company might get into the local-advertising busi-ness. Karl agreed, and Brubaker put the wheels in motion.

He contracted with a local advertising firm, Tailford Associates, to pre-pare a sales brochure, and began looking for sales help. He hired Steve Piller, a young graduate of Bowling Green State University, who had some experi-ence selling radio advertising in Toledo.

"I was making $750 a month in radio, and I jumped at Brubaker's offer of $1,250 a month," Piller, currently vice president for sales and local stations, said. "I got a 66 percent pay raise, but I didn't have an office. I worked out of a small conference room at Buckeye's office," which at the time was located at 1122 North Byrne Road, near Secor Road in West Toledo. He took the Tailford brochure and hit the streets.

He encountered a considerable amount of rejection before Grant Hollenback, advertising manager at The Andersons, a local family-owned grain, retail and rail conglomerate, decided to take a chance on this new medium.

"He had done some local broadcast advertising for the local retail store, and was not happy with the results," Piller said. "I took out a map of Buckeye's footprint and drew a 'golden triangle' around the store in Maumee, and pointed out how we could target Andersons' advertising to customers who lived near the stores."

With over-the-air broadcast, The Andersons' message was beaming across a large swath of Northwest Ohio and Southeast Michigan at a much higher cost per thousand viewers reached (the standard metric by which broadcast, cable and radio advertising is measured). Cable offered both a much lower cost per thousand and access to more viewers who were likely to patronize the local stores, Piller pointed out.

"The Andersons was the first advertiser we had. When I went back to the office and told people, Jim Dryden (head of engineering at the time) kissed me," Piller laughed.

Another big early advertiser was Video Connection, a video-rental business started in 1978 by John Day in his spare time while working as a district manager in *The Blade*'s circulation department. "I chose Buckeye because it's a visual medium, we were a video business, broadcast was too expensive, Buckeye advertising was something new and people were drawn to it," Day said. "Buckeye produced my spots, and we never had a problem with them."

Day began franchising Video Connection and had the foresight to sell the firm in 1995 to Movie Gallery just ahead of the growth in popularity of video-on-demand on cable and, later, streaming video over the Internet. Movie Gallery soon went bankrupt. Day now operates a new firm, Transfer Me to DVD, which puts movies, videotapes and still pictures on DVDs. He still advertises on Buckeye.

After The Andersons came onboard, Buckeye's next tasks were figuring out the mechanics of showing the spots at the proper times, providing an affidavit of performance and billing the client. At the time, no advertising-insertion equipment existed, so John Ctvrtlik, a young engineering technician, was pressed into service to monitor all programming into which advertising was to be inserted, and when he heard the audio tone the programmers transmitted at the beginning of a local avail, he pushed a button to run the local ad spot.

Ctvrtlik, now senior system engineering technician, would then create a handwritten log listing the time, date and program on which the spot ran. As the number of advertisers grew, monitoring and logging necessarily increased. Ctvrtlik would leave an entire week's worth of logs for Piller's review.

"By that time I had my own small office and an IBM Selectric typewriter," Piller said. "Each weekend my wife and I would come to the office, take the logs and type an affidavit for each advertiser and draft an invoice. I did it all: selling, scheduling the ads, documenting proof of performance and invoicing.

"Selling advertising (in those early days) was really pretty tough," he added. "The first avails on ESPN were billiards and *Top Rank Boxing.* A lot was simply selling the perception. Now we sell *Monday Night Football.*"

As Buckeye's partners grew to some dozen advertisers, the back-office work was getting too burdensome to let Piller sell effectively, so Vickie Opperman, who had joined Buckeye in 1979 and was fielding customer calls in the Showtime department, was transferred to Piller's department in early 1982 to do all ad scheduling and handle the growing number of affidavits and invoicing. Opperman, now Vicki Halamay, is still with the ad-sales department as billing specialist and responsible agent for affidavits.

Gradually, Buckeye was able to implement automated advertising-insertion equipment. Today, this equipment stores all advertising spots, each with a unique identifier that ties the commercial to the advertiser's specific schedule. The equipment receives the signal sent by the programmer to indicate that a local avail is starting, then picks the correct spot, runs it and creates the log, which is later printed out as the affidavit of performance for the advertiser or agency.

The equipment also creates the invoices and automatically inserts free public-service announcements into unsold local avails. Today, some one million advertising spots and roughly 1,000 public-service announcements are inserted each month.

Piller hired additional ad-sales help. Larry Jacquemotte and Jim Lorenzen came from WLQR, a Toledo radio outlet. Later would come Rick Watson, Jim Garner, Stu Roberts, Tony Maroun, and Glen Cerney among others. Today the department stands at eight salespeople in Toledo and three in Sandusky, plus eight on the administrative staff.

Cerney first became associated with Buckeye in 1984 when he started doing play-by-play announcing for Jacquemotte, who was producing Mud Hens games as well as University of Toledo football and basketball games. Cerney had sold his part-interest ownership in radio station WKIQ FM (now WRQN) and was working on a master of arts degree in Radio, TV, and Film at Bowling Green State University. Upon graduation in 1985 he joined Buckeye's ad sales team and continued to do the sports announcing.

He moved to St. Louis in 1988 to run KCLC FM, a non-commercial radio station at Lindenwood College, but for the next eight or nine years would fly back to Buckeye to broadcast many UT (men's and women's) basketball games as well as UT football, high school basketball state tournament games, Goaldiggers hockey and "a ton of Mud Hens games," he said.

Cerny, who now is executive director of university broadcasting at New Mexico State University in Las Cruces, where he is in charge of the National Public Radio and Public Broadcast stations, was hired to establish the special production unit that produces Aggie athletic telecasts, and does play-by-play of football, men's basketball and occasionally baseball and softball games.

"My philosophy has always been to hire very experienced, competent media-sales people. They are selling perception," Piller said. "They have been great people and have been a great addition. Most took a pay cut to join Buckeye because they could see the potential."

Jacquemotte was named sales manager, and he and Piller decided Buckeye needed a production department given that most local companies had not done much television advertising and couldn't efficiently create TV spots. Production of commercials and promotional spots had been done at Creative Images, a local audiovisual company owned by Dave Peterson. Jacquemotte moved out of sales and into production and struck a deal with Hart Associates, a Toledo advertising and public-relations firm with production capabilities, to produce spots for this new breed of cable advertisers.

In the early 1980s, in addition to ads, Buckeye ventured into developing local programming. First was *Toledo Beat*, which targeted a younger audience and was a product of Creative Images.

Another early program was *Limelight Tonight,* a compendium of social and civic events in and around Toledo. It was hosted by Paul W. Smith, a young radio announcer. Today, Smith, a native of nearby Monroe, Michigan, is host of the morning drive-time show on WJR, the powerful Detroit Cumulus radio station. In 2013, he was inducted into the Radio Hall of Fame. (See Chapter 9 for more on local programming).

In 1986, Buckeye moved its headquarters to the larger facility at 5566 Southwyck Boulevard, and soon, about a quarter of the second floor was carved out for the company's own production facilities.

"Starting in-house production was a strategic decision," Piller said. "I believe that he who owns production owns the client relationship." Today, Buckeye's production department is responsible for about 80 percent of the TV advertising produced in Toledo, much of which is also aired on the local broadcast stations, Piller estimates.

Jacquemotte moved out of ad sales into full-time production work. He hired Scott Sandstrom from Hart, as well as Ron Schulz, who had been with Creative Images, which Buckeye relied on less as it ramped up its own facilities. Both Sandstrom and Schulz are still with Buckeye's production department.

Having spent five years with Hart, Sandstrom joined Buckeye in March 1991. As was so often the case in Buckeye's formative years, and remains so today, a person's job description tells only part of the story. Although Sandstrom was hired as a videographer, he found himself wiring and setting up equipment in the one linear-editing studio in the nearly complete production suite being constructed in the Southwyck building.

He and Schulz wrote virtually all the ad scripts, as well as performed the editing, scheduling and shooting tasks, and given that there was only one edit suite, they had to schedule work carefully—while one was out on a shoot, the other could work in the suite.

In those days, the duo used three-quarter-inch videotape for their spots. When they were done, the tape had to be physically transported to the head end on Angola Road so the commercials could be shown at the right time.

As Buckeye began deployment of fiber optics, it installed a line from Southwyck to the head end, enabling the commercial spots to be stored on a server at Southwyck, which the master control operators at Angola Road could then access, transfer the spot via fiber and place it in proper rotation.

"This greatly reduced the time from production to air," Sandstrom said, as the client and editor could work much closer to the deadline for starting the rotation on a channel. It also saved time and money spent transporting tapes and eliminated tape expense.

"Buckeye was one of the first cable operators in the country to go tapeless," Sandstrom added. As a result, the production department played host to a number of other cable operators, equipment vendors and ad agencies that wanted to see the company's breakthrough and figure out how they could adapt it to their own needs—or, in the case of equipment vendors, determine how they could develop a larger market for their products.

Buckeye was once again ahead of the industry curve when its production department in 1987 eliminated ¾-inch video tapes in favor of a new digital medium, Beta Cam SP. Sandstrom told of the production staff being guests of the Detroit Red Wings at an NHL hockey game in the mid-2000s: When the hostess in the suite learned where the group was from, she said, "Oh, you guys are the ones who went with Beta Cam SP while others were still using three-quarter-inch tapes. We've heard about you."

Also in the mid-2000s, Buckeye became the first local medium to show a regularly scheduled High Definition commercial. "One of the local broadcasters showed one as a test," Sandstrom recalled, "but we were the first to run one on a regular schedule."

Today the company has moved, with the rest of the industry, to the use of File Transfer Protocol, using a Web-based server. Commercial spots are uploaded to the FTP server and assigned a password and code; the end user then can download the spot from anywhere in the world.

For example, a Toledo auto dealer currently uses a Florida ad agency, but Buckeye shoots all local video for that agency to use in preparing the dealer's commercials. The video is uploaded to the FTP server and downloaded by the Florida agency. When it puts the commercial together, it uploads it to the FTP server and assigns it a password and code, then gives local broadcast and cable outlets this information. The local outlets pull down the commercial and run it at the appropriate time.

"It's useful for distances," Sandstrom said, "but sometimes it can be faster to take a disc to a nearby advertiser than to code commercials' identifying information for the FTP server."

As industry technology progressed, Buckeye continued to grow. With the advent of set-top converters, which would enable the transmission of many more channels, and the staff required to roll out such a major change, the company was in need of more space. In 1998, the production department moved into 5522 Southwyck Boulevard, a building just south of the company headquarters' parking lot.

Buckeye had rented space in the building starting in 1994 for some Information Technology personnel, and in 1996 advertising sales moved into leased space on the first floor. The next year, Buckeye leased additional space for some marketing employees, then bought the structure and remodeled it in 1998.

The company needed additional production staff to meet increased demand, so it hired another videographer, an editor, a scriptwriter and a scheduler. Schulz moved into production of graphics, which were becoming an increasingly bigger component of TV spots. Here, too, Buckeye continued to add staff as the workload increased. Today the production staff numbers five, as well as additional administrators from the sales staff who schedule production shoots and commercial time, and provide affidavits to clients.

The production department has branched out beyond TV commercials, shooting training videos and other, longer productions. Among its work was a sales video for Intel Corp., the enormous producer of semiconductors. "The talent they used was local," Sandstrom said, "so several creative types came to Toledo to direct the shoot."

The staff also has produced promotional spots for *Monty Python's Flying Circus* at the Stranahan Theater and for *American Idol* singer Clay Aiken; it also brought a Playboy Bunny to the Southwyck production studio to shoot a promo spot for the Playboy Channel when it launched.

It also put together the *Lake Erie People's Choice* awards, a Grammy-style show honoring local entertainers. The production, staged annually from 1998 to 2000, packed the auditorium at Lourdes College's Franciscan Center, and was emceed by Jerry Anderson and Chrys Peterson, local broadcast-news talent.

There was also *Impulse Show*, with Tracy Rinehart, Alicia Walsh and Ellen Joyce sharing hosting duties. This program promoted Pay-Per-View events when those were new to the Buckeye system.

Finally, the department also shot behind-the-scenes interviews at the Jamie Farr Classic, a local golf tournament started in tandem with the eponymous native Toledoan who found fame as a star in the TV sitcom *M*A*S*H*. These were shown only on Buckeye, before the tournament received any national television coverage. It likewise produced a 12-minute training tape for Dana Corp. that won a national award in 1997.

BUCKEYE BITS

I Beg Your Pardon; I Can't Understand You

Paul W. Smith, who was part of early programming on Buckeye CableSystem as host of *LIMELIGHT Tonight,* as well as appearing in many promotions and training videos, once figured out a novel way to get himself, a Buckeye executive and some ad-agency people to New Orleans in style.

Smith, Buckeye president and general manager John Karl, Buckeye ad agent Jim Cooper and two others were bound for the Sugar Bowl in the Crescent City for the 1984 University of Michigan-Auburn University showdown. They had plane tickets for seats in coach. When Smith learned of this at the airport, he decided to do something about it.

"I had done a lot of flying and had become sort of a master at upgrading," he said. He approached a gate agent. "Excuse me," he said. "Can you help me?"

"Do you have a problem?" the agent asked, a harried look on her face.

"Well, yes, I do have a problem. The problem is, you can't understand me because I don't speak English," he said, in perfect English.

"Pardon me?"

"See, I told you," he said. "It's very difficult. You don't understand me because I don't speak English."

The agent was befuddled. "Wait a minute. What is it you're saying?" she asked.

"Oh, boy—this language barrier is much worse than I thought," he said, then gestured to his four companions. "I don't speak English, and I was thinking that if we're seated in the back of the plane—I think you call that the economy section—it might be more difficult for us, because we don't speak English, than if we go to the front of the plane, I think you call it in English, I think you call it first class."

He laughed as he recounted the story. "She must have looked at me for 30 or 45 seconds, mouth agape, dumbfounded, and finally said, 'Wow, that's the best one I've ever heard. Go get your friends' tickets, and let's go.' And she moved all five of us into first-class seats."

The flight was uneventful, and the group watched the Wolverines lose to Auburn 9–7.

Chapter Five

"You Couldn't Get a Dial Tone in Sandusky When That Call-in Show Was On"

In Toledo and Points Beyond, Buckeye Extends Its Reach

In the late 1970s and into the '80s, the cable industry was in a state of flux, with systems buying one another and consolidating into a handful of behemoths such as today's Time Warner and Comcast. Most of this purchasing and consolidation was financed by heavy borrowing, and the resulting debt service caused many conglomerators to cut back on customer-service expenses.

One such system, Tele-Communications, Inc., or TCI, served parts of Tennessee. Its niggardly attitude toward customer service so angered its subscribers that they cried to regulators for something to be done. One of those irate customers was the mother-in-law of then-Senator Albert Gore Jr. of Tennessee, who was one of 11 co-sponsors of the Cable Television Consumer Protection and Competition Act (a.k.a. the 1992 Cable Act), which imposed strict regulation and cost controls on the industry. (The now-defunct TCI was acquired by AT&T and later by Comcast.)

The Blocks took a more conservative approach to expansion, choosing to finance growth internally: building into unserved areas, extending lines into new developments within areas already served and acquiring two existing cable firms.

In 1980, The Cable System, Inc., a new subsidiary of The Toledo Blade Co., purchased Monroe Cablevision, Inc., in Monroe, Michigan, about 25 miles north of Toledo, and in 1981, the Block organization purchased North Central Television, Inc., in Sandusky, Ohio, about 70 miles east of Toledo.

Both the Monroe and Sandusky firms later became subsidiaries of Block Communications, as the holding company was renamed in 2000 in recognition of the 100th anniversary of the family firm's founding.

Monroe Cablevision had been established in 1970. The board of directors comprised of three Monroe businessmen and an attorney: John Holman, Charles McIntyre II, Dr. Robert Graham and Thomas Griffin Jr., respectively. Griffin was named secretary-treasurer, according to a Sept. 24, 1970 article in the *Monroe Evening News*, that city's daily newspaper. The paper today is known simply as the *Monroe News*. Ultimately, some 20 Monroe residents would jointly own the system.

City Council granted the firm a 15-year franchise on April 15, 1970. Its first office was at 12 East Front Street; the company later moved to 428 South Monroe Street. Bill Aubry, who was with Buckeye in its earlier days, had left the firm to become manager of the Monroe system. When the Monroe entity was sold to the Blocks, he was named vice president of Buckeye and general manager of the Monroe firm, and once again was a part of the Block family of companies. Following his retirement in 1990, Florence Buchanan, who had been in Buckeye's marketing department in Toledo, was transferred to Monroe to take the helm. She later became executive vice president and general manager.

After Monroe came into the Block fold, it began to emphasize local programming—not just traditional video programming, though. In 1984, the firm approached Monroe County sheriff Charles G. Harrington about instituting an emergency warning system. The company bought and installed equipment in the sheriff's office that permitted law-enforcement officials to take over the video and audio on all 36 cable channels to deliver a message in the event of an emergency.

At the time, Harrington said that the warning system was operational only in Monroe and not on any of the other cable systems in the county, because Monroe Cablevision was the only one that approached the department with the concept, according to a March 29, 1984, article in the *Monroe Evening News*.

Now, though, the federal Emergency Management Agency (FEMA) requires such warning systems, known as the Emergency Alert System (EAS), nationwide. In addition to cablevision, EAS is used by broadcast, satellite and other wireline-communications pathways. The first nationwide EAS test occurred November 9, 2011, according to the FCC, some 26 years after Monroe Cablevision rolled out the concept locally. Today the system is universal and is tested monthly.

Monroe programming included such features as a talk show, *All Points Bulletin,* hosted by a Michigan state police trooper, which focused on people with some type of broad influence on the community. The first show, in October 1993, featured the president of the Dundee High School Students

Against Drunk Driving (SADD), a state police recruiter and a Department of Natural Resources officer who spoke about hunting safety.

Another production featured students from Bright Horizons, a class taught by local resident Barbara Baumgartner and sponsored by the *Monroe Evening News*. Bright Horizons inculcated self-esteem, communication skills and poise in youths from ages 5 to 19. The students were featured in 30-second spots discussing a range of topics: pets, recycling, crime, their hometowns, sex.

The programs, called *Keen Kids* or *Teen Kids* depending on the age of those featured, were shown during cable-channel commercial breaks; they were filmed by Ron Schulz, with assistance from Buckeye's Carolyn Wright.

Other programs were not locally produced but found an audience regardless. In the early 1980s, *Fire Away*, produced by the National Fire Protection Association and partially funded by FEMA, provided fire-prevention and firefighting information to professional firefighters but was available to all subscribers. Another, *The Job Show*, was produced by the Public Information Services Division of the Michigan Employment Security Commission in the early 1990s, according to an article in the Feb. 28, 1990, edition of the *Monroe Evening News*.

In Sandusky, five area businessmen had formed North Central Television, incorporating it on June 29, 1967. Its first franchise was granted March 11, 1969, by Perkins Township, followed by agreements with the City of Huron, Huron Township and the City of Sandusky, besting another bidder seeking entry into the Erie County area, according to an Aug. 26, 1981, article in the Sandusky *Register*, that city's daily newspaper.

The founders rented an office at 232 Fulton Street in Sandusky to offer the area the relatively new cable-TV service, and built a 440-foot tower on farmland near Billings and Parker Roads in Margaretta Township, south of Castalia.

After several months at the Fulton Street location, North Central Television moved its operations to the Boeckling Building at 105 West Shoreline Drive, a facility along Sandusky Bay that had formerly served as headquarters of Cedar Point, the popular amusement park on a spit of land running northwest into Lake Erie on the other side of the bay.

Cable employees could gaze, perhaps wistfully, at Cedar Point's Ferris wheel and roller coasters as they worked. The building housed a small call center and customer-service lobby to accommodate its first 100 customers in the Perkins Township franchise area.

Having operated the fledgling business for a few years and in need of an infusion of capital, the founders turned to Jay Wagner, the general manager of a local radio station, WLEC. Wagner belonged to a local investment club, which agreed to put up some operating funds—on the condition that Wagner agree to run the business.

He had joined WLEC in 1947 as sports and programming director and became general manager in 1952. In 1971, he resigned and took the helm of the nascent cable firm. The initial investors retained 51 percent ownership; the investment club owned the balance.

Wagner followed by about a year a young engineer, Bob Heim, who left WLEC to join North Central Television as an engineer and who was instrumental in running the company's technical operations until he retired in 2004.

In the early years, North Central experimented with local programming, including a local news show that was filmed daily in the Boeckling Building. The tape would be taken to the tower and head end on Billings Road and cablecast over the system. In 1974, the company parked a trailer at the tower and shot the show live from there.

Tom Whaley, who joined North Central in 1973 as a cameraman, produced the news shows both in the Boeckling Building and the trailer. From 1974 to 1977, he hosted a popular trivia show in which he would ask questions about local events, people or history and show pictures of local scenes, and callers would try to answer the questions or identify the pictures to vie for prizes such as pizza and other merchandise donated by merchants.

"It was extremely popular, and you couldn't get a dial tone in Sandusky when that was on," said Whaley, who now owns TW Teleproductions in Sandusky. "People still stop me on the street and ask why we don't do the trivia show again. I think with the Internet and search engines, it wouldn't work in this day and age, but it was certainly popular back then."

Also in those early, experimental days, North Central cablecast a religious talk show, *Life in the Son,* hosted by the Reverend Dan Detzer, and a call-in talk show on general topics hosted by a local man, Bill Swain, Whaley said.

In 1979, Whaley and Ken Walters established Bay Area Productions, leased a channel from North Central and every day produced the trivia show, a sports talk show and a morning talk show. They also covered high-school sports.

In 1982, the *Sandusky Register* took over the channel's lease from Bay Area Productions, producing a daily news show from the paper's newsroom, as well as a call-in sports show. The paper even produced a bingo show, but "the attorney general sent us a cease-and-desist order, so we had to stop that," Whaley said.

Other efforts at local programing in those days covered a variety of topics; show titles included *Coffee Club, Trophy Fishing, Ideas on Parenting, From a Black Perspective, North/Coast Live, Luxurious Living* and *Movin' On,* according to a Nov. 29, 1981 article in the *Register.*

The Blocks bought the firm and changed its name to Erie County Cablevision, Inc. Wagner stayed on to run the company, but in September 1985, eyeing the need to rebuild the aging system and considering that Wagner expressed a desire to retire, Buckeye sent its manager of administration, Patrick Deville, to Sandusky, naming him vice president and general manager. Wagner stayed for about 30 days, then served as a consultant until December 31, 1989.

Buckeye began consolidating and, in Toledo, complementing some of the operations of the Sandusky system. For example, if demand on the phones in Sandusky got too high, unanswered calls would roll over to Toledo, where Buckeye's much larger customer-service staff could handle them. The company also tied Sandusky's billing system into the robust billing system in Toledo.

Rebuilding the Sandusky system began in 1985 with replacement of the older cable and an increase in channel capacity from 12 to 62. The Billings Road tower was replaced with a new 400-foot tower, plus a new head end and warehouse, at 1616 West Strub Road, south of Sandusky, an area much closer to the bulk of the firm's customers. That tower initially had antennae capable of receiving a multitude of broadcast stations, mainly from Cleveland, but in the early 2000s Buckeye struck a deal with Time Warner Cable to feed the signals via fiber from Cleveland to the Strub Road head end, from which it was retransmitted to customers' homes.

Today, the tower is used only to hold a mobile radio antenna for a local business and an antenna by which Erie County Cablevision receives the off-air signals from WOIO, the Cleveland CBS affiliate broadcasting on Channel 19 and WUAB, which broadcasts My Network TV, a programming service, on Channel 43. Both are owned by Raycom Media, Inc.

In 2000, Buckeye moved its administrative offices and customer-service operations from Shoreline Drive to 409 East Market Street.

After the rebuild was complete, the smaller system enabled Buckeye to field-test in customers' homes some of the new technologies on the horizon—such as Tocom boxes, the first set-top converters Buckeye was exploring—before committing a large capital outlay to deploy the software and hardware in the larger system in Toledo.

In other respects, Erie County operated independently. Technicians, installers, construction crews and customer-service personnel initially worked autonomously, though gradually operations were woven together. In emergencies, the two firms would share whatever resources were needed to overcome the problem.

A tornado on July 12, 1992, devastated much of the Erie County cable plant, wiping out service to most of the eastern part of the city and south to Bogart Road. It was important to replace the damaged cables and electronic equipment to get customers back in service as quickly as possible. City officials were slow to issue permits, though, and Ohio Power Co. had to replace scores of 80-foot-tall utility poles to which Erie County cable lines were affixed, so many temporary solutions were needed, Heim said.

At one point, cables were placed across the Galloway Road overpass over State Route 2, and crews used plastic ties to secure them to the bridge railing, a fix left in place for several weeks. Finally, Heim said, the poles were replaced and the cable lines were put in their permanent location.

Today, Erie County Cablevision operates in 12 franchise areas. In addition to the original four franchises, customers in Bay View and Castalia, as well as Margaretta, Oxford, Groton, Berlin, Milan and Townsend Townships now avail themselves of the hybrid-fiber coaxial cable system that offers more than 300 analog, digital and high-definition channels.

In addition to expanding its customer base by acquiring the cable firms in Sandusky and Monroe, each year Buckeye spent hundreds of thousands of dollars building new cable plant in new developments, pushing service into hospitals, hotels, apartment and condominium complexes and closing gaps in existing service areas.

After it obtained the Holland franchise in 1982 and another in Spencer Township in 1987, Buckeye focused on building plant in existing franchises in western and southern suburbs as new housing developments went up.

The next franchise activity involved the Lost Peninsula area of Erie Township in Monroe County, Michigan. The Lost Peninsula is a unique geographical area that juts north out of Toledo into Michigan, with the Ottawa River to the west dumping into Lake Erie at the north end of the peninsula. It became part of Michigan as a result of the 1835–1836 Ohio-Michigan War, sometimes called the Toledo War.

Conflicting laws passed by Ohio and the federal government in the late 1700s and early 1800s created confusion over Ohio's northern boundary. Both Ohio and Michigan claimed a one-mile strip along Ohio's northern line, and when Michigan prepared to join the Union in the early 1830s, it listed the disputed area as its own.

However, the Ohio Congressional delegation was able to delay Michigan's statehood bid. Starting in 1835, both sides passed legislation attempting to force the other side to give up its claim to the land. Neither side would, so Ohio Governor Robert Lucas and Michigan Governor Stevens T. Mason both raised militias, as reported on the website of the Michigan Department of Military & Veterans Affairs.

Other than some verbal taunting and a few shots fired into the air that resulted in no injuries, no military action ensued, and it all came to naught in 1836. Michigan, facing financial difficulties, capitulated to Congress and President Andrew Jackson and gave up claim to the land, receiving the Upper Peninsula in return.

The new boundary line was drawn straight east to Lake Erie, crossing the Lost Peninsula land just north of the present-day 149th Street in Point Place, leaving the area marooned from its home state, reachable by land only via Toledo.

Today the area is a respectable mixture of summer homes and permanent residents with a couple of restaurants and a marina with some 500 docks, though it had a checkered history during Prohibition as a staging area for rum runners bringing illegal liquor from Canada to the United States.

Lost Peninsula residents had been requesting cable-TV service for some time when in 1987 Buckeye began planning to extend it to them. First, however, a franchise had to be negotiated with Erie Township, solely for the Lost Peninsula.

Even though its residents for the most part shop and work in Toledo and subscribe to Toledo news media, the Federal Communications Commission nevertheless deems Monroe County part of the Detroit Designated Market Area (DMA). As part of its planning, Buckeye repeatedly tried to get the FCC to transfer the area from the Detroit to the Toledo DMA to alleviate possible programming problems under terms created by the FCC rules governing the importation of broadcast signals from another DMA.

However, the FCC was unwavering, and the Toledo bedroom community remains in the Detroit DMA. As a result, residents have a slightly different channel lineup than either their Toledo neighbors or other Buckeye customers in Michigan.

The franchise finally was signed May 26, 1988, and construction began.

Further expansion followed on the heels of the fiber-optic system rebuild, with service extended in 1999 to Middleton Township and the city of Northwood in Wood County, Allen Township in Ottawa County, and the village of Waterville and Monclova and Richfield Townships in Lucas County.

North of the border, Buckeye had been fielding requests for service to the Bedford area of Monroe County for years. However, with Toledo-area expansion moving rapidly, and few residents close to the border in Monroe County, Buckeye management preferred to devote capital to the denser areas of Toledo's suburbs rather than spend money to build large expanses of cable plant through vacant land before reaching residential concentration farther north in Temperance and Lambertville, Michigan. In addition, another operator was already providing service, reducing Buckeye's market potential. The move just didn't make economic sense.

Bedford residents had endured a number of owners of the cable firm over the years, each of whom seemingly wanted nothing more than to keep the system operating inexpensively as they sought a buyer.

One popular story has it that the first operator, making an initial foray south from its established operations in Michigan, conducted research to gauge the market. The study mistakenly showed the Bedford Township area extending as far south as Alexis Road in Toledo, an area with much denser housing, including a number of apartment buildings—a larger number of potential customers than actually existed.

Realizing the potential was not as great as originally anticipated, the initial operator soon sold, as did succeeding firms, some of which are no longer in business.

The township, long a bedroom community to Toledo, was rapidly growing, but somewhat north of the state line. Just north of the border were an airport, several businesses, a factory and farms—not a good mix for a cablevision business that needs housing density to show a fair return on investment.

As more and more residents moved from the Buckeye service area, development crept closer to the Ohio line. Additionally, former Buckeye subscribers moving north experienced service they considered substandard to what they had in Ohio, and requests for Buckeye service intensified.

Finally, in early 1999, Buckeye executives set up a series of exploratory meetings with officials of the townships involved. To break the ice at the first meeting in Bedford, one of the Buckeye executives, cognizant of the sports rivalries between the Buckeyes of The Ohio State University and the University of Michigan Wolverines and Michigan State University Spartans, joked that he had called the Ohio Secretary of State that very day and gotten special permission to change the company's name for that day and that meeting from Buckeye Cablevision to the Wolverine and Spartan Cablevision Co.

Humor aside, a franchise was negotiated successfully, and service to Bedford, as well as to Whiteford, Ida and Summerfield Township areas of Monroe County and Riga Township in Lenawee County, began in December of that year.

By that time, the incumbent operator had sold the existing system to Comcast, which served areas in Detroit and north of Monroe, with its closest plant separated by some 25 or so miles from Bedford Township. While Comcast operations were superior to those of its predecessors, it was operating an aging plant overshadowed by the modern fiber-optic plant Buckeye was building.

Talks began between Buckeye and Comcast to investigate a sale or trade of Comcast's recently acquired Bedford system for Buckeye's Monroe Cablevision. Over the course of several months, the two struck a deal in which Buckeye would absorb all existing Comcast plant in Bedford, Whiteford, Ida, Summerfield and Riga Townships, adjacent to its existing systems, while Comcast would acquire the Monroe Cablevision system, adjacent to its systems in Detroit and north of Monroe. Economies of scale would ensue for both companies.

The transfer was effective March 29, 2002, and Buckeye began replacing the aging coaxial system with its modern hybrid fiber coaxial system spreading through its Toledo area and its original Bedford Township area. Ms.

Buchanan, who had been executive vice president and general manager, was transferred back to Toledo and was named marketing vice president after the retirement of Ellen Jackson, for whom this book is dedicated.

Buckeye acquired no additional franchise areas until 2013, when continued residential growth west of Sylvania and subsequent plant extensions by Buckeye made it economically feasible to extend service to Berkey, a village of a few hundred residents in western Lucas County.

While earlier expansion plans required a number of meetings with local government officials to negotiate a franchise agreement, in 2007 both Ohio and Michigan had passed statewide franchising laws that mandated, among other things, that no new local franchises could be granted.

Existing franchises would still be honored but could not be renewed upon expiration. Buckeye, being a local company, preferred to deal with local people and keep its existing franchises intact.

However, the company had to obtain an Ohio statewide franchise upon passage of the law to continue to operate in several townships where service extended only short distances and only a few residents subscribed. These were mainly along border roads, where the houses could be served by extending a drop of the backbone cable plant that had been built on the other side of the road to serve the adjacent area.

Previous state law required a franchise in a township only after the cable provider had more than 500 customers. Both Buckeye and Erie County Cablevision had several townships with fewer than that number, including one with only two homes served.

Ohio's statewide franchising law repealed that part of the old law and mandated that *any* service to a township required inclusion in a statewide franchise. The mechanics of the law are such that an operator obtains a franchise to serve the entire state, but must list specific political subdivisions—townships, villages and cities—it actually serves. To extend into a previously unserved area, the operator need only amend its existing service area of the statewide franchise, a process that requires filing an application and takes no more than 30 days.

The initial filing in early 2008, done under the name of Block Communications, Inc., rather than separate filings for Buckeye and Erie County, brought under the company's Video Service Area (VSA) Allen Township in Ottawa County and Lake Township in Wood County. In the Sandusky area, the townships of Berlin, Groton, Oxford and Milan in Erie County, plus Townsend Township in Sandusky County, were included in the original VSA.

Subsequently, as franchises have expired, Riga Township in Lenawee County, Michigan, and the City of Waterville in Lucas County, in the Toledo portion of the system, were brought under the statewide documents, as were the City of Sandusky and the villages of Bay View and Castalia in the Erie County portion.

Later changes brought Waterville Township in Lucas County and Middleton Township in Wood County under the State VSA before they expired to save Buckeye's customers some money each month.

Under the statewide franchise law, when a new applicant files to serve an area, the franchise fee is zero until the local franchise authority adopts a resolution (in townships) or an ordinance (in municipalities) establishing a franchise fee. That fee is then applied to any new applicants seeking to serve the area under a VSA.

Time Warner Cable applied to the state Commerce Department to add both Middleton and Waterville Townships to its state VSA. Trustees of both townships set a fee for Time Warner that was less than the resolutions governing Buckeye's existing franchises. Rather than put itself at a competitive disadvantage, Buckeye merely filed the proper paperwork and moved those two townships away from the existing franchises and saved the average Buckeye customer roughly $1.50 a month compared to what they were paying at the time the change was made.

(Under Ohio law, cable companies do not keep any franchise-fee receipts; they merely collect the fee from the customer and pass it on to the local franchise authority [LFA], whether it is under a local franchise or a state VSA. The cable operator is assessed an annual regulatory fee by the Ohio Commerce Department, based on the number of subscribers in areas served through the State VSA. This is paid by the operator and is not part of the franchise fee paid by the customer. The Michigan statewide franchise law mirrors the Ohio measures in these issues, except the Michigan Public Service Commission regulates cable firms.)

To expand into Berkey, Buckeye filed paperwork in April 2013, approval was granted and Buckeye now had the legal right to extend its cable there.

In August 2013, Anthony Wayne Schools were in negotiations with Buckeye TeleSystem for phone service. Since much of the physical plant traditionally had been built by Buckeye Cablevision with capacity leased to Buckeye TeleSystem, the cable firm decided to add the Village of Whitehouse to its service area since it would be working in the public rights of way.

Even though the village had requested Buckeye service in the past, the company had no immediate plans to provide cable service in 2013. Nevertheless, that same month Buckeye filed paperwork to add Whitehouse to its VSA in case anyone might question why its trucks were working there; approval was granted on September 11. Under Ohio law, no time frame for offering cable service is specified; the firm merely is required to notify the village officials 30 days prior to the initiation of service.

Prior to passage of the statewide video-franchise law, obtaining franchises was a cumbersome process of meetings, hearings and negotiations with the local franchise authority. From the earliest days of cable franchising nationwide, interest groups tried to exert pressure on LFAs for all sorts of amenities: free service; provision of a local studio for the community's use; video production equipment donated by the operator; formation of cable committees to oversee operations of the cable company and programming suitability; customer-service offices in the individual franchise area; and a host of other demands.

Buckeye always tried to maintain uniformity across all franchise areas and not grant a demand to one that it couldn't provide system-wide.

Many of the franchises expired in the late 1990s and early 2000s, so as Buckeye was planning the fiber rebuild in the mid-1990s (See Chapter 6), it decided to renew all franchises for another 20 years. It did so to ensure, given the high projected rebuild costs, that its operations could continue without interruption and that there would be payback for the substantial investment.

Buckeye officials approached Toledo City Council first, given that Toledo was the largest franchise, and negotiated an agreement that was signed July 15, 1997, effective August 1. It expires July 31, 2017, and will have to fall under the state VSA at that time.

The Toledo agreement served as boilerplate for the other franchises, and one by one Buckeye approached the LFAs. While franchise personnel at other cable firms in Ohio with whom Buckeye executives had personal relationships told horror stories of being raked over the coals during such negotiations, Buckeye's franchise-renewal efforts went smoothly by comparison— a tribute to the firm's almost religious devotion to excellent customer service and being a good corporate citizen and community supporter.

Buckeye would send the boilerplate franchise agreement to the LFA along with a letter explaining the planned rebuild as the impetus to renew even though the current agreement, in many cases, had some time to run. Similarly, Buckeye would offer to have its executives attend LFA meetings at any time to answer questions. In all, the 16 franchises involved at that time were renewed with only one dissenting vote. Many LFAs did not even request a meeting; they merely signed the agreement and returned it.

The city of Northwood, in Wood County, exhibited a similar situation, though for an initial franchise instead of a renewal. Because of repeated requests for service there, in late 1998, Dave Huey, at the time Buckeye's president and general manager, and I attended a meeting one evening of council's public utilities committee. We explained our policy of uniform franchise agreements, took a copy of the boilerplate franchise document and answered a few questions posed by committee members.

We offered to meet with the full council at its convenience to explain more fully the operations and answer any questions. We heard nothing for several weeks and began to wonder if a problem had arisen. I was pleasantly surprised, then, when I came to the office early the morning of January 15, 1999, and found a voicemail message left the previous night.

"Tom, you can start building. Council signed the franchise tonight." The caller was Charles Kozina, the chairman of the utilities committee.

BUCKEYE BITS

I Asked You to Move That Pole

Among the more unusual outages Buckeye has experienced was the result of a developer using a chainsaw to cut down a utility pole to which the cable lines were attached.

In 1987, the developer was in the process of creating St. James Woods, an upscale residential area in Sylvania Township. He had arranged for Toledo Edison to remove some poles that were interfering with his work, and he became irked when, he felt, the utility did not remove a pole in a timely manner.

He called Edison and warned it that if the pole were not removed by a certain time that day, he would remove it himself.

When his arbitrary deadline passed, he fired up his chainsaw and felled the mighty pole across Bancroft Street, bringing down electrical wires and Buckeye's cables. An Edison spokesman said the pole was scheduled to be removed in a month and that it would seek restitution from the developer, whom it claimed was well aware of the timetable.

Cable Works Fine as a Clothes Hanger

During cable's halcyon days in the mid- to late 1970s, the industry was experiencing rapid growth. Not only were the choice and quantity of programs expanding, but signal quality was improving, which was especially noticeable compared to the picture delivered via antenna.

All sorts of innovations in customer conveniences were being introduced: the ability to discard unsightly "rabbit ears" from set tops; weather-sensitive rooftop antennae; remote-control devices that really made couch potatoes out of viewers; and converter boxes that enabled TV aficionados to schedule taping of a program in advance.

Customers literally chased cable trucks down the street, not only in Toledo but in cities around the country, begging to be hooked up. Over the course of several years, Buckeye was signing up some 1,000 customers a month.

It's understandable, then, that construction crews were under tremendous pressure to build cable as rapidly as possible. The more miles of cable, the more customers could be brought into service.

Thus, it wasn't always in the best interests of the construction crews to do everything correctly—just to do it quickly.

After a house in St. James Woods, an upscale development in Sylvania Township west of Toledo, had been occupied several years, the homeowner called Buckeye to inquire when the company might be removing its cables from his basement.

Years earlier, a construction crew had dug a trench to put a cable along one street which would then turn to go down a second street. In their haste, workers failed to observe a nicety called a public-utility easement. An easement is a strip of land, usually 8 to 10 feet wide, that the developer dedicates along the property for utilities to place electrical, cable, telephone, gas, water and sewer lines.

This Buckeye crew failed to stay within the easement and instead cut 45 degrees across the corner of the property rather than going to the corner and making a 90-degree turn.

The builder had faced such transgressions occasionally, having been delayed while crews returned, unearthed improperly placed cables and dug a new trench where they should have been in the first place. This time, he decided he'd had enough.

He carefully excavated around Buckeye's dual cables, poured the foundation around the wires and left them running through about 10 feet of one corner of the basement. The woman of the house had been using the two sturdy parallel half-inch cables as handy racks to hang laundry.

Finally the homeowner began to worry about liability and called Buckeye to have the cables removed.

I Could Have Been in Jail

When the Persian Gulf War started early in the morning of Thursday, January 17, 1991, I was in New Orleans attending the annual session of the National Association of Television Programming Executives (NATPE).

A late Friday flight from the Crescent City brought me back to Toledo, and I went to my Angola Road office early Saturday to clean up some of the work I had shunted aside before I left town.

Having had no contact with anyone in the office since Wednesday, I wasn't aware that Allan Block feared that communications installations might be likely terrorists' targets and as a precaution ordered guards posted at the Angola Road complex.

I found an armed guard at the Angola entrance. I had no company identification with me, but explained who I was and why I was there. The guard recorded my driver's-license information, noted my license plate and said he would sign me in as a visitor.

As I sat at my desk opening a stack of mail, it suddenly dawned on me that I was extremely lucky he didn't ask to search my car.

In the trunk was my son's rifle, which I planned to take to a gunsmith after I was done with my Buckeye duties to have some work done on it.

Had he found it, under the circumstances I might still be wearing those shiny, lockable bracelets securing my wrists together.

Chapter Six

"We Spent the Money to Continue the Business"

For Buckeye's Service Area, a New High-fiber Diet

The cable industry was advancing rapidly in the 1980s and '90s, with many new channels, new electronics, pay-per-view technology, new transmission methods and many other refinements, additions and changes. Buckeye was not alone in trying to figure out the best course forward.

Executives realized the one-way dual-cable coaxial system would have to be replaced if the company were to be able to stay competitive and offer all the new services customers wanted. But at what cost, and which technology?

Planning began in the early 1990s to replace the dual-cable coaxial plant and its inconvenient A/B switches with fiber optics for a number of reasons: signal clarity, bandwidth capacity, lower maintenance costs and fewer amplifiers and power supplies, all of which are subject to failures.

Buckeye was already deploying some fiber optics, having replaced microwave links to three hub sites with fiber-optic lines in the mid-1970s. Signal attenuation, or loss of intensity, in coaxial cable requires an amplifier about every quarter-mile to boost signal strength. Each time the signal passes through an amplifier, though, a certain amount of "noise" is introduced, degrading the signal. After passing through approximately 30 to 35 amplifiers (known as a "cascade"), the signal becomes unwatchable.

With fiber optics, only the capability of the electronics at the end of each fiber determines the quality of the signal at the end, so the distance a signal travels can be much, much greater with no reduction in quality. With fewer amplifiers, too, a fiber system is subject to far fewer equipment failures. In short, fiber-optic transport has significantly enhanced video quality, signal reliability and overall network availability—and because of the nature of the technology, it also has all but eliminated the limitations previously imposed by coaxial amplifier cascades. Such a system also improves reliability, as it's less dependent on commercial power—the fewer electrical devices in the field, after all, the fewer power outages.

From its humble beginnings—430 miles of single cable in the Ohio Bell leaseback system in the late 1960s—Buckeye in the 1990s operated some 1,900 miles of dual-cable system—3,800 cable miles. To reach the far ends of its expanded coverage area in Toledo's suburbs while providing a clear signal free of long amplifier cascades, Buckeye in the early '70s established three hub sites: one at Flower Hospital in Sylvania, one at St. Charles Hospital in Oregon and one at a tower the company constructed on land it bought on Creekside Avenue in North Toledo near Sylvania Avenue and Lagrange Street.

Microwave links fed the signals from the Angola Road head end to each of the three hub sites, where coaxial cable fanned out to subscribers' homes. This arrangement enabled the transmission of good signals over much greater distances than long amplifier cascades could have managed had every area been wired directly from Angola Road.

In the mid-'70s, Buckeye decided to replace those microwave links, which are subject to signal degradation and loss in certain weather conditions, with fiber optics. It was, in fact, the first cable company in the country to implement frequency-modulation fiber optics to deliver entertainment TV and data transmission from the system head end to scattered hub sites. It was also among the first to use amplitude-modulation fiber optics to provide a feed-and-return link between the head end and the hub sites.

But the industry was changing. The number of programs was mushrooming, for one, and the carrying capacity of the old dual-cable system was limited, necessitating an upgrade. In the early '90s, Buckeye decided to replace the coaxial-cable system with a hybrid fiber-coaxial system (HFC), which entailed deployment of fiber hubs and rings on a backbone to ensure redundancy and greater reliability.

From the hubs, redundant fiber rings would be extended to neighborhood "nodes," each serving about 500 homes. Fiber would feed the light-borne signal to 14 hub sites, where it would be converted from an optical to an electrical signal, and then again to a unique optical conversion—all to facilitate transmission from the hub-ring optics to the node-distribution optics.

Unlike a light-borne fiber-optic signal, the resulting electronic signal was visible on a TV set. The shorter coaxial runs would carry program signals to subscribers' homes; having each node serve only 500 residences would limit amplifiers to a maximum of four in a cascade, providing much clearer signals while reducing maintenance requirements and possible outages.

This design was advantageous in several ways. Fewer amplifiers meant fewer power supplies hanging on poles, where they were subject to bad weather, traffic mishaps, vandalism and failures. A sizable portion of the coaxial plant was located in backyard easements rather than in street rights-of-way; this led to service problems, particularly at night when residents weren't pleased with technicians showing up in their backyard at 3 a.m. to repair an outage. Powering would now be centralized at each node, too, eliminating some 10,000 pole-mounted devices.

However, such a rebuild would be costly. Early estimates put the figure at about $130 million, including the outside plant and necessary lasers and other electronic equipment. The cost of replacing the drops—the lines from the pole or pedestal to individual customers' homes—was estimated to be about $8 million of that.

Meanwhile, in Washington, Congress was rewriting the Communications Act of 1934, which, with subsequent amendments, regulated all forms of communication: radio, television, telephone, microwave, satellite and others. In 1974, the U.S. Department of Justice had filed an antitrust lawsuit against AT&T, which had been the sole telephone provider in most of the country. In 1984, fearing it might lose the case, AT&T signed a consent decree breaking itself up into seven regional Bell operating companies (RBOC's) plus the long-distance carrier, which retained the AT&T name.

The RBOCs then began casting about for additional revenue sources. One potential money spigot was the cable-television business, a likely venture because they faced upgrading existing plant, some of it almost a century old, and the improved plant would permit the transmission of video signals, with certain limitations.

With that history in mind, legislators were leaning toward removing some of the barriers to competition and allowing telephone companies to enter the cable business, and vice-versa. The Cable Television Consumer Protection and Competition Act of 1992, commonly called the 1992 Cable Act, moved in that direction, but it wasn't until the Telecommunications Act of 1996 that the barriers were breached totally.

Estimates to build a fiber plant that would support telephone traffic would add about $50 million to the initial estimate. Once again, though, the in-grained entrepreneurial spirit first exhibited by Paul Block Sr. in the late 1880s came to the fore.

Toledo, like other Rust Belt cities in the late 1980s and into the '90s, was experiencing rising unemployment and crime, and its manufacturing base, closely tied to the auto industry, was eroding as firms closed or moved south. More importantly, the cable industry was undergoing consolidation as large firms such as Comcast, Time Warner and Charter were gobbling up their smaller brethren, many of which were small to midsize family-owned cable-vision providers.

The Block family was receiving frequent inquiries about the possibility of selling Buckeye to one of the big boys. Could the family continue to operate? The third generation was now running the enterprise—a critical period in many family-owned businesses, as the younger cohort often loses interest, seeks other opportunities or decides to sell and enjoy its gains in a life of leisure.

Cable always has been a capital-intensive industry and Buckeye was no exception, carrying debt to provide the equipment needed. Yet when the time came to commit to the fiber rebuild in the mid-'90s, no one in the family considered any other course of action, Allan Block said.

"Why would you get out of your better business?" he asked. "You can't get out of the better business to keep the one that isn't so good"—that is, the newspaper division, which even in the 1990s was being buffeted by rapid change.

Huge as that $180 million figure was, the Blocks decided to do it. As Allan Block pointed out, there was no certainty that the resulting plant would be able to supply telephone service effectively and competitively, "and in 1997, no one knew what the Internet would be. It wasn't guaranteed that Internet transport would be a good business. You had to make the gamble before you had the certainty."

Years later, he acknowledged that "we had to do it to survive" as a cable business. "It was a choice between spending the capital or selling," he added. "We don't own this business to sell it. We own this business to continue it. My grandfather wanted his business to continue"—a principle handed down to succeeding generations, he noted.

The family's roots in the community were also a prime consideration. "I'm proud that I've stayed in the town that I was born in," Allan Block said. "When you grow up in a place, you become part of the team that community represents. If you get a chance to stay on the team and fight for that team, that's a wonderful thing. I'm essentially fighting for the team that I've always fought for. I'm serving the community that I've always been a part of, going back to my being born here."

The $180 million marked the largest single investment the various Block enterprises have ever made. And while Block is privately owned and doesn't make its finances public, the Buckeye companies—Buckeye CableSystem and Buckeye TeleSystem—have increased in value significantly over the worth of Buckeye CableSystem before the fiber rebuild and entry into the telephone business, though by exactly how much is impossible to determine.

For one thing, cable-company values were depressed in the early 1990s, as planning for the fiber rebuild was starting, because the 1992 Cable Act burdened the broader industry with a host of onerous regulations. In addition, most systems faced a major upgrade of their physical plant to handle the new services coming down the technology-innovation pipeline—the Internet,

telephony, more channels, video on demand and on-screen channel guides—
as well as a general sense that many more currently unimaginable things
were on the way.

While many cable companies upgraded their plant for cable, got it operating smoothly and then ventured into the telephone business, Buckeye plowed
ahead with both the upgrade and phone entry simultaneously. Dave Huey
would later say that this dual effort was the most stressful experience of his
Buckeye career.

The company began to gear up for the monumental task ahead of it.

James Dryden, vice president/engineering, who was nearing retirement
age and had been through two other system-rebuild operations, decided it
would be counterproductive and create additional problems for the company
if he would retire in the middle of such a massive undertaking, so he suggested that Allan Block bring someone else in; Dryden would then step aside
and help bring the new hire up to speed on the company and the project.

Joseph D. Jensen, a Utah native with a bachelor's degree from Brigham
Young University and a master's from Purdue, both in electrical engineering,
was recruited in 1996 to head up the undertaking. He was named executive
vice president and chief technical officer of Buckeye CableSystem and president of Buckeye TeleSystem, with responsibility for the technical platform
and architecture of the Buckeye network.

Jensen brought with him the unique combination of training and experience the company needed. He had joined AT&T Bell Laboratories in 1980 as
a member of its technical staff and held design responsibilities on the 5ESS
Central Office Switch development. In 1985, he moved to Rockwell International (which had no connection to the Rockwell Construction Co. formed by
Buckeye to rebuild the Ohio Bell leaseback system and then the dual-cable
system) as manager of systems engineering for its Network Systems Division. He later spent time at Ameritech (now AT&T once again) as director of
data, access and transport systems for the company's entire five-state region.

At Ameritech, he was involved in technology planning and product development for voice, data and video products, a perfect fit for the vision Block
had for the emerging telecommunications company—not your father's cable
company any longer.

Intensive planning occupied about two years: investigating equipment,
determining what design to use, settling on who would design it, questioning
where the large numbers of contractors could be found and scores of other
tasks.

One of the early, and most critical, jobs was working with Toledo Edison
on pole attachments. Buckeye's dual-cable plant was attached to some
61,000 poles, and federal, state and industry rules and regulations stipulate
the amount of weight on each pole, the spacing between electric and communications lines and a number of other technical requirements.

(With various cablevision expansions and Buckeye TeleSystem needs, the two Buckeye companies are currently attached to almost 87,000 poles owned by, in addition to Toledo Edison: AT&T; the city of Bowling Green; Ohio Edison Illuminating Co.; Hancock-Wood Electrical Cooperative; Verizon Communications; Frontier Communications; Consumers Power; American Electric Power; Detroit Edison; and Embark [Century Link].)

The problem was figuring out how to operate the dual-cable plant so customers would experience no interruption in service while at the same time building the new fiber-optic plant in the same space on the poles. The design called for lowering the existing plant out of the designated position for communications wiring, where space limitations necessitated it, and supporting it on hooks called J-Hooks below the existing plant until sufficient fiber-optic lines and associated electronics could be put in place to activate a node and thereby place a neighborhood in service with the new cable plant.

Toledo Edison had engineering specifications that would not allow such attachments, even temporarily, and Buckeye's engineering staff held countless meetings starting in late 1995 and going deep into 1996, trying unsuccessfully to get Edison's engineers to waiver.

By a stroke of luck for Buckeye, though, Toledo Edison had been in merger talks with Ohio Edison, located in Akron, and that merger was completed in 1996. A new leader, Jim Murray, was sent to Toledo from Akron to become the first regional president of what was to become First Energy. Engineers began meeting with the new staff.

These meetings culminated in a session shortly before Christmas at Edison headquarters on Madison Avenue in Toledo. Participants included Murray; Don Brennan, Edison's operations director; Huey; Jensen; Dryden; and several other Edison and Buckeye executives.

"I remember discussing the issue at length," Murray said. "Don (Brennan) and I suddenly realized that while Toledo Edison's engineering specifications prohibited what Buckeye wanted to do, Ohio Edison's did not. Don and I said, 'Let's just change the regulations to agree with Ohio Edison's. That'll fix everything.'"

"Consider it an early Christmas present," Murray said at the 1996 meeting. The Buckeye executives left the gathering eagerly anticipating the project now that this major hurdle had been cleared.

"I believe that was the start of a long and mutually rewarding relationship between the two companies," Murray said.

"Had Edison refused to let us J-Hook the old plant on a temporary basis while we built the new plant, we would have been faced with a significant challenge," said Jim Brown, Buckeye's current principal engineer-architect and at the time senior manager/engineering operations. Though he couldn't put an exact cost on an Edison refusal, "it would have easily been in the hundreds of thousands of dollars and many months of delays.

"We would have had to manage pole applications and deal with make-readys (paying for necessary changes in pole position by other utilities) for all of our attachments. We did have an application process anyway, though thanks to Edison these were handled as bulk applications (for blocks, or groups, of poles) as opposed to individual pole applications.

"In the case of new attachments, all poles would have had to have been looked at individually for available clearances for another attachment" and would have required make-ready work, he added. "This would have been a significant labor commitment, expense and added project time."

While talks with Edison were going on, however, planning continued. Brown, Dryden and others investigated equipment and designs, which already had taken more than two years. Design, too, had been progressing.

The original thinking was to have all fiber branching out from the NOC to the various end points, but in the early 1990s, Huey was thinking ahead to when Buckeye might want to get into the long-distance access business (carrying the long-distance traffic from a business to the long-distance carrier). At the time, that was the only telephone business a cable company could enter, but there were rumblings that cable legislation then making its way through Congress might open up local traffic as well.

With that in mind, Huey engaged a consulting firm to prepare preliminary plans to make Buckeye's plant ready to be a competitive access provider (CAP) if the decision were ever made to go that route. The plan called for three sonic rings of fiber optics on a backbone, to be able to offer redundancy rather than have all fiber fan out from the head end. The plans were put in a file for possible future use.

When Jensen came on board in 1996, he pulled out those plans and expanded upon them, adding to the sonic rings to make the system even more robust.

This would make the transport more secure in case of an equipment failure, traffic could be rerouted almost instantaneously via another ring. It also was done with an eye toward future business customers who demand the capacity and redundancy, Jensen knew from his earlier experience in the telephone business.

Because of the project's scope and size, Buckeye hired two engineering firms—local Benchmark Technologies, and an arm of Motorola, which supplied much of the electronics Buckeye had used for years—to do much of the design. In the end, the outside firms were responsible for roughly two-thirds of the design; the rest was handled by Buckeye's in-house staff.

At the same time, Rich Hurd, the senior construction coordinator, was walking out the entire system with Edison technicians to see what make-ready and pole replacements would be needed should the Edison dispute be resolved.

"I had to walk every inch of the plant (some 1,900 miles) and check every pole," he said. The National Electrical Code specifies pole-attachment regulations regarding the distance between electrical and communications lines, and if the space allotted to communications wouldn't permit additional lines, other occupants—either the electric or other communications companies— would have to move their lines to allow proper distances, or the pole would have to be replaced. All such costs would be Buckeye's responsibility.

The walkout, while tedious and time-consuming, turned up no major difficulties. "I also had to walk out the Bedford plant when we went to rebuild that," Hurd, who retired in 2003, said of the company's swap with Comcast Communications for the plant that Comcast recently acquired in Monroe County. (See Chapter 5)

While all this was going on, the parts of the existing coaxial system that could be used in the new system—from the proposed nodes to the area addresses to be served by each node—had to be checked by technicians to make sure they would work with the new service's higher frequencies. Replacement of aerial plant was not as big a problem as it would be in the newer areas, in which the cable was buried. Since two coaxial cables were in use, the hope was that if one were bad the companion piece would be viable.

Optimal locations had to be found for the 15 hubs (the Sandusky head end was later converted from a stand-alone facility to another hub on the Toledo system) and 623 nodes, and a contractor, David Allen, a telecommunications consultant who was also a real-estate broker, was hired to contact the landowners in those locations and negotiate easements. This was a lengthy yet vital task. Working with Buckeye's design department, Allen developed a list of two or three potential locations for each node.

The hubs are rather substantial buildings, roughly the size of a mobile home, and had to be sited first. Generally, they were located on school or other public property, or at a business.

The ideal site for the nodes, each approximately the size of a large freezer, was close to electricity, for immediate power, and to gas lines, for eventual connection for the backup generators planned for each node. At the same time, Allen had to concentrate on securing locations quickly, as construction was proceeding apace.

Keeping in mind Buckeye's operating philosophy—mandate, really—to be a good neighbor, Allen would visit each site and try to pick an area that would be least obtrusive to the surrounding residents or businesses. He had to be cognizant of utility and highway rights-of-way, as those would be the most efficient locations.

However, road rights-of-way were less desirable because of the possibility of a traffic mishap knocking a node out of service, as well as the damage winter road salt can cause to electrical components. Yet the equipment had to be located where a technician could access it quickly in an emergency—and the proverbial 3 a.m. backyard visit mentioned earlier is hardly ideal.

Where an easement didn't exist, Allen said, he concentrated primarily on commercial establishments, businesses and schools, with residential property as a last resort. He would send a letter, then visit each property owner personally and explain, with pictures, what the equipment would look like and where Buckeye hoped to place it. "If anyone objected," he said, "we backed off and went to the next possible location."

He also had to meet with government officials in each jurisdiction to explain the process and see if they had any qualms. After a site was agreed upon, a permanent easement had to be prepared, executed and filed in the county recorder's office.

It all took a great deal of time, though Allen says that most property owners were cooperative when they realized what was being planned and saw that Buckeye was trying to work with them to overcome any objections—by painting the structure a requested color or by hiding equipment with landscape shrubbery where necessary, for example.

Buckeye's technical operations crews had to go through the entire 1,900 miles of existing coaxial plant prior to the rebuild to check all cable and drops for suitability for fiber optics' higher frequencies.

All the retrofitting was done by technical operations crews and workers from Metro Fiber and Cable Construction Co., a Buckeye subsidiary formed as part of the fiber-upgrade project. The aerial plant would be all new; Buckeye hired several subcontractors to accomplish this mammoth task on time.

No such enormous project is ever without its fits and starts, of course. Work began in 1997 but soon fell behind schedule and ran over budget. Buckeye was spending hundreds of thousands of dollars, but no customers' homes were being converted. Much of the work done by some of the contractors was of less than sterling quality.

Huey turned once again to Chip Carstensen, just as he had for Buckeye's customer-care overhaul. By that time, Carstensen had been named senior manager of technical operations, and to right the listing ship, on November 2, 1998, he was named vice president of rebuild/technical operations, with full responsibility for the massive fiber rework, as well as continued oversight of field operations for the existing plant.

As often happens on huge infrastructure projects, "silos" began to emerge, with those in charge of the various aspects—design, materials procurement, construction, etc.—not communicating well with one another.

"I demanded total authority over the entire project" to eliminate those silos, Carstensen said, adding that he told Huey, "That means what I say goes, and I don't want to go double-clutching back to you for decisions. And if I fail, go ahead and fire me."

Huey and Allan Block agreed, and "I determined to complete the project on budget, on time and on spec," Carstensen said. People told him he couldn't do it, that he'd have to settle for two out of the three.

"I said I want it on budget and I want it on spec first," he said. "If we flexed anything, it has to be on the time. We would not compromise on doing it on specification. Why? Because we were going to have to maintain it after it was built."

Once Carstensen was fully in charge, he said, "we adopted a motto of 'Rebuild It Right,'" and that became his guiding principle for the next several years.

Within 60 days he was able to double both the number of contractors and the previous production, "and that gave Dave (Huey) confidence," he said. "It took another six months to get it really humming."

Luck was on his side in the form of a succession of mild winters, which permitted much more construction than a typical northern Ohio winter would. Between 1999 and 2002, the National Weather Service at Toledo Express Airport recorded average high temperatures above normal. The seventh-warmest March on record occurred in 2000; the second-warmest November was in 2001; the sixth-warmest November was in 2003; and 2002 was the fourth-warmest year ever recorded in Toledo. November 2001 was the least snowy November on record, with no snowfall whatsoever—optimal conditions for construction, both aerial and underground.

Among Carstensen's early jobs was recruiting and training those additional construction crews. He had made some inroads by hiring a small number of crews, and the earlier subcontractor agreements included requirements about customer-service standards.

"There was a lot of rebuilding (of cable plants) going on, and there were a lot of cowboys out there," said Carstensen, who later would be president of Block Communications until his retirement in 2015. Those cowboys were people who had experience in cable building and would travel the country looking for the next job. Workmanship quality was less important than simply securing the next paycheck.

Many of the contractors who hired those workers were slow to pay; workers might have to wait 90 to 180 days. "It was a cascade of contractors," Carstensen said. "You'd get a big contractor who'd sub to a smaller contractor, who'd sub to even smaller contractors, and by the time the cascade got done and you were the low man on the totem pole, you'd wait six months for your money."

Common sense indicates there was little incentive to do outstanding work. If workers didn't get paid on time, some would simply move on to another part of the country and another job. "We set it up so we paid everybody, and we paid on time, and the word got around that we (had) the money and they didn't have to worry about getting paid," Carstensen said.

Carstensen decided to pick a large company to serve alongside Metro as the other prime contractor. He selected a Findlay, Ohio, firm called American Digital Technologies (ADT), owned by Tony Tate, to ride herd with Metro over the other contractors and workers to ensure standards would be met. "I insisted (ADT) have an office and warehouse (near Metro) in Toledo," Carstensen said, so it would be more readily available and responsive to the assignment.

He tasked ADT with vetting and hiring crews and then training them to Buckeye's standards "down to how to put a bug nut on a fitting"—one of the more elemental tasks in constructing a cablevision system.

This kind of standardization was a monumental undertaking. The contractors hailed from several states, and at one point, some 58 separate crews were working in Buckeye's service area, moving from public rights-of-way to the backyards of the more than 217,000 homes passed by the firm's cable at the time.

Roughly 25 percent of subscribers' homes had to be rewired, at Buckeye's expense, to replace aging and unsuitable interior wiring. Even though in many cases subscribers did some of their own wiring using inferior cable, Buckeye bore the expense to bring the entire system up to date so that every customer would have good-quality pictures—or as good as a variety of older television sets could display, at any rate.

Approximately 90 percent of apartments, condominiums, hotels and motels (multiple-dwelling units, or MDUs) were rewired, said Jim Wolsiffer, now director of technical operations, who at the time was a member of a technical operations crew, or tech ops. The only MDUs not overhauled were those in which the building or complex owner, for whatever reason, refused to let the work progress.

Two subcontractors were brought on to do the complex MDU rewiring. First, each unit of the MDU had to be visited by a crew, which hung on every door an explanation of the work to be done, the reason access to the unit was needed and a timetable. A vacant apartment, if there were one, would be used as a staging area where tools and materials could be stored.

In most cases, the contractors arranged with the MDU's on-site manager to provide a master key that would enable workers to gain access to units when a resident wasn't home—and although this process soon became routine, one macabre incident underscored that this was far from ordinary work.

A subcontractor crew entered one apartment, but, seeing the tenant asleep, left. In subsequent checks throughout the day, the man was still reclining. It wasn't until the next day, when he still hadn't moved, that the crew realized he was dead. They called the rescue squad—and afterward, the building manager inexplicably chastised the crew for calling the squad and bringing undue attention to the complex, Wolsiffer said later.

Crews replaced all substandard drops, the cables that go from the main-line taps on poles or in pedestals to subscribers' homes. Virtually every drop in East Toledo was replaced, as the earlier system inspection had found the area plagued by poorly shielded cable.

Of course, activating the new system had to be coordinated with decommissioning the old system in such a way that no customers would be out of service. Buckeye engineers knew that after the new system was in place, many customers would face the problem of their in-house wiring and electronics not being suitable for the resulting higher frequencies. In such cases, the company performed any needed upgrades at no charge to the customer. Early estimates had pegged that aspect of the project at $1.5 million.

As part of early planning, Buckeye had made preparations to construct a new head end, termed the Network Operations Center (NOC), and in February 1996, the 17,415-square-foot state-of-the-art facility, which cost some $5 million to construct and contained approximately $17 million in electronic equipment, opened.

The building, situated in front of the small, decades-old existing head end and right beside Angola Road in Toledo, was designed to withstand a Category 5 tornado and to be so well-grounded that lightning could never penetrate it or affect the electrical system and equipment inside. All reinforcing steel in the floor, roof and concrete walls was welded together, creating a giant steel cage that was then grounded at several positions on all sides of the building.

A 600-kilowatt diesel-powered generator was installed to provide power in the event Edison power was ever interrupted. The generator, almost as big as a train locomotive engine and sounding quite a bit like one when running, stood on a rubber-cushioned concrete pad separate from the rest of the floor in the NOC to eliminate any possible vibration problems.

A second generator, this one capable of supplying 2,000 kilowatts, was installed in June 2012, and a third 2,000-kilowatt unit followed in early 2014, at which time the original 600-kilowatt generator was decommissioned.

The generators are tested by running them for 30 minutes every week, and twice a year they're load-tested, during which the electrical use of the entire building is transferred off Edison power and put onto the generators. Each generator has a tank that holds 2,650 gallons of diesel fuel; those 5,300 gallons will run the generators for 48 hours at 50 percent load, according to Kevin McCormick, Buckeye's real estate and purchasing manager.

Total demand for the building is between 50 and 60 percent of the generators' capacity, said Doug Ward, vice president/network and field operations. Thus, if necessary, the generators could be run one after the other, supplying almost 66 hours of electricity with the fuel on hand.

In the event of an emergency, a local fuel supplier and a backup supplier in Detroit are under contract to refill the tanks as needed. The generators have been pressed into emergency service a couple dozen times since the NOC opened; the longest such period was about 24 hours, Ward said.

The one-story structure was intended to serve both Buckeye CableSystem and Buckeye TeleSystem, and designed to accommodate future switching equipment and telephone operations in the southwest portion of the building; cable equipment and operations would be at the northwest end, with offices for both lining the east side. To ensure uninterrupted service, redundant fiber-optic lines were laid to and from the structure, buried deep in concrete branching out east and west on Angola Road.

The original fiber backbone, roughly 50 miles long, was designed for redundancy, so that any damage to the fiber from a traffic accident, for example, would not interrupt any communications or video transmissions. The signals would simply transfer to another part of the redundant ring, and the customer would not notice any interruption of voice, video or data.

Since that original design, the fiber backbone has increased to 2,147 sheath miles, with 1,881 in Northwest Ohio and Southeast Michigan and another 266 in the Sandusky area. ("Sheath miles" indicates the number of miles from start to finish of a fiber route. The term is distinct from "fiber miles," a much greater number given that each sheath can contain up to 192 individual fiber strands. Thus, one mile of 192-count fiber would constitute one sheath mile but 192 fiber miles. Buckeye's system today consists of 94,436 fiber miles today, according to Gary Kasubski, senior manager, net-work design engineering.) In total, Buckeye operates 3,476 sheath miles of plant, including both fiber and coaxial cable, with 3,013 miles in the Toledo area and 463 miles in the Erie County area.

As nice and modern as the NOC structure was, both the phone and video businesses grew so fast that it soon became necessary to expand it, and an 18,133-square-foot, two-story addition, sheathed in handsome blue glass, opened in February 2001. The additional building and equipment represented a sizeable Buckeye investment in what to this day is Toledo's most advanced communications facility.

Moving the existing plant, altering poles and erecting new cable had already started when construction of the first hub began on July 22, 1997, at Arlington School at 700 Toronto Avenue in Toledo.

The hubs supply service to approximately 20,000 homes each, and the redundant routes designed into the fibers feeding them mean that none of the hubs should ever suffer a service outage caused by a cut cable, traffic acci-dent or electrical problem.

The contractors had to make two passes through the entire 1,900-mile system: one to lower the existing plant into the J-Hook arrangement that Toledo Edison's Jim Murray approved in 1996, and a second to build the new plant. Work occurred in 217,000 backyards over the course of the re-build, which started in 1996 and was completed in early 2002. A complete rebuild of the Erie County system was started in 2003 and finished two years later.

Buckeye had an intensive quality-control program in place; its crews regularly inspected all contractors' work. Given the immensity of the project and the speed with which it was completed, though, some mistakes and damage to private property were inevitable. Buckeye, forever cognizant of its reputation as a responsible corporate citizen, implemented an equally intensive damage-control and remediation program. The goal was to settle damage claims as quickly as possible, in the landowners' favor. Fritz Byers, the company attorney at the time, noted at the Buckeye board's 2002 year-end meeting that it had finished the rebuild without a single lawsuit having been filed against it.

BUCKEYE BITS

The Chopper Isn't Coming; It's Been Hijacked

Engineers realize—as do most people, in fact—that the best-laid plans can go awry, and sometimes for the strangest reasons.

None were stranger, perhaps, than during the 1975 planning for the microwave link to the proposed northeast hub on Creekside Avenue, near Lagrange Street and Detroit Avenue. There, work was mysteriously interrupted due to a jailbreak at Southern Michigan Prison at Jackson—a daring escape reminiscent of *Breakout,* a movie released earlier that year.

That film, starring Charles Bronson, Robert Duvall, Randy Quaid, Jill Ireland, John Huston and Sheree North, revolved around a plot in which a woman hired a bush pilot in Brownsville, Texas, to fly a helicopter into a Mexican prison and pluck her husband out.

Buckeye had contracted with a helicopter firm in Plymouth, Michigan, to fly the route from Angola Road to Creekside. The chopper was to pick up three people working on the project at the former Wagon Wheel Airport in Lambertville, Michigan.

The Buckeye party consisted of Chris Barker, chief engineer; John Nicholas, assistant chief engineer, and Jim Dryden, at the time foreman with Rockwell Construction. The plan was to have the helicopter hover at the height of the proposed tower on Creekside to determine if the trio could see any physical obstructions between there and the top of the Angola Road tower. They were then supposed to fly the straight-line route back to the Angola tower to make sure it was a feasible track for the microwave path.

Standing at the Lambertville airport, now known as Toledo Suburban Airport, for the scheduled 12:30 p.m. pickup on Friday, June 6, 1975, the threesome waited . . . and waited . . . and waited.

Barker tried calling the Plymouth firm at 1 p.m. to find out where the chopper was but couldn't get through. He then called the Buckeye office and asked the receptionist there to keep trying to reach it. Several minutes later, she called back.

Return to the office, she told them; the helicopter would not be coming. It had been hijacked and used in the daring escape at the Jackson lock-up. The pilot was ordered at gunpoint to fly into the prison, land, pick up someone and fly out quickly—a real-life *Breakout.*

"We all had a laugh, thinking it was a joke," Barker told a *Blade* reporter at the time. "But she assured us it was no joke."

The pilot, Richard Jackson, was ordered to land at a waiting car several miles away, where the hijacker and the escapee, who was in his second year of a 10-year term for fraud, sprayed mace in Jackson's face, then ran to the waiting car. However, in the confusion, the convict missed the ride and spent the next 30 hours wandering the countryside before he was apprehended in a Leslie, Michigan, bar, two miles north of the prison.

The Buckeye trio, who had used the Plymouth firm for other surveying jobs, chartered a second survey helicopter for the next day. Luck was not with them, though, as the helicopter—the same one used in the jailbreak—was grounded because of mechanical problems and no other craft was available.

Finally, on Monday, the helicopter met the group on schedule.

"Don't worry," Dryden joked to the pilot as he boarded, "none of us has any guns."

The pilot was the same man who had flown into the prison four days earlier. "That's OK," Jackson replied, "cause I have one under the seat. I was never so scared in my life."

The Creekside tower site was tangentially involved in another underworld escapade when Detroit mobsters killed a man in the Motor City, then buried his body across the road from the site.

Otherwise, the Night Shift Was Fairly Quiet

A would-be thief got a surprise early in the morning on November 6, 2011, when he tried to break in to Buckeye's Southwyck headquarters to steal televisions from the lobby.

About 4:10 a.m., he took a large rock from the landscaping in front of the building, smashed the glass beside the entry door, crawled through the shattered glass, went through the outer lobby, broke the window beside the door to the customer lobby and began removing TV sets from the wall, putting them next to the broken window.

He didn't know that the building wasn't unoccupied or that it had a number of security cameras trained on the entrances. He was also ignorant of the fact that the security system was monitored around the clock from the computer center in the back of the building.

The quick-thinking computer operator on duty, Sally Lavoy (now the asset administrator in the IT department), saw the first window shatter and immediately called police, then called the other employees working overnight and instructed them to go to the second floor and lock themselves in an office or conference room. The operations center where Lavoy was working is a secure area, so she considered herself safe.

The first Toledo policeman to arrive crawled through the broken window into the outer lobby, and as he approached the second broken window, he drew his gun and ordered the thief to stop. The scofflaw threw a television set through the broken window at the officer, jumped over the customer-service counter and started through the customer service-area toward the rear of the building.

As the officer tried to unlatch the gate to follow, his weapon discharged accidentally. A bullet hit the floor and ricocheted up through a cubicle wall in the customer-service area before lodging in a second cubicle wall.

Paul Block, Sr. as young man. Courtesy of Block Communications, Inc.

From left, Paul Block, Jr., William Block, Sr., and Allan Block. Photos Courtesy of Toledo Blade, Block Communications, Inc.

Flatiron Building, top, in New York City, site of the office of Paul Block, Inc., early 1900s; Buckeye Network Operations Center, Toledo. Flatiron Building photo used by permission W. W. Rock/National Geographic Creative, Network Operations Center. Courtesy of Buckeye.

Initial office, top, at 1122 N. Byrne Road in 2014 photo; Southwyck Boulevard office occupied in 1986. Byrne Road Office Photo by author, Southwyck Office. Courtesy of Buckeye.

Workmen erect first satellite receive dish at Angola Road in 1978. Toledo Blade
Photo Reprinted with permission.

Receive antenna being hoisted onto Angola Road Tower, 1978; Inset, Lamar Gossett, of Covington, KY, carrying antenna, being pulled to top of tower. Toledo Blade Photos Reprinted with permission.

Barbara Hoover delivers news on 6th Grade Report in 1974. Toledo Blade Photo Reprinted with permission.

BCSN Pregame interview at St. John's Jesuit High School. At desk, from left, Ken Watlington, Tom Cole, both of BCSN, and Doug Pearson, St. John's football coach. Photo by author.

CATV Area Being Expanded

Coaxial Cable To Begin Carrying TV To Home Sets In Toledo Tomorrow

Will Relay Signals Picked Up By New 350-Foot Tower

Community Antenna Television (CATV) will become a reality in Toledo tomorrow when subscribers of Buckeye Cablevision, Inc., receive the first programs brought into their homes by coaxial cable.

The beginning of operations by Buckeye coincides closely with the March 1 target date established several months ago by the Ohio Bell Telephone Co., which engineered and wired most of the system.

Leo Hoarty, system manager, said the CATV service currently is available in an area bounded by West Central Avenue on the north; Secor Road on the west; Nebraska Avenue on the south, and Detroit Avenue on the east.

Representatives of Buckeye are calling on residents of the area to provide them with additional information about CATV and to invite them to subscribe to the service.

Buckeye Cablevision is a corporation owned by The Toledo Blade Co. and Cox Cable-

—Blade Photo

LEO HOARTY
To manage cablevision firm

vision Corp., of Atlanta, Ga. The Blade is the major stockholder of Buckeye Cablevision. Cox Cablevision Corp. is a wholly owned division of Cox

Broadcasting Corp. Cox Broadcasting also is associated with Kaiser Industries in joint ownership of the Kaiser Cox Co., of Phoenix, Ariz. in the manufacture of electronic equipment for cable vision systems.

The start of CATV operations comes shortly after completion of a 350-tower (978 feet above sea level) off King Road between West Central Avenue and West Bancroft Street in Sylvania Township.

Although CATV service is currently limited to the one operational area, Mr. Hoarty said that Ohio Bell crews already are at work engineering and wiring other sections of the Toledo metropolitan area. Service will be available to residents in those areas as work is completed. It is estimated that the entire system will be completed within 12 to 15 months.

Besides Toledo, Buckeye has permits granted by city councils to operate its cable vision system in Maumee, Sylvania, and Perrysburg. In addition, applications for permits are pending in other Toledo area municipalities.

Turn to Page 5, Col. 1

Announcing initiation of service, March 15, 1966. Toledo Blade Article Reprinted with permission.

Bill Aubry in 1966 photo in front of demonstration trailer parked at Door and Secor. Courtesy of Buckeye.

John Bylow unloads cables from Buckeye mobile unit (converted Blade Circulation truck) preparatory to cablecasting game in 1972 photo. Toledo Blade Photo Reprinted with permission.

2014 Photo of the Rev. John Roberts, Buckeye's first customer. Photo by author.

Assemblage of Satellite receive dishes at Angola Road tower site in 2014. Photo by author.

Advertisement from early 1970s. Courtesy of Buckeye.

Top row: First remote, called CableSystem Controller, and Disney Channel set-top descrambler; Middle Row: Showtime Channel set-top descrambler and first Tocom converter box with Impulse Pay-Per-View set-top descrambler box; Bottom: Worldgate keyboard. Courtesy of Buckeye.

Paul W. Smith in early ad for remote controller. Courtesy of Buckeye.

Dennis Robedeau, right, and Ken Vedder prepare gear for BCSN trailers prior to athletic events. Photo by author.

Panels where thousands of fiber optic lines terminate in Angola Road Network Operations Center. Photo by author.

Neil McCormick operates camera at athletic event in 1972. Toledo Blade Photo
Reprinted with permission.

Scott Sandstrom, senior editor and videographer with Buckeye Production department, holding jacket from his days as a University of Toledo student working on the university's Channel 10/B. Courtesy of Frederick Laginess.

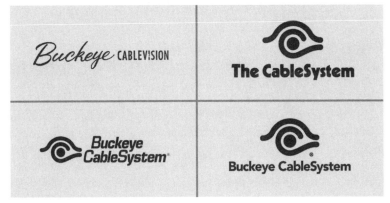

Buckeye logos through the years: Top Left, 1970; top right, 1975; lower left, 1996; lower right, 2004. Courtesy of Buckeye.

Buckeye presidents: Top Row from left: Wayne Current, John Karl, Dave Huey; Bottom Row: W.H. "Chip" Carstensen, Bradley Mefferd, Jeff Abbas. Paul Block, Jr., pictured elsewhere, was the second president. Courtesy of Toledo Blade, Buckeye.

Special 50th Anniversary Logo. Courtesy of Buckeye.

Some 500 dishes fastened to billboard for Buckeye dish buy-back program, initiated to get customers to return to cable from satellite-dish service. Courtesy of Buckeye.

Paul W. Smith in Limelight Tonight advertisement. Courtesy of Buckeye.

Chapter Seven

"We'll Do Whatever We Can to Help Toledo Reach Its Full Potential"

Voice, Video, Data, Home Security:
Fiber Optics Boost Buckeye's Capabilities

On April 21, 1998, the James Stegeman family of South Toledo became the first customer of Buckeye CableSystem's new fiber-optic 125-channel analog and digital cable system—at that time a state-of-the-art telecommunications network that Buckeye predicted, accurately, would be an infrastructure for the twenty-first century.

The new system offered the Stegemans and the more than 130,000 other Buckeye customers who would be converted over the next four years a package that served up more choices, greater clarity and reliability, and access to many new services, such as high-speed Internet and interactive TV, as well as many more in the ensuing years.

With an advanced analog converter and remote control, the modern system offered an interactive program guide containing several days' worth of program listings and automatic VCR scheduling to tape programs, and enabled the viewer to watch one program while taping another. It was a significant change from the limited dual-cable system with 38 analog channels, no remote control and an A/B switch that had to be changed if you wanted to watch channels on the second cable. And it was worlds beyond the 10 channels the first customers had in 1966.

While users of the existing system had access to premium channels like HBO and Showtime, priced between $8 and $10 per channel per month, the new one offered a programming tier called SuperChannels, which offered *Bravo, Food Network, Great American Country, SPEEDVISION, ESPNews,*

Game Show Network, Romance Classics and *Turner Classic Movies*—all for
$2.99 a month.

SuperChannels also included 32 digital-music channels, which Buckeye
boasted would deliver CD-like clarity and quality, and could be accessed
even while the TV was off. If the set was on, the screen displayed the song,
artist and information about purchasing a CD containing the music. Each
channel featured a different genre of music—jazz, classical, rock, blues, hits,
dance and more—according to Ellen Jackson, who was director of marketing
and programming at the time.

While the programming additions made possible by fiber optics were
important, the most significant feature for many customers was the introduction of high-speed Internet access. On July 1, 1999, Buckeye rolled out a
modem service offering 512 kilobits per second (Kbps), some 20 times faster
than the then-prevalent dialup access through traditional telephone lines,
which were typically 28.8 or 56 Kbps.

In the non-rebuilt areas, customers were supplied with a modem utilizing
telephone lines for transmission, which was replaced with the modern two-
way modem as each area was switched to the fiber system.

The initial fiber-borne service was 512 Kbps downstream (from the Internet to the customer) and 128 Kbps upstream.

While that was a tremendous breakthrough and very popular, faster upstream and downstream speeds followed regularly. Starting in November
2010, Buckeye customers could get 50 megabits per second (Mbps) downstream and 3 Mbps upstream; by February 2012, those speeds were 110
Mbps downstream and 5 Mbps upstream. The 50 Mbps upstream was increased to 60 Mbps in March, 2013, and to 66 Mbps in August of that year.

In December 2013, the 5 Mbps upstream speeds for both the 66 and 110
Mbps advertised services were increased to 10 Mbps. The 110 Mbps is
approximately 220 times faster than the original 512 Kbps, which seemed
unbelievably fast to customers at the time.

In reality, the speeds are roughly 10 percent higher than advertised, Joe
Jensen, executive vice president/chief technology officer of Block Communications, said. "It boosts customer satisfaction when they get more than they
pay for" when they run speed tests and see the greater performance, he said.

Buckeye introduced Buckeye Express—the formal name for its high-
speed Internet service—in mid-1999, and by January 2000 had enrolled
1,785 customers. Buckeye Express was offered in Sandusky starting in August 2001; by the end of the year, 15,057 customers in both Toledo and
Sandusky had signed up. Growth thereafter was continuous: subscribers
numbered 22,565 at the end of 2002; 37,702 at the end of 2004; 98,157 at the
end of 2007; and 107,761 at the end of 2009.

By early 2015 some 130,000 customers got their Internet access via
Buckeye's fiber-rich plant.

The rebuild upgrade that made it all possible was the largest single project in the 31-year history of Buckeye CableSystem, in the 115-year history of Block Communications and its predecessors—and by the Block family.

"This is a big gamble," Allan Block said at the May 6, 1997, rebuild kickoff announcement. "But I was born in Toledo, I live in Toledo, and I expect to die here. We have great faith that there will be a dynamic economic future for the Toledo metropolitan area. As a locally owned and operated company, we will do whatever we can not only to help restore Toledo's economy, but to allow this community to reach its full economic potential and greatness."

The project has done much to put Toledo in an unparalleled competitive position, according to Doug Born, vice president of the Regional Growth Partnership (RGP), the area's primary economic-development agency.

Mark Arend, editor in chief of *Site Selection* magazine in Norcross, Georgia, agrees that the availability of fiber-optics is an important economic determinant for companies planning to expand or relocate. "(Fiber availability) was more of an issue before fiber became so ubiquitous. When it wasn't so available it was a major factor, but now it's just expected," he said. "However, data centers do locate in places that are fiber-rich."

One of the first, and largest, customers for the new fiber was the Northwood data center of TNS, the United Kingdom-based market-research and business-analysis firm that operates in more than 80 countries worldwide.

"Having Buckeye's fiber was very important to us," said Brian McGuire, director of IT services at the Northwood installation. "We were the primary data center for TNS, and we had 700 to 800 phones, plus the high-speed Internet, which was vital to our business."

"Fiber has become a critical staple in modern office, industrial and integrated-distribution operations," Born said. "Its presence is essential (for companies) to be connected to related facilities in a real-time format, as well as to customers and suppliers. In short, access to fiber has become an assumption in site-selection circles and is considered basic industrial/commercial infrastructure much as electric, water and public sewer. The reverse of this is that sites that do not have fiber are at a significant disadvantage unless arrangements for extending service can be readily finalized."

When companies are looking for a place to locate, in other words, they naturally give a close eye to the available connectivity. Buckeye's multimillion-dollar investment in Northwest Ohio's communications future has therefore been a major draw for businesses looking for a home.

"The infrastructure always comes first," Joe Perlaky, formerly a business-development specialist with the RGP and now a grants administrator with the University of Toledo, said in 1997. "Without the infrastructure, there's no development. So I think it says a lot about Buckeye that they're willing to make this major investment in the community's infrastructure, well before they get any rate of return on it."

"Anything this community can do to become more wired and connected is a positive," Mark V'Soske, who retired in mid-2014 as president of the Toledo Area Chamber of Commerce, said when the project was announced. "It's building the infrastructure that can help existing companies grow into the tech area, and attract new companies."

In addition to the community-wide economic-development edge Buckeye's system offered, the upside for residential customers was significant. In 2009, the company began entrée into Fiber to the Home (FTTH), replacing the coaxial-cable drop with a fiber-optic line running all the way into the customer's house.

(In industry lexicon, FTTH, FTTP and FTTX are more or less the same, contingent upon the specific use. FTTH means fiber to the house or home; FTTP stands for fiber to the premises; and FTTX indicates fiber to the "X"— business, residence or a stand-alone point where service is needed, the end point where the optical signal is converted to an electrical signal capable of reception on a television, modem or other device.)

In its quest to provide FTTH economically, in 2009 Buckeye conducted the first nationwide test of a new concept that quickly and seamlessly removes the coax cable center conductor and dielectric material, providing operators with a conduit through which they can easily deploy fiber optic cable without costly new construction or excavation and upgrade of existing lines.

The technologically unique approach used a proprietary lubricant under pressure to separate the dielectric within the coax cable from the outer aluminum shield. The dielectric and center conductor are pulled out, leaving an empty conduit for easy placement of fiber optic cable.

"The process is highly efficient, and the most significant legacy cable upgrade technique developed to date," Joe Jensen, Block Communications' chief technology officer, said at the time. If it proves out, he said he could foresee the technology as "an innovative tool that will allow us to deploy a cost-effective fiber-to-the-home architecture in areas currently served by a traditional buried hybrid fiber coax (HFC) network."

However, the firm that held licenses on the process was unable to further develop it and subsequently turned the technology over to another firm, which in 2015 is in the process of advancing it. Nevertheless, Buckeye once again was on the leading edge in trying a new technology.

The first FTTH test was installed in early 2010 in Jensen's home; other customers were able to schedule installation appointments starting that May. By mid-2014, more than 800 homes and about a dozen commercial customers were being served by FTTP.

This technology has several advantages—growth high among them, said Gary Kasubski, senior manager, network design engineering. "The FTTP drop opens the door to unparalleled capabilities regarding the amount of services that can be supplied," he said. New technology is focusing on Internet Protocol Television (IPTV), which will "change the way we deliver signal across our system," he added.

Ultimately gone will be the analog channels, as well as the QAM channels. (QAM stands for "quadrature amplitude modulation" and refers to the equipment that creates the formats by which digital channels are encoded for transmission to the home. Such modulation equipment allows 3 high-definition channels or 10 to 12 standard-definition channels to be transmitted in the bandwidth of a 6 MHz broadcast channel.)

"Everything will be delivered via Internet Protocol at ever-increasing speeds, which mandate a better delivery method," said Kasubski, who joined Buckeye in 1981 and has held a number of roles in both technical operations and engineering. "We're (currently) researching which would be the best and most economical way to achieve this."

From the customer's perspective, increased system reliability is one obvious advantage of the new technology. Traditionally, the coaxial-cable plant delivers the signal to each home with active RF (Radio Frequency) devices or amplifiers in cascades. Before the introduction of fiber optics, these amplifiers, as noted earlier, were subject to noise interference and failure, and could be in cascades of up to 30 or 35 amplifiers—a recipe for trouble. Fiber has reduced the maximum number of amplifiers in a cascade to five, but each still is a potential failure point.

With the new FTTP deployment, by contrast, just one active device feeds a given customer, Kasubski said. "Going forward, as we continue to improve delivery methods, we will be offering services over PON (Passive Optical Network), meaning that there are no active (transmission) devices between the launch equipment and the customer."

Cost per mile to construct fiber is about the same as with the old coaxial plant, ranging from roughly $45,600 per mile in rural settings to roughly $66,000 per mile in urban areas, Kasubski said, while the FTTH drop to the customer's home costs about $350 more than for a coaxial drop. A number of variables enter into the equation, he said, so it is difficult to make a precise apples-to-apples comparison. For instance, the company constructs fiber in bundles ranging from 12 to 192 fibers depending on housing density and a number of other factors. Thus, splicing costs vary greatly.

And while customers will have more services, faster delivery and better system reliability, the advantages to the company include less power consumption, Kasubski said—up to 95 percent savings over traditional coaxial cable.

"Also, there is no noise (interference) generated by line equipment or amplifiers, nor are there any ingress signal issues with the fiber delivery as there are with coax," he added. "Signal ingress" occurs when another RF signal, such as that of a mobile radio or from a broadcast radio or television aerial, gains entry to Buckeye's system through a faulty connector or a break in the shielding around the coaxial cable.

FTTP deployment also has led to a drastic reduction in service calls to customers served by the new method. From the initial testing and tweaking of the original employee hookups in 2010 to mid-2014, the field technicians had received exactly one service call from the almost 900 customers, according to Jim Wolsiffer, Buckeye's director of technical operations.

That problem, in the Perrysburg area, involved a fiber-optic line that needed to be disconnected and the connections cleaned. It affected 32 homes at most, Wolsiffer said, manifesting itself in distortions, especially on modem services, and did not result in complete loss of services.

An additional advantage, Kasubski said, is that with FTTP, it's possible to deliver quality service to customers whose properties sit far off the existing trunk lines. With coaxial cable, if a customer's house sits at great distance from the road, often an additional utility pole or poles would have to be installed, and distribution cable built partway back to the home before a cable "drop," the pencil-sized cable that actually goes into the house, could be placed. In some cases, customers were asked to pay some of the additional costs. This added sometimes tremendous expense—and the problem disappears with FTTP.

Going forward, the company plans to implement FTTP in expansion areas not currently served by Buckeye's coaxial cable in any part of the delivery system. An FTTP installation typically adds several hundred dollars to Buckeye's cost for an average residential hookup, though the customer sees no additional charge beyond the standard rate-card figure for a standard installation. But FTTP's lower service, powering and maintenance costs, coupled with the new, faster services available to the customer, make it a good step forward, Kasubski said.

One potentially groundbreaking service enabled by the robust fiber-optic network was announced late in 2014, when Buckeye and *The Blade* rolled out Buckeye1, a unique partnership with Apple in which subscribers to Buckeye's 50 Mbps Internet service received an Apple iPad Mini preloaded with apps to access Buckeye and BCSN sports programming, read *The Blade* electronically and order items such as pizza from advertisers, merely by touching an icon on the screen.

Buckeye1 marked Apple's first collaboration with a local Internet/media firm, as well as the first time Apple delivered a preloaded device with a specific media connection. "Apple, in spite of its success and size, still is willing to deal with innovators at the level we're at," Allan Block said at the time.

Company officials had approached Apple about a year earlier with the idea, which piqued the interest of the California firm and was the impetus for it to develop the specialized apps. One of those, the BCSN Watch App was introduced early in 2015 for Apple and Android devices. It features BCSN archived content on demand plus the live streams of all programming.

And looking to an uncertain future (See Chapter 13), Buckeye in late 2014 introduced Buckeye Brainiacs, a program under which the company will take care of customer-owned electronic equipment, such as computers and smart phones, that use Buckeye Express.

The service concentrates on four areas: malware removal, computer and tablet optimization, in-home networking support (including all devices connected to the network), and customer education, said Rick Mlcek, vice president/operations and treasurer, who heads up the project.

Brainiacs requires an initial one-year contract and costs $10 a month for unlimited help requests; when a problem can't be fixed over the phone, a technician will go to a customer's home. After the first year, customers can continue the service month to month.

Buckeye continues to offer free support service for problems related to the delivery of any of its products, including Buckeye Express, video services and residential telephone, as well as on any equipment owned by Buckeye. "If the cable or Internet goes out, we'll still come for free," Mlcek said. "(Brainiacs) will take care of the customer's own equipment connected to Buckeye Express."

Buckeye also established Brainiacs pricing for individual service calls for customers who don't wish to sign up for the monthly fee, he added. Those prices are significantly lower than rates for similar services offered by commercial computer stores, he pointed out, but noted that unlimited service calls offered under the $10 monthly plan likely will result in significant savings for the consumer.

"Buckeye Brainiacs is a service for the customer who, for example, bought a new computer and has difficulty connecting a printer and needs help installing a new printer driver, or whose computer has been infected with a virus and he or she doesn't know how to remove it," Mlcek said.

"In the past, because it wasn't Buckeye's equipment, we were hesitant to undertake such an operation, but we felt that we should support everything our customers want to do with our core service, Buckeye Express. Whatever interacts with our service, we'll support it for them," he said. Customers also can take equipment to Buckeye for repairs if that's more convenient than having a technician visit their home.

Buckeye is one of only a handful of cable firms nationwide to offer such a service.

While Buckeye had been in the traditional home-security business (telephone-line-based burglary, fire and flooding alerts monitored by a central station that would summon aid if needed) for seven years from late in 1999 to 2007, the new, fully developed fiber-rich plant enabled the company to re-enter the home-security market in a more robust way that offered more than just an alarm service.

The rollout in mid-2014 of Buckeye Smart Home ("Smart" standing for Security Monitoring and Automation in Real Time) meant that in addition to traditional fire- and burglar-alarm service, customers now had the ability to monitor their homes or small businesses from afar.

The Security aspect offers round-the-clock monitoring by an Underwriters Laboratory-certified station for burglary, fire and medical emergencies, while the Home Automation feature enables customers to control their thermostats, lights and appliances from anywhere by using a device such as an iPad, smartphone or computer, according to Phil Giordano, Buckeye's director of residential security, who joined the company in August 2013. Customers also receive alerts if their basements begin to flood or carbon monoxide reaches a dangerous level.

The Video Surveillance portion offers customers the ability to check on the children's babysitter or pets remotely, or just check various areas of the house. The system also allows residents to view anyone at the door.

Each service is accompanied by personal access to a portal with which the customer can set specific preferences. For example, the system can send a video clip to a mobile device whenever the back door opens, enabling the customer to see when his children get home safely from school, or change the temperature on the home thermostat when the motion detector first senses movement after a certain time in the morning.

Equipment includes a router and touch screen with a backup battery, cellular backup and siren, three door or window sensors, a yard sign and window decals, as well as a motion sensor, carbon-monoxide detector, smoke detector, lamp module, appliance module and other warning devices, indoor and outdoor cameras, keypads, remote locks and more, depending on which services the customer desires.

Buckeye's earlier foray into home security began in December 1998 when it acquired Corporate Protection Services (CPS), a 12-year-old Toledo firm started by Perrysburg resident Kim Klewer, who earlier had been a manager on the corporate-security staff of Owens-Illinois.

CPS had a robust corporate clientele, including the worldwide facilities of Nestle, the well-known Swiss food company; the Detroit Institute of Arts; the former Medical College of Ohio (now part of the University of Toledo); Owens Corning; BP Oil; and Roadway Express. It was working to develop a substantial local residential client base, and Klewer and his staff stayed on to run the business after Buckeye's purchase.

Buckeye's intent was to meld its cable business with the residential alarm capability and provide residents with voice, video, data and alarm services via Buckeye's fiber-fed single coaxial cable going into the house.

In the summer of 2003, management decided to concentrate on the residential side of the business, and on January 1, 2004, spun off the commercial side to Klewer, who named his new company Asset Protection Corp.

Barry Webne, an Ottawa Hills man with an accounting background and a fair amount of management experience, was put in charge of the now totally residential operations of CPS, which had been rolled into the Block empire as a subsidiary of Buckeye.

One part of Buckeye's strategy was to create a program for developers and builders in which Buckeye and CPS would do a complete installation on new homes, either free or at very low cost, making the homes ready for any level of the four services envisioned. Homebuyers would then be offered a promotional deal on the hope that they'd become loyal, longtime Buckeye customers for both communications and residential-security services.

Despite repeated attempts by Buckeye executives to get Webne to detail the costs for the security portion of the concept so the company could roll out a comprehensive plan, he always had more pressing issues, he said, which delayed progress on the plan.

After an exhausting interval, it became evident what was occupying Webne's "valuable" time: He was cooking the books and had embezzled more than $1 million from the company. On February 5, 2008, in U.S. District Court in Toledo, he was charged with one count of mail fraud. On April 23, he pleaded guilty; on October 20, he was sentenced to five years and three months in prison and ordered to make restitution for the $1,138,334.90 he had embezzled.

Brian Rex, who had been treasurer of Buckeye CableSystem and was named first treasurer of Buckeye TeleSystem when it was established, began delving into the CPS operation to assess the damage and recommend a recovery plan.

After several months spent examining every transaction since Buckeye bought CPS, Rex recommended that the company shed the operation altogether due to a number of operational problems, not the least of which was the fact that self-contained monitoring stations lacked the desired economies of scale to operate profitably. The firm was sold in 2007.

In the end, though, Buckeye was able to roll out Smart Home in 2014 with more robust features than the old CPS concept, including remote surveillance and off-site home-system control. It's also a Buckeye product rather than a separate entity, as CPS had been.

Among the additional advantages of the fiber-rich system was the ability to add many more channels and to conserve bandwidth to enable even more programming and other high-tech services. To foster such attributes, Cable-

Labs, a nonprofit research-and-development creation of the cable industry, began promoting something called switched digital video (SDV).

With traditional cable service, each channel goes to each home, whether anyone is watching or not. With SDV, homes are divided into service areas, which closely parallel the node-service areas. Equipment in each node enables the signal to pass only to those homes in which someone wants to watch a particular channel. Thus, the bandwidth occupied by that channel is available for different programming in other homes in that service area. In short, unwatched channels are not transmitted but are available if someone wants to watch them.

Planning for SDV began in 2008, said Jim Brown, principal engineer-architect, and it became available to customers on December 6, 2010, with 85 channels. By the start of 2014, some 230 channels were SDV, of which 60 percent were standard-definition and the remainder high-definition.

Networks such as ESPN, CNN and others, which are fed from satellites, always had been transmitted in digital format, with cable companies "down-converting" them to analog so they could be seen on analog TV sets. Broadcasters also transmitted their over-the-air signal in analog format, but the FCC ordered all broadcasters to convert to digital broadcasting and cease analog programming no later than June 10, 2009.

A substantial number of customers still had analog TV sets, so rather than forcing them to add converters at extra expense, Buckeye down-converted from digital to analog all broadcast stations and other programming on the channels that were part of the 72-channel Standard Service package.

The initial phases of SDV conversion cost more than $3 million, but as bandwidth needs increase, Buckeye can deploy additional QAM equipment to encode digital channels for transmission to homes. Remember, such equipment enables 3 high-definition channels or 10 to 12 standard-definition channels to be transmitted in the bandwidth of a 6 MHz broadcast channel.

Buckeye currently uses equipment that provides 16MHz transmission in each 6 MHz of bandwidth. To go to the next level cost roughly $750,000. Buckeye completed an intermediate step—reclaiming the 72 channels still being transmitted in analog to provide additional bandwidth—in 2014 in the Northwest Ohio/Southeast Michigan portion of the system; the Sandusky system followed suit in early 2015.

SDV conversion means that each television set now needs a DTA (Digital Terminal Adaptor). Customers with old analog TV sets can't receive any signal without one, and an estimated 20 percent of all sets in operation are analog, according to Buckeye in-home customer surveys.

Because more and more programmers are encrypting their signals, even customers with digital TV sets but no premium services that require a converter to unscramble still will need a DTA for those encrypted standard-service signals. DTAs are not compatible with switched digital video, however; a DVR is required.

Buckeye spent some $20 million on the DTA project and began providing all subscribers with two DTAs at no charge, with additional units available for $1.95 a month. Operating a sophisticated communications system entailing fiber optics, coaxial cable, an array of electronic equipment, trucks, test equipment and computer systems that serves more than 100,000 addresses across six counties is not for the fiscally fainthearted.

The firm also spent some $6 million in the early part of the 21st century on cable cards—software and devices installed in every set-top box. This concept of 'separable security' was promulgated by federal regulators who yielded to the demands of electronic equipment manufacturers which wanted to be able to produce converter boxes for retail sale.

The federal edict mandated an authentication process that would allow the customer to go to retail providers and purchase a convertor of any brand and still be able to receive encrypted programming from the cable provider.

While the FCC foisted this on the cable industry, the satellite dish firms, ATT, and Verizon were not included in the federal edict. Within several years of the FCC directive, the consumer electronics providers stopped making CableCard-compatible devices, yet Buckeye and the other cable system operators were required to continue the use of the CableCard in leased equipment.

The concept fell out of favor with equipment manufacturers largely because agreement could not be reached on a two-way version of the Cable-Card specification, and in late 2014 fewer than 500 Buckeye customers still used them, and that number falls by more than 100 each year, Jensen said.

The regulatory framework was allowed to die quietly as both the equipment manufacturers and the FCC wanted to put the embarrassment behind them. Nevertheless, Buckeye was required to spend the $6 million required by the FCC diktat. The amount the entire cable industry was forced to spend on this federal fiasco is inestimable.

Even after the $180 million fiber rebuild was finished, Buckeye has spent an average of $28 million a year to upgrade electronic equipment and add new services as it strives to maintain its position as the area's premier provider of voice, video and data.

Such commitment underscores Allan Block's sentiment, so firmly expressed in Chapter 6: "I'm proud that I've stayed in the town that I was born in. "When you grow up in a place, you become part of the team that community represents. If you get a chance to stay on the team and fight for that team, that's a wonderful thing. I'm essentially fighting for the team that I've always fought for."

BUCKEYE BITS

Needed, Ready or Not

Buckeye's first fiber-splicing trailer was pressed into emergency service even before fuel had been added to power the electric generator needed for heat, lighting and fiber-repair equipment.

The company had been subcontracting its fiber splicing and repair, but as more and more fiber was built, it finally became economically feasible for Buckeye to purchase its own fiber trailer, at a cost of roughly $30,000. A fiber trailer has the necessary workspace and special equipment to allow for complete fiber work in a temperature-controlled, well-lighted environment.

In fiber splicing and repair, a technician takes down damaged fiber span from a pole; the repair loops permit enough slack in the line to pull it thorough slots in the trailer's walls. The tedious job of splicing fibers, as many as 192 in a single bundle and thinner than a human hair, then can be done in relative comfort and security.

The trailer was delivered late in the afternoon of Friday, January 27, 1995; Buckeye staffers decided to fuel and equip it the following Monday.

Two days later, however, was Super Bowl Sunday—and just before kick-off, a garage fire damaged the main feed that provided cable service to all of East Toledo. Ordinarily, summoning a subcontractor to do the repair work, especially on a Sunday, would have taken hours. Super Bowl Sunday might have proven nigh-on impossible to rouse a subcontractor, in fact.

Jim Wolsiffer, a technician at the time and now director of technical operations, was among those who raced to the Angola Road warehouse, filled the trailer's fuel tank, moved the necessary equipment inside and headed to the fire scene.

Working quickly, the crew spliced the fiber, mounted the line back on the pole, and had good signals going to the hub at St. Charles Hospital, which supplies service to East Toledo and Oregon. They worked until late evening, but most of East Toledo was back in service by game time, with only a few unlucky areas not restored until after it was over.

When Super Bowl XXIX began, only those few fans without service in East Toledo were aware that anything had happened. The rest saw Steve Young, San Francisco's quarterback, pass for a record six touchdowns as his 49ers became the first team to win five Super Bowls, routing the San Diego Chargers, 49–26.

The Kids Figured Out How to Do What?

With new technology comes new problems, as Buckeye engineers and administrators have occasionally learned.

In 1987, Buckeye introduced the Tocom Converter to provide customers with additional channels, pay-per-view and other enhancements to their cable service. The company rolled out Tocom systematically, and regularly cablecast a training video to show subscribers how to use all the new features. The converters had remote controls that enabled the viewer to change from the A cable to the B cable without having to walk across the room and flip a physical switch—a real improvement at the time.

The converters also had a button on the front to allow physical switching between the cables, as well as two other buttons, one each for channel up and channel down.

When Tocom was introduced, only 14 percent of cable viewers in the country had access to such technology, which also enabled a cable provider to scramble the signals of premium channels such as HBO and Showtime, eliminating the need for separate tuner boxes for each premium channel.

Such scrambling also offered greater security than the individual boxes, and as a result Buckeye considered yielding to a small (but vocal) number of customers who for several years had demanded access to adult programming. After many months of study, negotiations with programmers and meetings with law-enforcement, court and government officials to assure them that such programming could be secured from juvenile eyes, Buckeye added the Playboy Channel in early 1989.

Only a few months had passed when Buckeye president Dave Huey received a call from Lucas County Juvenile Court Judge Andy Devine, asking for a meeting. Two youths were in Judge Devine's court to answer for some errant behavior. In talking with the youths and their parents, the judge perceived that the juveniles had figured a way to bypass the security feature and tune in to the Playboy Channel.

Judge Devine asked them for a demonstration, and the boys showed him that by hitting the three buttons on the front of the Tocom in a certain sequence and for varying lengths of time, you could defeat the scrambling safeguard and get Playboy in the clear.

How they stumbled on this, and how they remembered it, was a puzzle to the judge—and he wanted an explanation from Buckeye.

Three company representatives—Huey, vice president of engineering Jim Dryden and marketing director Ellen Jackson—paid a visit to the court to meet with the judge.

However, Huey said later, there was more to the boys' trick than just pushing buttons. It turned out that someone had developed a chip that could be inserted in place of the Tocom converter's existing chip and get past the encryption. The rogue chip was being sold clandestinely from parking lots and in bars, Buckeye learned.

The manufacturer who supplied the converters devised a remedy that rendered the converter inoperative. When a customer then called and said his converter wasn't working, Buckeye retrieved it. If it had the illegal chip installed, the company gave the customer a choice: pay damages or face federal charges.

Paul Szymanowski, treasurer, was put in charge of the theft program. He said he made one large mistake. "We sent out letters explaining that we had evidence the customer was stealing signal, a violation of federal law, and that they (customers) should contact us to arrange a settlement or face federal charges and a lawsuit.

"We sent the letters all at one time," he said of the 350 or so customers who had been caught. "It seems like they all called at once, and I was deluged with incoming calls and phone messages. It was hectic," he remembers.

In all, most paid the $300 for the theft and damaged converters, but about 50 to 60 lawsuits were filed, he noted. In some cases, miscreants settled at that point but a few fought it out in courts. They lost and liens were placed against assets, including houses in some cases.

In one such instance, some 20 years later a homeowner tried to sell the house he had inherited from his father and found a lien Buckeye held against the house, a result of his father being caught with an illegal chip in the late 1980s. When his father died, the house transferred to the son and the lien was not discovered. But when he tried to sell the house in the mid-2000s, the lien came to light and he had to satisfy it before title could transfer to the purchaser.

Chapter Eight

"They're Leaders in Technology and Communications"

The Company's Trophy Case Gets Increasingly Crowded

Given the Block family's long business traditions of integrity, community support and fair treatment of employees, a certain amount of recognition was bound to come to the family and its ventures—and Buckeye CableSystem has garnered both state and national acknowledgment of its good works.

In June 2010, Buckeye was named one of the top 10 best employers in Ohio by the Best Companies Group in conjunction with the Ohio State Council of the Society for Human Resources Management (SHRM).

Companies from across the state were judged on categories such as leadership and planning, corporate culture and communications, role satisfaction, work environment, relationship with supervisors, pay and benefits, and overall engagement.

To be considered, a company had to complete an extensive questionnaire about benefits, policies, practices and other general data, and supply personal contact information for all employees. SHRM staff then contacted employees randomly for confidential question-and-answer sessions. The employee results counted as 75 percent of the overall score. SHRM then tallied the results numerically and weighed them against other entrants based on number of employees.

Buckeye finished among the top 10 Large-Sized Companies, those with more than 250 employees. The other category, Small/Medium-Sized Companies, encompassed those with between 15 and 249 employees. Buckeye was the only winner from Northwest Ohio in either category.

Other winners in the Large-Sized Companies category included Southern Ohio Medical Center, Deloitte, Northeastern Ohio Universities College of Medicine and Pharmacy and the stock brokerage Edward Jones.

"We're extremely proud of the award and feel it is the result of years of hard work and positive attitude by everyone involved: employees at all levels, management and owners," Chip Carstensen, Buckeye's president and general manager, said at the time.

The company scored a 93 in overall engagement—that is, 93 percent of respondents reacted favorably to the criteria established by SHRM and the questions they were asked. SHRM also cited Buckeye's Idea Power Program as among the reasons for the honor. Under that program, Buckeye employees are eligible for monetary awards for submitting suggestions that are later implemented: operational improvements such as safety or service upgrades, or money-saving practices. The group also cited Buckeye's incentive programs that expose employees to healthy lifestyles, safety practices and online training.

In July 2004, just six months after Allan Block launched BCSN (See Chapter 11), the Ohio House of Representatives honored him for combining "civic concern and commitment with selfless initiative to become a dynamic leader in the Toledo area" in starting the 24-hour channel focusing on local sports.

Jeannine Perry, a State Representative at the time, who presented a printed copy of the resolution at a ceremony in Toledo, said she got the idea to introduce the resolution while attending a luncheon earlier that year in Columbus with some Toledoans at which BCSN came up in conversation. "I heard nothing but good comments about it, and thought it appropriate that Mr. Block get some recognition for his foresight in doing something positive for the community," she said.

Later that same year, *Multichannel News,* a leading trade publication, picked Buckeye as its national Innovator of the Year based on its "commitment to serving its subscribers via BCSN."

"With a strict focus on local sports, the 24-hour BCSN . . . has brought to television hundreds of local high-school and college sports events that previously could only be seen live from the stands," *Multichannel News* said.

BCSN also was the subject of articles in *CableWORLD*, another national trade publication, as well as earlier pieces in *Multichannel News* and several local newspapers.

In 2011, Buckeye was singled out by the national trade publication *Communications Technology* as System of the Year for its accomplishments in technical advances, customer service and other areas.

Communications Technology chose Buckeye after studying the system and surveying customers and other industry sources for several years unbeknownst to company executives, said Debra Baker, the magazine's editor.

"Buckeye CableSystem is at the forefront of cable technology, offering the same kinds of residential and commercial services as do larger MSOs (Multiple System Operators) and maintaining majority market share in a competitive broadband environment," Baker said at the time. "Its dedication to customer service has won it kudos from its local constituency in survey after survey."

The criteria for the honor, set by the publication, included a demonstrated push to upgrade and improve technical operations, innovation in testing and development, high customer satisfaction, advanced services deployment and success in nontraditional markets.

"We have an engaged management team," said Joe Jensen, at the time executive vice president of Block Communications in charge of cable and telecommunications operations. "We make decisions and we move forward. We have to do everything the bigger companies do, but with less money and fewer people."

Buckeye was recognized for the achievement at an awards luncheon December 8, 2011, in New York.

Other recent honorees have included systems operated by Comcast, the country's largest cable operator with 22.5 million subscribers at the time, and Cox Communications, the fifth-largest operator with almost 5 million subscribers when it was recognized. By contrast, Buckeye had approximately 150,000 customers when it won the award.

In 2007, Owens Community College honored Buckeye CableSystem and its sister company, Buckeye TeleSystem, with its Community Partnership Award for outstanding dedication and service to the college, citing the instrumental roles the two companies played in developing and enhancing the school's technology and high-speed communications.

Buckeye CableSystem also provided the technical ability to televise around the state and provide video streaming for global Internet distribution of the hands-on demonstrations at the opening celebration of the college's Center for Emergency Preparedness. The network at the center gave area fire and police departments the ability to conduct distance-learning exercises on a variety of simulated terrorist incidents, emergency hazards and natural disasters. The more than four-hour event was carried live on Buckeye CableSystem.

The college's partnership with the two Buckeye companies continues in several ongoing initiatives that have significantly furthered academic excellence, including establishing a cable-television distribution system in all campus buildings, a spokesman for the college said at the time. Coordinated by Buckeye CableSystem, the network provides television signals into the College's classrooms and student common areas.

In addition, Dr. Christa Adams, who was president of Owens at the time, noted that the companies had established a partnership to develop and implement Ohio's Third Frontier Network—later renamed the Ohio Super Computer Network—the nation's most advanced fiber-optic network for research, education and economic development. Because of these collaborative efforts, the state of Ohio established its Ohio Super Computer Network hub on Owens' Findlay-area campus, about 45 miles south of Toledo.

Owens had established the Community Partnership Award in 2004 to honor individuals or organizations that have supported the college directly or indirectly by providing time, skills and energy to assist it in providing access to a quality affordable education.

The Buckeye companies were selected because they "are leaders within the technology and communications industry," Adams said.

The company's programming and other ventures had long been recognized for their high quality and community spirit. In the 1970s, a show called *Sixth Grade Report* won a Gabriel Award for outstanding youth-oriented programming, presented by USA-UNDA, a Catholic fraternal organization for broadcasters and allied communications. Named after the Biblical angel Gabriel, the patron saint of broadcasters, it was a major award at the time. (See Chapter 9)

Sixth Grade Report competed with programming submitted by 225 popular broadcast television and radio stations and was the first cable production to win a Gabriel Award. It also received the All-Ohio Golden Mic Award from the American Legion Auxiliary for an outstanding youth program.

Also in the early 1970s, Buckeye's programming was honored nationally when the National Cable Television Association (now the National Cable Telecommunications Association, NCTA) named it a national winner for public-affairs and news programming among cable systems with more than 15,000 subscribers. That award honored a program called *Are You Listening?*, a taped, nationally syndicated 16-part series that dealt with such topics as welfare mothers, drug addiction, police work, women's liberation and abortion.

At the 1974 Broadcast Industry Conference at San Francisco State University, Buckeye received an award for excellence for community-service programming such as *Ecunews,* a religious-news show produced in cooperation with the Ecumenical Communications Commission of Northwest Ohio.

Of course, recognition by one's peers is perhaps the most noteworthy kind, and both Buckeye and Erie County Cablevision have been honored with more than 80 Image Awards by the Ohio Cable Telecommunications Association (OCTA).

These were presented in a number of categories to member companies at the association's annual meetings between 1988 and 2012. In addition to awards for various video productions, commercials and public-service announcements, the association recognized employee achievements in community service, exemplary customer service, outstanding field work and executive performance.

BCSN scooped up a good portion of those awards in later years, including seven of the 23 handed out in 2012, the final year of the statewide program. Other Buckeye productions and commercials received an additional four awards, meaning the company garnered nearly half of all awards that year. Four years earlier, Nancy Duwve, who headed BCSN from its initiation to her retirement, had been presented with the Executive Leadership award.

Individual employees have sometimes received community recognition, which of course reflected favorably upon Buckeye. In 1991, the Safety Council of Northwest Ohio bestowed upon Larry Keith Daniel, a technician, its Good Samaritan Award for his part in rescuing a driver involved in an auto accident on Interstate 280. Another technician, Randy Anderson, was feted a year or so later by the Safety Council for his role in helping at the scene of another wreck.

Both awards were handed down at an annual dinner the Safety Council holds each year, at which several dozen people are recognized for outstanding actions to help others.

The Block family's strong support of the communities in the 11 states in which it operates is exemplified by the cable companies in Toledo and Sandusky, and in Monroe, Michigan, while that system was part of the Block stable. The family has long decreed that each company donate a certain percentage of operating profit back to charities and institutions in the areas in which each operates. The executive in charge of contributions can expect to be chastised if the full amount budgeted is not given away. The guidelines for donations are fairly broad—education is important, as is anything that improves the quality of life of area residents.

In Toledo, Buckeye has long supported the Toledo Opera Association, Toledo Zoological Society, Toledo Symphony, Toledo Ballet Association, the Toledo Museum of Art, the Public Broadcasting Foundation of Northwest Ohio, Lourdes University, Owens Community College, the University of Toledo, Bowling Green State University and similar institutions.

Over the years, the company has returned millions of dollars to the community, making a concerted effort to award each franchise area its fair share. Every year the company donates to some 300 organizations.

In 1992, Buckeye developed a program of CATS grants (CableSystem Assists Teachers and Students) to help teachers at the grassroots level. The funds were earmarked to go directly to teachers for classroom projects or items they deemed important. Buckeye limited the program to elementary schools, as educators stressed that the years up to third and fourth grade were the most important of a student's development.

The grants totaled up to $150 per classroom, with certain limitations based on building size. The only restriction was that the money had to be used for the direct benefit of the students—a teacher could not use the money to defray the cost of a seminar he or she wished to attend, for example.

Teachers would write an application, and a Buckeye committee would decide which ones showed the most merit based on the number of students involved and the overall educational value. The program existed from 1992 to 1998, during which time Buckeye received 3,322 teacher applications and awarded more than $430,000 for 3,136 projects involving 248,500 pupils in 127 schools. (Those figures may represent the same students benefiting from separate grants in more than one year.)

Buckeye allocated funds for a wide array of things: art supplies, musical instruments, computers, software, even gerbils to teach students about pet-care responsibility. Often, school budgets were far too tight for many of the teachers' preferred projects—one told Buckeye that her school system allocated 68 cents per pupil per year for classroom supplies.

The program had many positive effects—some of which wouldn't be evident for years, others whose benefits became clear much sooner. One year, teachers in a Toledo inner-city school approached Buckeye with a request to pool all the money allocated to the school rather than have it blocked out in $150 grants to individual teachers. Surveys they had conducted found that the students' homes had little, if any, reading material available, and the teachers wanted to buy books they could give to the pupils to take home.

The idea of giving one lump sum to the school ran counter to the original idea of funds going to individual teachers, but Buckeye relented.

The same teachers approached Buckeye the next year with the same request, but with an added bonus: They reported that largely because of the book-giveaway program the previous year, they had reached the school's three-year reading-achievement goals in just two years. Buckeye execs choked back tears as they realized what an impact the CATS program was having.

In another outreach project aimed at helping students, in December, 2014, Buckeye began a trial program with two Toledo high schools to provide free Buckeye Express to 25 students to enable them to take on-line courses at the University of Toledo.

In addition to the Buckeye Express service, Buckeye also provided at no charge Buckeye Brainiacs, its service which offers maintenance and support for computing devices, plus free installation if needed.

Under the program, the school system provided laptop computers to each student and Buckeye furnished the free service for the duration of the 2015 spring-semester trial.

The program was the outgrowth of talks between school and Buckeye officials about how best to bridge the "digital divide,"—the disparity between the haves and the have-nots as far as connectivity is concerned—and how to influence high school students to take college-level courses.

Part of the impetus was a number of studies touted by school officials that pointed to a correlation between at-home Internet access and higher graduation rates.

In addition to support of education, the company's rather broad contribution guidelines emphasize community-wide endeavors. As part of that mission, Buckeye and Erie County have adopted an employee-directed contribution program. At the start of each year, the company earmarks $100 for each employee to give to a charity or group of his or her choice.

The only stipulation is that the employee or a family member must be actively involved in the recipient organization. The employee completes an application detailing his or her involvement, and if it's approved—few have ever been denied—Buckeye writes a check to the group, as well as a letter explaining the donation and naming the employee. Both are given to the employee to hand-deliver to the group.

Recipients of employee-directed contributions have included scout troops, Sunday-school classes, school plays, club sports and robotics-building competitions. These contributions have totaled almost $200,000 and have gone to more than 700 organizations.

The animating spirit behind the program was to encourage employees to take an active part in their communities and to show employees that such involvement is important. Although no exact figures have been compiled, the estimated value of the time employees donate to community organizations is in excess of a half-million dollars every year.

In addition to cash contributions, Buckeye annually donates roughly $100,000 in in-kind contributions each year. Production and editing time for promotional material for charitable groups, commercial time for groups to run their promotional material and auction items such as certificates for free Buckeye services are just a few of the ways the company helps the communities in which it's active.

BUCKEYE BITS

Worms Ought to Be a Good Business for a Cable Company

In early 1991, one Buckeye executive had been given a temporary assignment that would require him to be in Columbus, Ohio's capital city, for about four months. He planned to rent an apartment there, driving from Toledo each Monday and returning home Friday night.

At about the same time, to improve drainage at the warehouse at 4818 Angola Road, Buckeye was digging a swale alongside the building back toward the ditch that ran along the railroad at the rear of the property.

There was general conversation about planning for the Columbus assignment, but no specifics about what it would actually entail.

Rose Fulton, in charge of the department that prepared converter boxes
for deployment into the field, asked one of the engineers about the executive's Columbus assignment. Thinking fast, and being something of a practi-
cal joker, he said that it was connected to the swale being dug to the east of
the building.

He told Fulton that Allan Block had determined that given Lake Erie's
prominence as a fishing mecca, there was a real business to be developed in
producing bait, particularly worms, for the recreational anglers who flocked
to the lake each year.

He told her that the executive was going to Ohio State University's agri-
cultural college for a four-month crash course in raising earthworms, and that
the swale was being dug for the worm beds that would be needed.

Block, the engineer said, didn't want anyone to know he was developing
a new business until it was operational, so he asked Fulton to keep it quiet.

A few others in engineering and the warehouse heard about the prank and
kept it going. The warehouse manager at the time asked Fulton if she could
clean out a substantial area along one wall of her department to make room
for coolers that would be needed.

Being a loyal, helpful employee, she went in on her own time on a
Saturday and moved a number of pieces of heavy equipment to clear an area
large enough for the massive coolers she expected to be installed.

Only a few people at Angola Road were in on the joke, but they took the
traveling executive into their confidence. Once, when he returned from Columbus early, he and the engineer were talking with Fulton. The engineer
asked the executive how his studies were going. The executive faked a
pained look, glanced furtively around as if to see who else might have heard
and said to the engineer, "How'd you find out about that? It's supposed to be
top secret."

Fulton chimed in immediately: "Don't worry, there are only a few of us
who know, and we're keeping it quiet. They had to tell me so I could clean
up the area over there for the coolers," she said, pointing proudly to the
vacated space along the wall.

The joke was kept alive for several months until Fulton happened to
mention worm farming to the company treasurer, assuming that someone in
his position would know about the project and that it was OK to discuss it
with him.

"I'm not sure, but I think someone's pulling your leg," said the treasurer,
who wasn't in on the gag.

Fulton was a good sport and had no animosity about the prank afterward—in fact, she joked about it for years. Her husband, Dick, is an avid
fisherman. "I remember I went home and told Dick that he'd have a lifetime

supply of worms, that he'd never have to buy worms from a bait store again," she said.

Fulton, who retired in 2008 as manager of the warehouse and converter department, also was the butt of another prank.

She was deathly afraid of mice. The converter department she ran was on the first floor of the warehouse, and adjacent to the department was a second deck for storage. The deck covered only part of the first floor; the uncovered converter department was open to the warehouse ceiling. The deck was high enough to restrict visibility from the first floor of anything or anyone on it.

One employee, an accomplished fly fisherman, knowing of Fulton's squeamishness, took a fly rod and a fuzzy lure that looked like a small mouse, and frequently went to the second deck and cast it down on her desk, or right beside it.

Once she had fled the scene in panic, the man would reel in his mouse, go calmly back to his office and wait a few days before casting about for another opportunity to tease Fulton.

No one is sure she ever knew the truth.

Highway Patrol to Headquarters: Why Do You Sound Like HBO?

Because some of the frequencies used for cable-TV channels are the same ones used by aircraft, law enforcement and other public entities for radio communication, coaxial cable used by cable firms is heavily shielded to prevent the electronic signals from escaping into the atmosphere.

As Jim Dryden, Buckeye's retired vice president of engineering and a former pilot, once joked, "You don't want to have a pilot making an emergency landing at Toledo Express and the only thing he can hear on his radio is HBO." Federal regulations therefore specify the security of the coaxial cable systems and related electronics.

One of the recurring problems Buckeye and other cable companies experience is signal theft by people who think they can get free cable by running a wire to a neighbor's house—or, more commonly, to a neighboring apartment. In such cases, typically, the fittings connecting two cables together, or connecting a cable to an amplifier, are not tight, or the cable has substandard shielding, enabling the signal to leak from the system.

Most cable firms spend large sums of money each year to maintain the integrity of their systems, and the Federal Communications Commission requires each company to fly over its entire system twice each year with a specially equipped airplane to measure signal leakage.

In the early 1990s, Buckeye uncovered one such case in an apartment complex along the Ohio Turnpike in Maumee. The Ohio Highway Patrol reported that when troopers tried to use their radios while driving on a certain section of the Turnpike, all they could hear was a TV soundtrack.

Buckeye technicians attempting to pinpoint the problem discovered that a tenant in the complex was helping his downstairs neighbor steal cable service by running a wire from his TV set out the window and into the window of the apartment immediately below.

Instead of using coaxial cable, even substandard coaxial, the enterprising crook used twin lead, the thin copper cable used to run from a rooftop antenna to TV sets in areas without cable. It therefore acted like a large transmitter along the Turnpike.

Buckeye technicians quickly put him and his neighbor out of their startup cablevision business.

III

What to Provide the Viewers, and at What Cost?

Chapter Nine

"We Experimented with Everything.
We Even Had a Fish Tank on Camera"

In Buckeye's Early Years,
Programming and Production Were Decidedly Ad Hoc

From its infancy, Buckeye has had a penchant for innovative programming, taking risks in uncharted waters to see what viewers might accept.

Soon after the system was up and running, the irrepressible Leo Hoarty ran an ancient film on Wolfgang Amadeus Mozart, the 18th century Austrian pianist and composer. "This was one of the first talking movies that was in the public domain, which was all he could get," Allan Block remembers. Later, in the early 1970s, Hoarty was able to obtain better public-domain fare, and began running all-night movies on Channel 5 and developed local programs. He bought equipment and hired crews to put together tapes of events in schools and churches, cablecast restaurant reviews and much more.

"I tried to build a television station on Channel 5," Mr. Hoarty said. "I did my best to copy what the TV stations did." His first manager of the channel was a man named Terry Hickson.

He telecast bingo games – Buckeye Bingo, in which customers could pick up bingo cards at an area supermarket and then watch the weekly televised program on which numbers were drawn. "It was the first audience participation show," Allan Block would say later.

"We even had a fish tank on camera," Hoarty said in his 2002 Cable Center interview. "We had a camera that scanned all the weather instruments so that people could look and see what the weather was." Beside the row of weather instruments was a slate on which announcements could be written.

After the camera scanned that, it began scanning the weather gauges again ad infinitum.

Jim Dryden, vice president of engineering, recalled some years later that the camera was rigged to show news on a teletype machine as it was being typed in real time. It also had a switch that, whenever the teletype machine failed (not an uncommon event), would rotate the camera to focus on the fish tank. A technician would then be dispatched to fix the teletype and turn the camera back to the incoming news. In one such instance, he recalled, an inebriated viewer phoned in disgust once the news was back on display. "Bring back the @*%#@ fish!" he demanded.

Hoarty cablecast FM radio stations as an added service for customers, carried Voice of America "because I personally liked it" and put on the BBC and Radio Moscow. He even rigged up antennae to "put all the favorite shortwave stations on, including two which I later found out I wasn't allowed to do."

In 1973, the New York Stock Exchange stock ticker was run in color across the screens of Channels 11 and 13. They were the two local VHF broadcast stations and the over-the-air signals would interfere with cable transmission, creating a ghost behind the cable signal and making them unusable for full-motion video. The two broadcast stations were shown on other cable channels and cable channels 11 and 13 were used for such features as the stock ticker and static messages.

"We experimented with everything," Hoarty said in 2014. "We (produced programs) at the zoo, we did a cooking series and we even had a Detroit writer come to town and write a series of programs for us."

That writer, Monroe, Michigan, native Vernon J. Sneider, was a novelist who wrote the 1951 book *The Teahouse of the August Moon*, which was adapted for a Broadway play in 1953 and awarded the 1954 Pulitzer Prize for Drama. It was made into a movie in 1956. Sneider also wrote the Broadway musical *Lovely Ladies, Kind Gentlemen* in 1970.

Hoarty couldn't remember how he made initial contact with Sneider. "I ran into him somehow and we got to talking," he said. "He was a very friendly guy."

A 1940 graduate of the University of Notre Dame, Sneider entered the Army and was part of a military government team that landed in Okinawa in April 1945. He became commander of Tobaru, a Japanese village of 5,000 people that was the basis of Tobiki Village in *Teahouse*. "He did a series of programs for us over a period of about a year" in the late 1960s, Hoarty said.

Buckeye's reputation as an up-and-coming innovator spread. "People came from everywhere to visit us," Hoarty said. "We were overwhelmed by visitors. Others wanted to get into the business but didn't know all they needed to, so they came to see our operation and ask questions."

Even the cooking show had a famous name connection—Martha Stewart, albeit not the publishing, broadcasting and merchandising mogul of today. This Martha Stewart, middle-aged in the early 1970s, according to Hoarty, had a New York TV show and wrote a column that was syndicated in several newspapers. A profile at the time described her as having "an extensive background in social work and network television."

Hoarty's daughter, the late Dorinda Lee Hartson, worked for her in New York. "Dorinda got Martha interested in Buckeye and me," Hoarty said. "Martha used our welcome to Channel 5 as some sort of test for her own shows on networks and big-city TV stations."

She came to Toledo and produced her own 16-part show, *Are You Listening?*, which was telecast for some six months on Channel 5 and was also nationally syndicated.

Other celebrities Hoarty remembered appearing on Channel 5 include Red Buttons, a comedian and Academy Award–winning actor, whose career peak spanned from the 1930s to the late 1960s. "I had dinner with him when he was in Toledo for something or other and asked if we could interview him," Hoarty said.

Another Channel 5 interview subject during that time, Hoarty said, was Dick Kazmaier, a 1948 graduate of Maumee High School who went on to star as quarterback, halfback and kicker for Princeton University's football team. Chosen an All-American in 1951, he also won the Heisman Trophy.

Channel 5 also was the viaduct by which "*Rambling Around*" was delivered to viewers. This show, hosted by native Toledoan Karen Martensen, was a series of interviews and site descriptions taped at such venues as Promenade Park in downtown Toledo, historic Ft. Meigs in Perrysburg, the Toledo Zoo, The Toledo Museum of Art, the airport, and various parks and neighborhoods in the area. The taped segments were shown twice each day.

Another early programming venture on Channel 5 was a series of motorcycle scrambles races at various sites in northern Ohio, according to a July 1, 1974 article in *The Blade*.

In 1972, a young graduate of Bowling Green State University, Pat Deville, was hired as one of two producers whose job was to focus mainly on developing local programming. Deville, who in 1985 became president of the Erie County system that Buckeye had purchased in 1981, said each producer was responsible for three or four shows a week in the early 1970s.

They used part-time videographers, usually college students, and had a refurbished *Blade* circulation truck as a mobile video unit. At least one of those videographers, Pete Gerken, went on to bigger things, including a top position with the United Auto Workers union. He later became a Toledo City Councilman and is, as of 2015, a Lucas County Commissioner.

Gerken, who was hired in 1972 as a production assistant after studying journalism at the University of Detroit, credits his Buckeye experience with building traits that helped him throughout his career, including in politics. "I learned a lot about what goes into a video production and what it takes to produce a show," he said. "It's a blend of a lot of moving parts all together, from scheduling, technology, people, timing, hardware, and if any one of those parts gets out of balance, the whole thing can crash.

"So it really taught me as a young man to keep my head up and my eyes open, and my mouth shut . . . sometimes," he laughed.

He recalls the primitive tasks in the early days, taking the mobile production unit to an assignment and rigging all the gear needed for the show. "We covered motorcycle races at Delta, and in order to get the kinds of shots we needed, we had to erect a 30-foot high scaffold in mud in the middle of the track, then bury the cables because they couldn't be on the ground or they'd cause trouble in the race," he said. "That was always a two-day effort."

Gerken also remembers carrying the 40-pound shoulder cameras around the Glass Bowl at the University of Toledo football games, dragging the necessary cables behind him. "It's a far cry from what they have today," he said, "but then it was a brand new technology."

The local-origination production team, headed by Michael O'Connor, set out on an ambitious course to develop unique programs such as *The Sixth Grade Report* and *Jabberwocky*.

The Sixth Grade Report was written and produced by sixth graders in various Toledo schools. Launched in 1973, the show rotated among the schools. Work started with a visit to each school on a schedule developed by producer and director Tom Ponrick, according to an April 28, 1974, feature in *The Blade* written by Cheryl Lutz. Ponrick would give the students a talk illustrated by a slide show. His presentation, which usually lasted an hour and a half to two hours, covered news gathering, news writing, on-air presentation and TV production.

The following week he'd return, and he and the teacher and students would map out which stories they'd work on and what pictures would accompany them. Students would be selected for the positions of anchor and the two or three reporters who would appear on camera. The third week, those children would go to Buckeye's studio, where the program would be taped for later cablecast. The program won a number of industry awards. "Cable's growing up," Hoarty said at the time.

Jabberwocky, also introduced in 1973, and on which Gerken worked until he left Buckeye in 1974, was an educational and entertainment program aimed at preschool and elementary-school children. Lee Drew, a teacher at Toledo's Maumee Valley Country Day School, was host of the half-hour program, three of which were produced each week and shown five times during the week.

Honors came Buckeye's way for programs including *For the People, By the People,* which tackled a number of general-interest topics; *Jobline,* which reported on area job placements and openings; *Perspectives,* on which the Reverend John Hiltz took a weekly look at the bases of Christianity; *Collage,* a review of art and literature; and *I Am Woman,* which explored women's issues.

I Am Woman was the first locally produced show entirely about women, Rosemary Johnson, its producer and director, told the *Toledo Times* newspaper. (A Bowling Green State University graduate, Johnson had been a camera operator on *Jabberwocky.*) The idea came from Deville, who thought it was important to have a woman in charge of the show.

Deville and Dan Myers, one of the camera operators, were the only men involved. Madalyn Carfuny served as assistant producer and director; Susan Schaeffer was the moderator; and Cynthia Drew operated the second camera.

"It was a big step for me," Johnson was quoted as saying in a Feb. 8, 1974 feature in the *Toledo Times* written by Judith Wagner. The show was unique "because it provide(d) a training ground for women in a male-dominated field." Among its episodes was a talk with Marigene Valliquette, an Ohio state senator, discussing the Equal Rights Amendment. Also featured were episodes on quilting, consciousness raising, houseplant care, daycare and women in science.

In March 1974, Buckeye cablecast what at the time was termed the largest Lenten services in Toledo at the time—a program spurred by the Ecumenical Communications Commission of Northwest Ohio, which approached head of production Michael O'Connor with the idea. A service conducted each Wednesday during Lent at Trinity Episcopal Church and cosponsored by Holy Trinity Greek Orthodox Church, St. Francis de Sales Catholic Church, St. Paul United Methodist Church and St. Paul Lutheran Church was videotaped and telecast on Channel 5.

To round out the local programming, Hoarty turned to sports, eyeing high-school football and basketball and the Toledo Mud Hens, a minor-league baseball team with a colorful history.

In 1970, the Mud Hens had been unable to get a local radio station interested in broadcasting their games, and that August, Charlie Senger, the team's general manager, approached Buckeye. He struck a deal for Buckeye to carry two games: an August 23 contest with the Louisville Colonels, a forerunner of the Louisville River Rats, and an August 30 battle with the Winnipeg Whips. One catch: The cablecasts would be audio-only, no video.

"I don't know how it will turn out," Senger said in an August 16, 1970, interview with *The Blade,* "but if it's well-received we may try to get all Sunday games in 1971 on both audio and video cablevision, and the rest on audio only."

Viewers were intrigued, and on April 25, 1971, a doubleheader between the Mud Hens and Winnipeg was tape-delay televised. Getting the rights to cablecast the games, and then producing them, was not without hassles, though. Buckeye had to obtain a waiver from the International League, the Mud Hens' governing body, which controlled broadcast rights for all games. Because the team hadn't been able to secure any local radio coverage, the league granted the waiver for the April doubleheader and eight more Sunday games during the 1971 season.

Production wasn't easy, either, but Buckeye pulled it off. "Considering the technical problems and the greenness of the crew, the show came off almost without a hitch," Norman Dresser, *The Blade*'s entertainment editor, enthused in a feature April 28, 1974. "The work was near network quality, except that it was in black and white instead of color," (He did add that "it may not be ABC's *Wide World of Sports* or NBC's *Game of the Week*.")

To cablecast the game, Buckeye partnered with some of the University of Toledo's video-production students; the crew consisted of 20 people and four cameras. Jack Taberner, brother of Orris Taberner, a popular local sportscaster at the time, provided the play-by-play and color commentary.

The production itself was very much a seat-of-the-pants effort. In the early years, Buckeye's work was sometimes looked down upon by local industry sophisticates—as one local-TV employee once muttered, "Well, they'll try that and find out how difficult it is."

However, "in two short years," *Blade* sportswriter Duane Schooley wrote in an October 29, 1972, feature on the production staff, "the cable outlet has shown action—live and via tape—of track, tennis, baseball and basketball, as well as a high-school football game of the week. "It's more than a onetime stab at local sports broadcasting."

Assistant chief engineer John Nicholas had assembled an ad hoc production outfit, utilizing the converted used *Blade* circulation truck as a mobile control room and figuring out ways to create workable equipment like the networks and broadcasters used, but without the high costs.

For instance, the roving camera in those days was a camera with a modulator and a one-inch TV reception monitor attached. "Without the monitor, the cameraman could not see the shot he is taking," Schooley wrote. The crew used three stationary tripod-mounted cameras at various points around the venue plus the mobile unit, which the cameraman carried on his shoulder.

"The upright (tripod-mounted) cameras have the usual viewing screen built in, making the roving camera a unique setup, perhaps the only one in the Midwest," Schooley observed.

"Compare us to the major network teams and we're dead," producer Michael O'Connor told Schooley. "But that doesn't mean we're any less idealistic."

Not only was Buckeye doing the games in black and white while the networks were working exclusively in color by that time, but the Buckeye crews were using cameras that cost several hundred dollars "and they're using ones costing $80,000," O'Connor said. "Also, most of our cameramen are just breaking in and theirs are professionals—seasoned veterans."

The four cameramen—John Bylow, Brian Naughton, George Young and Neil McCormick—were guided from the production truck by O'Connor and assistant director Mike Malone. Jim Detwiler and Keith Tice handled the announcing and color commentary.

The production crew would arrive at the venue four hours ahead of the scheduled start time, roll out hundreds of feet of cable, make all the connections so everything would work as expected come game time, test the audio and video signals, talk with coaches—and then keep their fingers crossed. Much could go wrong, and sometimes did.

For high-school football games, for example, Buckeye tried to map out the schedule during the summer so each City League team (plus Whitmer High School, a Toledo institution which at that time was not part of the league) could be covered at least once during the season. As the season progressed, it was sometimes necessary to reschedule a game at the last minute to show a more interesting contest.

That in itself created problems, as not all venues were equipped with adequate power and lighting—and even if they were, sometimes the crew would show up and find that others had appropriated the only available power outlets. Often, power problems of one kind or another resulted in a poor picture or no video signal at all—an unwelcome surprise that the crew generally discovered as the game was about to start.

Much of the production work in the early days involved Creative Images, an audiovisual company owned by Dave Peterson and located in a nondescript red brick building on Summit Street just north of downtown Toledo.

An early video editor and cameraman was Ron Schulz, a 1982 graduate of Bowling Green State University who had returned to Toledo after a couple of months in Los Angeles testing the job market. A family friend suggested he check if Creative Images had any openings, and he was hired as a freelancer to run a camera at a Mud Hens game in August 1982.

When Schulz went in to collect his pay for that gig, Peterson asked him to edit a tape. He did, and continued to hang around several months doing occasional editing and camera jobs before being offered a full-time position. Creative Images did projects for various advertising and public-relations agencies but mostly did work for Buckeye, promoting new channels the company was adding and shooting sporting events.

Its production van was Peterson's camper. After a while, Schulz decided it was too crowded for efficient work. "I asked Dave if he planned to use it as a camper anymore or could I convert it to work better as a production truck," he said.

Peterson assented, and Schulz took out the bed and table to make more room for equipment. He placed the audio board atop the bathroom sink; the operator would sit on the toilet to work the controls. Setup was cumbersome and usually took four or five hours.

"We would pull the van as close to the door as possible and string all the cables, place the three cameras and test everything," Schulz said. He stayed at Creative Images for two years, followed by stints at two Toledo broadcast television stations. Peterson later sold the camper and bought a used ambulance that he converted into a production truck.

Schulz, who joined Buckeye in 1988 and is now senior editor and videographer, recalled that in the early days he produced commercials for a growing number of companies that were finding cable advertising to their liking, working from a small production studio on the second floor of Buckeye's new Southwyck headquarters.

Buckeye did larger projects through an arrangement with Hart Associates, a Toledo public-relations and advertising firm which at the time had a more elaborate production and editing facility in the former First Federal Savings and Loan Association office in downtown Toledo.

Most remote events were tape-delay cablecast, but sometimes an event was produced live, with the signal sent via microwave from the venue to Buckeye's head end on Angola Road. On those occasions, the crew rented a portable microwave transmitter and receiver unit from Ball State University in Muncie, Indiana. That meant a crew had to drive to Muncie, take the unit to the event and return it the next day—a costly, time-consuming affair.

Microwaving from Bowling Green State University proved particularly troublesome because of the distance from Buckeye's head end, and the fact that microwave requires line of sight for the signal to be received.

The crew planned to put the portable transmitter on the roof of Anderson Arena, the basketball arena near the north side of the campus, for basketball games, and on the roof of the Ice Arena several hundred yards east of Anderson for hockey games, "but we had to figure out where to put the receiver," Schulz said. "We considered the rooftop of the (former) Ramada Inn on Reynolds Road but ruled that out as impractical."

He remembered that he could see Toledo office buildings from his fourth-floor dorm room when he was a student, and wondered if Buckeye's 355-foot tower on Angola Road might work. "I climbed the tower with a pair of binoculars and about half way up, I could see buildings on campus.

"I went to Art Iron (a Toledo metal fabricator), got some scrap steel and crafted a mount for the tower," he said. He climbed the tower with a pulley and rope, pulled up the homemade mount and fastened it to the tower, then pulled up the receiver dish and affixed it to the mount.

Cold weather created problems with the electronic gear, so he wrapped both the receiver on the tower and the transmitters on the roofs of both the Ice Arena and Anderson with heating pads, the kind easily purchased at any drugstore. "That also meant we had to pull extension cords up to provide electricity for the heating pads," he said, chuckling at the memory.

Schulz's inventiveness wasn't limited to building a satellite-dish mount more than 100 feet up the Angola tower. It also came into play in 1987 when the crew planned to shoot the first North American Open Singles Championship squash tournament at the Toledo Club, an exclusive members-only club near downtown. "Spectator seats were limited, and the Toledo Club didn't want to give up a seat for the camera," Schulz said—so he built a camera stand for one corner of the court where it wouldn't occupy a seat or interfere with anyone's view.

Peterson said that BGSU basketball games proved especially tricky because the nearby Oak Grove Cemetery stood between Anderson Arena and the Angola Road tower. As its name implies, the cemetery is home to a number of tall oak trees.

"There was only one spot on the roof where there was a gap in those trees to allow the signal to go to Angola," Peterson recalled. Someone would have to lug the transmitter up a catwalk beneath the roof and crawl through an access port on the roof, place the transmitter in the designated spot and then aim it toward the tower, where a Buckeye engineer would monitor the signal strength and report via phone to the crew member on the roof for final alignment.

"One time I went to the roof of Anderson in minus-17-degree weather," Peterson said. "There was real high wind and snow and the roof was so icy, I told my people to stay inside, that it was too dangerous. They came out and helped anyway—that's how dedicated they were," he said, praising the actions of Schulz, Jeff Larkin, John Diener, Dennis Robedeau and James Sweet, among others.

On another occasion, the crew placed, aligned and tested the transmitter well ahead of game time, then tested it again about 45 minutes before the start of the game, Peterson recalled. "It was a snowy and windy day, and the receive dish on the Angola Road tower had been blown slightly sideways," he said. "I drove to Angola Road, climbed to the dish, which was mounted at 125 feet, and aligned it." He did this by turning the dish slightly, then hollering down to Chris Kasner, the engineer on duty, who would report the signal strength and tell him which way to turn it further.

"We got it properly aligned about five minutes before game time," he said. "I was so exhausted. I just sat there at the 125-foot level in all that wind and snow for about 20 minutes, just to catch my breath. I had good people working for me, so I let them handle the game while I was on the tower."

In the 1980s, drawing on its earlier experience of taping a few Mud Hens baseball games, Buckeye approached Gene Cook, who by then was general manager of the team, to inquire about cablecasting some live games. Peterson recalled doing only 10 Hens games, albeit in color, the first year because

Cook was worried that televising the games would hurt attendance at the park.

The young crew filmed Christmas concerts at a few Toledo-area churches, and also taped the June 1987 opening of the Hippoquarium at the Toledo Zoo, editing the tape in the converted ambulance en route to the Buckeye head end so it would be ready for cablecast at the advertised time.

In 1984 and 1985, the crew cablecast the first two Children's Miracle Network local fundraising telethons live, the first from the former Medical College of Ohio. It was staged in the Dana Center, and "we had to do two (microwave) hops back to Angola—from the Dana Center to the top of a taller building on the MCO campus, then back to Angola," Peterson said. The second telethon was held at Southwyck Mall.

Some of the new programming did not require a lot of work by Buckeye staff, however. In October 1973, Buckeye added Channel 100, only the second cable firm in the country to embrace the new service, according to a Dec. 1, 1973, article in *The Blade*. With Channel 100, owned by Optical Systems of Los Angeles, subscribers received a black encryption box to place atop their TV sets and were then able to tune into movies, blacked-out sporting events and other programs. Each week, two movies were shown, each appearing four times on weekdays and five on Saturdays and Sundays. Subscribers could watch a movie as many times as they wished.

Channel 100 was offered for $6.50 a month. It showed mostly movies rated G and PG, but did offer some R-rated films late in the evening. It never offered X-rated movies, and the technology allowed for parental blocking.

Buckeye offered the service until January 1, 1980. In October 1977, it had added Showtime and found viewers were much more interested in it than in Channel 100's fare. Buckeye added the Movie Channel in April 1980; PASS, a regional sports channel out of Detroit, in April 1985; and HBO in August 1987. Pay-Per-View, by which a customer could order movies, concerts, and other events and pay on an individual basis, was added in 1989.

Each of those premium channels required a converter box, so any customer subscribing to all four would end up with a stack of converters on top of the TV, along with the cumbersome A/B switch to toggle between cables.

In 1984, Rose Fulton, who had been hired in August 1978 as a customer-service representative, was assigned oversight of the preparation of all converter boxes for field deployment. She would grow with that job as the system was upgraded and Tocom converters added in 1987, followed by a plethora of converters by several manufacturers and finally the whole-house Digital Video Recorder (DVR) in February, 2012. (She retired in 2009 as manager of the warehouse and converter department.)

Much earlier, Buckeye had ventured down another business path as well: On September 9, 1971, it ran an ad in *The Blade* announcing, "We are now accepting ADVERTISING and SPONSORS." The ad meant exactly what it said: Buckeye was *accepting* premade ads brought in by merchants. The company didn't establish a formal ad-sales department until the early 1980s. (See Chapter 4)

No records exist of how many ads Buckeye took in at the time, but at least one was highly successful. Pam Koontz, director of marketing operations, remembered placing an ad seeking her lost dog. "We were living in Maumee at the time and had recently moved to a new house," said Koontz, an assistant production director under O'Connor at the time. The dog got out and couldn't find its way back to the new house, but someone saw the ad and called her to say they had found it.

Much of the early programming had come to a halt in 1974 as the FCC began to limit the growth of cable systems; Buckeye had to cease construction and downsize a bit. Deville, who had been hired in 1972 as a producer, was laid off, as were many others, but he found work with WTOL, the CBS affiliate in Toledo.

Buckeye, and the entire cable industry, began experiencing rapid growth due in part to the advent of satellite-fed programming, and Deville returned to Buckeye in 1977 to run Channel 100, having earned a law degree from the University of Toledo in the meantime.

After Channel 100 was discontinued at the start of 1980, Deville was contemplating what his future might hold. An August 1979 graduate of the University of Toledo College of Law, he was in Columbus in February 1980 taking the state bar exam with an eye toward becoming a practicing lawyer when Buckeye, like much of the cable industry experiencing rapid growth and planning for more, called to offer him the title of manager of administration, in charge of human resources, labor relations and dispatching.

Another major local venture emerged in the early 1980s, when Michael Drew Shaw, who hosted a morning talk show on a local radio station, had lunch with John Karl, Buckeye's president, and O'Connor, the production manager, to discuss possible programming ideas.

Shaw, who also was part-owner of Blue Page Productions, an audio-video production company, had done opening and closing segments for movies Buckeye had shown, as well as voice-overs for station breaks on the cable channels.

The result of those discussions was *LIMELIGHT Tonight,* intended to be similar to nighttime broadcast talk shows. Five half-hour shows were taped live each week at Ricardo's, a restaurant on the ground floor of One SeaGate, Owens-Illinois' sparkling new 30-story headquarters on the Maumee River. (The building has since been renamed the Fifth Third Building; OI moved to the Toledo suburb of Perrysburg, and the Cincinnati-based Fifth Third Bank moved its Toledo operations into the facility.)

LIMELIGHT featured interviews with local celebrities such as radio and TV newscasters talking about their careers and backgrounds, local entrepreneurs discussing new business ventures and the occasional national celebrity if the crew could intercept one when he or she was in town for other engagements.

Among the national figures who made an appearance on *LIMELIGHT Tonight* were actors Burt Reynolds and Carol Channing, and Charles Nelson Reilly, an actor, standup comedian and TV director.

One natural guest was native Toledoan Jamie Farr, who frequently promoted Tony Packo's, a popular East Toledo restaurant, in his role as Corporal Klinger on *M*A*S*H**. Tony Packo Jr., co-owner of the restaurant, was a frequent *LIMELIGHT* guest.

"We'd set up chairs on the (dance) floor (of Ricardo's) and could have 50 to 75 in the audience for live tapings. We would do five half-hour shows, taping three on Tuesday and two on Thursday, then show them nightly Monday through Friday the following week," Shaw said.

That week's worth of shows would be cablecast back-to-back in a two-and-a-half-hour segment on the weekend. The weeknight shows were cablecast at 11 p.m. to provide an alternative for people who didn't want to watch the news on broadcast stations, he said.

Because the dance floor where the show was taped was close to the bar, revelers and other noise were an occasional feature of tapings. "We'd sometimes joke at the beginning to 'cue the blender,' because invariably someone would order a drink requiring the use of the noisy blender and it would cause a minor interruption," Shaw said.

"We had to move through the tapings quickly, as Ricardo's had live entertainment and needed the dance floor later in the evening," Shaw said. Featured entertainment at the time was Polyphony, a local band headed by Joe Perlaky, who would later become economic development director for the city of Oregon and who is currently project manager for various grant programs at the University of Toledo.

Shaw was host of the show as well as its producer; Doug LaRue, who later had a career in Hollywood, was the director.

"I was still doing my morning show on radio, and it got to be too much," Shaw said. So after about a year, a young Monroe, Michigan, native and Toledo radio announcer to whom Shaw had been a mentor was hired to be host, and Shaw became producer-director along with Tom Brady, a local advertising and public-relations specialist.

The new host was Paul W. Smith, who today is the morning host on Detroit's WJR radio and an industry giant; at the time he had a morning television show on Toledo's Channel 24, and an afternoon radio show. For several years, he had done instructional tapes for Buckeye when the firm rolled out a new product.

Creative Images' Schulz, who did production work for the show, remembered one especially unusual incident. "One night someone outside walked up to the floor-to-ceiling windows behind Paul W. and proceeded to eat a big chunk of raw liver," he said. "Paul W. didn't see it, but it broke the rest of us up."

LIMELIGHT Tonight was canceled near the end of 1983. Shaw owned the name and format, so when independent broadcast station WUPW went on the air on Channel 36 in 1985, he pitched the program to station management, which ran it for two years as a one-hour show on Sunday nights.

Another Creative Images project was *Toledo Beat*, which debuted in August 1982, the same time Buckeye began carrying MTV. It consisted of interviews with musicians, which were then edited into five-minute segments and inserted weekly in a break offered in MTV programming. "We got interviews with a lot of nationally known performers," Peterson said. "KISS, Bon Jovi, Aerosmith, Gene Simmons, Eddie Money and Ted Nugent, to name just a few."

Most of the segments were taped in the small recording studio on Summit Street, but the crew would go farther afield if necessary. Eddie Money was performing in Detroit, "so we went up there and spent a couple hours with him," Peterson said. The Nugent interview was taped at his concert at the Sports Arena, along the Maumee River in East Toledo. *Toledo Beat* lasted about a year and a half.

One unusual performance—though not part of *Toledo Beat*—came courtesy of Jerry Reed, the singer, guitarist, songwriter and actor who appeared in more than a dozen films, most notably 1977's *Smokey and the Bandit*, in which he played a truck driver hired to run a trailer full of beer from Georgia to Texas with a pesky sheriff in hot pursuit.

Buckeye had launched the Nashville Network in March 1983, and staged a party for employees, advertisers and community leaders at Luke's Barn, a large former structure at the Lucas County Recreation Center in Maumee.

Paul W. Smith emceed the event. "I said, 'And now, Jerry Reed!'" Smith remembered. "The doors opened and he came in driving a big Mack truck cab. He had a microphone in the cab, and he started singing. The crowd went wild."

Standing on the side step of the cab was Creative Images' Peterson, filming the dramatic entrance. Reed then performed a two-hour concert, which was taped in its entirety and later shown on Buckeye.

Another earlier venture into local-origination programming was a joint effort between Buckeye and *The Blade*. Paul Block Jr., *The Blade*'s publisher, was mulling the idea of marrying newspapers and television.

I was night city editor of *The Blade* in 1978, working from 6:30 p.m. until 2 or 3 a.m., whenever the first edition was completed and went to press. Block's secretary called me at home early one afternoon and said that the publisher would like to talk to me but could not wait until I came to work.

She asked if I could come in at 4:30 to talk to him. With a certain amount of trepidation, wondering what I had done wrong, I agreed.

Instead of a trip to the woodshed, I had an enlightening two-hour discussion with Block about the future of newspapers. He explained that he could see the day coming when newspapers no longer would be a viable business model. He pointed to the high cost of newsprint, delivery trucks, printing presses and the human labor accompanying all those functions—"plus we're 24 hours behind the electronic media," he said.

"I see the day coming when there will be a large screen like a television hanging on everybody's living-room wall, and we'll deliver the news to them electronically via Buckeye Cablevision," he said – prescience of today's Internet. In 1962 a scientist at the Massachusetts Institute of Technology had drafted a series of memos discussing his vision of an interconnected set of computers which would grant users anywhere in the world rapid access to data and programs residing anywhere on the network. No one knows for certain that Block, ever the curious scientist, was aware of this research, but it stands to reason he was. Further, it stands to reason that Block, ever the visionary, saw the future potential of such data transmission.

"The customer will be able to read the news on that screen and print out any stories he wants to keep, saving us the printing, paper and delivery costs," Block said, showing extraordinary intuition for 1978.

He ruminated about the idea for some time, and surely discussed it with other executives.

Leo Hoarty, in a 2014 interview, said that John Willey, *The Blade*'s associate publisher, had occasionally talked about the possibility of using cablevision to deliver *The Blade* in some form. Block now intended to bring that idea to fruition.

In early 1981 we renewed the conversation, revisiting the early idea that subscribers would have a large wall screen on which they would read the news we delivered electronically.

"My job," Block said that day, "is to contact some of my scientific friends and see about getting that big screen for the living-room wall developed.

"Your job," he said, nodding toward me, "is to go out to Buckeye and see how we can put the newspaper on cable."

Others in the news-gathering and electronics industries were sniffing around the edges of the concept of efficiently putting text on television screens, and I was sent to a seminar in Chicago at which that topic was discussed.

Upon my return, I met with engineers and management of Buckeye and with Lee Gagle, who at the time represented the information technology staff at *The Blade*. We laboriously put together a plan, began looking seriously at character-generator equipment (which creates alphanumeric symbols for transmission via a television signal) and earmarked two channels, 11 and 13, to use for the experiment.

We picked those channels because they were the two VHF broadcast stations in Toledo at the time, and the over-the-air signals would interfere with video cable transmission, creating a ghost behind the cable signal and making them unusable for full-motion video.

After setting up a test editing desk at Buckeye's Byrne Road headquarters—connected via closed circuit through the head end on Angola Road and by the regular coaxial-cable plant back to Byrne Road, where I could watch it on a TV set beside the desk—I spent several months learning the equipment and experimenting with what might make the best presentation.

It was nothing like today's on-demand Internet. There were no graphics, just words and numbers on the screen. We were limited to 256 characters per screen, and we, not the viewer, determined how long each screen would be displayed. This was critical, as stories had to be up long enough for slow readers to finish but short enough that fast readers didn't get bored and tune out.

Viewers could not summon a particular story, or even a general category such as news, sports or weather—we determined what would be shown and when.

We came up with a pie-shaped 30-minute clock—the first 10 minutes local news, the second 10 national news and the third international and sports news. The sequence would repeat the second half-hour. The 256-character news pages were interspersed with classified ads.

The Blade promoted sales by offering print classified customers the opportunity, for a small increase in price, to have their ads on television the same number of days they appeared in print. While the text was on the screen, elevator music played in the background.

All the editorial and advertising material was typed in on a special machine in The Blade Building downtown, while the electronic equipment that translated the keystrokes into television pictures was at the Angola Road site. The two pieces of equipment were connected by a special phone line.

The service launched in July 1981 as *The Blade InstantNews*. Ron Boeckman, a young reporter who was attending law school at the University of Toledo, was its first full-time editor. Other newspapers were nosing around the concept, but *The Blade* was among the first in the country to launch a viable product.

It was all very elementary, limited by lack of sophisticated equipment that didn't enable us to have color graphics or motion for ads. Every story had to be manually entered, keystroke by keystroke.

The field in general was so new, as was the equipment—which was virtually being adapted and upgraded as it was being manufactured—that sometimes we felt we knew more about it than the vendors did. On one visit by an engineer from the character-generator manufacturer in Silicon Valley, Gagle performed a couple of operations that changed the onscreen display in an unusual way—something we had been doing for several months. "How did you *do* that?" the engineer asked, unaware of what his own product could do.

It was a start, and we continued to add features and improve the product.

Because interest in the concept was growing, albeit slowly, the wire services, notably Reuters, began to convert their typical teletype format to make it more easy to translate to a format that could be used on TV screens. The Reuters news service also made its stock ticker available for such use, and we scrolled it continuously across the bottom of the screen on one channel.

We converted that channel for classified ads and the stock ticker, and regular experimentation with timing and topics continued to improve the news channel. We added lottery numbers and local high-school and college sports scores. At the bottom of each screen, temperature, barometric pressure, wind speed and direction, precipitation and humidity data scrolled, with each readout on the screen for about five seconds.

Block, trained chemist that he was, paid as much attention to the minute details of his latest news-delivery experiment as he would to an experiment in his home laboratory. His scientific bent came into play with the barometer readings which popped up in rotation every 25 seconds or so.

The barometric pressure was measured by a chip on a circuit board mounted in an equipment cabinet in Buckeye's Angola Road head end, and the readings often fluctuated greatly. The cause, we discovered, was the large amount of heat-generating electronic equipment in the room. The facility was environmentally controlled to such an extent that whenever a door was opened or closed, the pressure would rise or fall, sometimes with each appearance on the screen of the barometer reading.

On one of his visits to the head end to see what could be done about this, Block mentioned to Jim Dryden, who had been named vice president of engineering, that the barometric pressure was adjusted to sea level, while Toledo is 511 feet above sea level—the pressure reading, he said, should reflect that.

Dryden, a private pilot, pointed out that sea level is used universally, because all pilots use that reading when taking off and landing. "And just how many airplanes do you have wired for cable?" Block asked. For once, Dryden, generally quick with a humorous retort to just about everything, was without a comeback.

The two problems were solved by adjusting the pressure reading to Toledo's elevation and polling the pressure sensor only a few times an hour, though it continued to rotate at five-second intervals with the other readings.

Dryden's offbeat sense of humor was a constant presence. In the early stages of *InstantNews,* Mary Block, Paul Jr.'s wife, became interested in the concept, particularly once we had introduced the Reuters stock ticker. One day, I was sitting at my desk at *The Blade* when the phone rang. It was Dryden. "Tom, on the phone with me is Mary Block, and she has some questions about the stock ticker. Mary, go ahead."

Mrs. Block, who was watching TV from her home on River Road in South Toledo, asked why the ticker sometimes moved rapidly across the screen, while other times it ran much more slowly. She asked if I could slow it to a consistent speed. Before I could tell her that the speed was not controlled by us but was governed by the trading activity on the New York Stock Exchange—on a busy day it moved faster as more trades were made—Dryden chimed in.

"Mary," he said, "stand at the right side of your set, and when you see a stock you're interested in, run like hell to the left side." I thought we both were goners—but she just laughed, listened to my explanation about trading activity, thanked us and hung up.

The Blade, which had converted from Linotype machines to computer-set type several years earlier, was installing a new typesetting computer. IT executives at the paper were able to have the software configured so that news stories already in the system could be transferred electronically to the *InstantNews* editor at *The Blade,* who could then edit them down to fit the 256-character format without entering each story a keystroke at a time. Classified ads still had to be manually entered that way, and this was done by printers, the composing-room employees, who worked overnight.

A consultant recommended establishing a small studio in the newsroom from which reporters could periodically tape video dispatches of news stories they were developing, but that concept was vetoed, only to be introduced three decades later. It was then that newspapers, facing the declining competitive edge Block had foreseen 30 years earlier, began to pair with local electronic media in joint ventures to gather and present the news.

By then, though, the dispatches were done live. A camera was permanently mounted in *The Blade* newsroom, and a reporter would stand in front of it and discuss with a TV anchor a story on which he or she was working.

Other *InstantNews* embellishments included introducing National Weather Service forecasts that were inserted automatically four times an hour, and adding equipment that allowed for graphics and color, which spiced up the advertising potential. Business ads were sold on 30-day contracts.

However, because of the limitations that prohibited viewers from accessing information whenever they wanted it, the service never really caught on, and the *InstantNews* classified-advertising experiment was dropped in the late 1980s.

Over the next several years, Buckeye carried a number of programs that required little or no production work by its own staff. These involved the

University of Toledo, the Toledo Fire Division, local groups and churches, and even live audio transmission of high-school basketball games.

In the early 1980s, Don Reiber, now an associate professor of communication at UT, used a $100,000 federal grant from the Department of Education to supplement $257,000 in university funds to upgrade video equipment and build a production studio and transmission facilities at the university's Scott Park campus, east of Westwood Avenue between Hill and Nebraska Avenues, about two miles from the main campus on West Bancroft Street.

The university had a contract with the Learning Channel, which at the time broadcast from 6 a.m. to 4 p.m. The Learning Channel signal was received on a large satellite dish atop the Learning Resources Center building at Scott Park, where staff would record the programs, then show them on Buckeye's Channel 10/B until midnight each day. To do this, a transmitter was placed on top of the building to send a microwave signal about two miles to Buckeye's head end on Angola Road.

The Learning Channel programming was supplemented by UT-generated programming, such as *About Your Health,* a monthly call-in show done at the nearby MCO campus. Dr. Richard Ruppert, MCO's third president, was the program's first host; Jim Richard, MCO's public-relations director and a former sportswriter for *The Blade,* produced it.

The university also produced a number of home football and basketball games, as well as *Rocket Country*, a weekly magazine-format show featuring coaches, athletes and other students. That ran about three years before being replaced by *Rocket Replay,* a recap following UT football and basketball games. These also were shown on Channel 10/B.

The university started producing a few sporting events on the road, such as a football game at Florida State University in Tallahassee and basketball games at Marquette University in Milwaukee and the University of Minnesota in Minneapolis. These were tape-delayed given that the necessary microwave equipment to show them live would have been too costly, Reiber said. He recalled the hectic pace of some of those productions, such as going to Oxford, OH, for a UT–Miami University basketball game, trucking all three cameras from the UT studio to tape the game, then hurrying back immediately afterward to be able to show the tape that same night.

Scott Sandstrom, currently senior editor and videographer in Buckeye's production department, was a UT student then, and he humorously recalled the time he and Reiber went to Muncie, Indiana, for a football game against Ball State University. They forgot that although Ohio is in the Eastern time zone while Indiana is in Central. They were an hour late getting there, and only through extremely fast work were they able to have the production truck and crew ready at game time.

Other university programming included *Japan, the Changing Tradition*, a 20-part series narrated by a UT history professor, and the production of cut-ins to promote Showtime and Movie Channel movies for Buckeye. "We also produced *Basic Keyboarding*, a 20-part series teaching how to type. It seems strange today, but in that day it worked," Reiber said.

The university produced four local programs on various topics each week, and these were shown on Channel 10/B at various times. Throughout, UT employed students for production staff. "They did not get class credit for their work," Reiber said, "but the relationship with Buckeye exposed students to a whole different world and gave them real-life experience."

The original UT production truck, fondly called Old Blue by the students, was replaced with a newer vehicle after the university renovated the Glass Bowl, its football stadium, and installed a Jumbotron animated scoreboard. The new truck was mainly used to feed signals to the Jumbotron, but also to produce a high-school football game of the week and two basketball games each week, which were shown on TV5. (See Chapter 10.)

Another new kind of programming not created solely by Buckeye was what has since become known as public-access. The 1992 Cable Act mandated that cable systems provide channels for the general public and for educational institutions and government entities to use for disseminating information of broad community interest.

This concept, called PEG (for Public, Education and Government) in industry terminology, is to be programmed by the outside entities themselves, and the cable systems are not permitted to have any editorial control over content, other than through broad guidelines that enable them to refuse pornographic programs or those otherwise judged objectionable.

In addition, channel capacity was to be earmarked for leased access, so if a particular group—a church or fraternal organization, say, or an advertiser—wanted to produce a program that didn't fit the loose definition of "broad interest," it could pay for time and have full control of the channel. Buckeye created the Community Channel to meet those requirements.

It's currently programmed 24 hours a day, seven days a week, with about 5 percent of the programming paid, while the rest is offered free under the umbrella of local general interest. Some 30 hours of original programming are shown each week, some of it repeated, according to Veronica Pinciotti, director of local stations. The channel cablecasts about 40 different religious or church-related programs each week.

Local events, such as the annual Hero Awards dinner of the Safety Council of Northwest Ohio, the annual downtown Holiday Parade, fireworks displays, half-hour holiday specials and the annual conference of Jehovah's Witnesses in downtown Toledo, are produced and shown on the Community Channel, Pinciotti noted.

For years, a local running group, the Toledo Roadrunners, produced regular programs featuring marathons, half-marathons and similar races, as well as general information for runners.

One unique programming concept began in 1991, when Toledoan Neil Little, who had been broadcasting high-school sports on a local radio station, leased a channel from Buckeye to cablecast his audio coverage of the contests, selling his own advertising to cover the lease cost. His wife, Jill, and Doug Allen, another Toledoan, provided the color commentary. That concept lasted several years.

In December 1991, Buckeye began showing every Toledo City Council meeting, tape delayed but in its entirety—a relatively new notion at the time. The idea came from Allan Block, who by that time was Buckeye's chairman. He remembered watching City Council meetings shown on tape delay in the 1970s on WGTE, the local public broadcast station, and thought it would be helpful to voters to be more knowledgeable about city issues.

The company negotiated a contract with WGTE to cover each session. When Buckeye began putting fiber-optic cable throughout the downtown area for its telephone business later in the 1990s, a fiber link was run into One Government Center, home of most of Toledo's and Lucas County's offices and the location of City Council chambers. That fiber link was used to transmit the signal back to WGTE's South Toledo studios, then to Buckeye's head end for delivery to customers' homes via the Community Channel.

In order to be fair to all, the politically connected Dave Huey, Buckeye's president and general manager, who had arranged the Toledo Council effort with city government, approached the other local franchise authorities. Buckeye couldn't do all Council meetings of each of the 27 franchise areas in which Buckeye operated at the time, but if they had a session scheduled on a particularly hot topic, he told them, Buckeye could arrange to show it.

One mayor, Louis Bauer of Rossford, jokingly told Huey, "We don't want you coming to our meetings. In Rossford, politics is a contact sport."

Politicians, never shy about seeking exposure, began to hog the podium during City Council meetings. After Buckeye began televising them, Council sessions ran 45 minutes to two hours longer than they had before, according to an analysis done early in 1992 by Jim Drew, a *Blade* reporter.

In an article published on February 28 of that year, Drew pointed out that of the 11 meetings before the coverage began, four broke the two-hour mark and three broke the three-hour mark. Of the first 11 afterward, all broke the two-hour mark, six lasted longer than three hours and two marathon sessions lasted a seemingly unendurable four hours.

One cablecast even went on into the next year. The tape-delayed cablecast of the Dec. 31, 1991 morning meeting began at 7:30 p.m. on December 31, 1991, and ended at 12:01 a.m. January 1, 1992, Drew said.

John McHugh, Toledo's mayor at the time, attributed the lengthening sessions to politicians' hunger for airtime. "A little more pontificating, more political positioning and everybody has to rebut everything that is said," he told Drew.

Councilmen, especially those with aspirations to become mayor, saw the programs as a "virtual feast of free publicity," Drew wrote. "And a bunch are eating their fill—in particular Carty Finkbeiner, Mike Ferner, Jack Ford and Peter Silverman." All four Councilmen later ran for mayor, with Finkbeiner and Ford winning. Finkbeiner served two terms, followed by a single Ford term—after which Finkbeiner won a third term.

Following the introduction of set-top converters in the late 1980s, Buckeye provided a channel to the Toledo Fire Division to show training tapes. A converter box was given to each fire station, and the programs were delivered encrypted to the stations. This was done for two reasons: one, because the Fire Division had to pay copyright fees, and two, because the sometimes graphic content was deemed unsuitable for the general public.

As part of Buckeye's efforts to offer the most value to the most people, in 2003 it contracted with a firm to develop software to enable each community and school district to have its own channel of Video on Demand (VOD), which it could program and schedule remotely, from a government or school office, or even from someone's home computer.

All a viewer would have to do was access the VOD menu and click on a community or school district. Each could program as many subcategories as they wished—for example, schools could set up separate categories for holiday schedules, menus, sporting events, scores, bus schedules, tutors available and more. They could even attach full-motion video clips if they had them.

Buckeye offered the service free; viewers could access it anytime, order programming à la carte and watch it whenever was convenient—stopping, pausing, fast-forwarding or replaying as often as desired. All the information already existed in the form of mailings, Web pages and bulletin boards, the theory went, and by entering it on the virtual channel, the government body or school could get one more way to reach its constituent audience. At the time, no other cable firm offered such a feature.

Each community and school was asked to designate at least one person for training in how to use the system; there were no restrictions on how many other people could be trained by that person. Buckeye then conducted a number of training sessions, supplied each group with a copy of the necessary software and provided a staffer to be available via phone if someone encountered a problem.

Although most franchise authorities and school districts sent someone to the training sessions, only a few made any serious effort to use the service, and after a year or two, most simply quit entering new information. Because the material available was outdated and of little value to the viewer, Buckeye simply discontinued the feature.

One of the more unusual programs shown was the August 31, 1997, taping of the Jeep Hometown Heroes Celebration. Chrysler was considering moving production of its iconic Jeep out of Toledo, where the vehicles had been made since they were introduced in 1942 to supply soldiers in World War II. Several thousand local jobs would be lost.

Local businesses, media, politicians, unions and others mounted a tremendous civic effort. Chrysler ultimately decided not only to keep Jeep in Toledo, but also spent $1.2 billion to build a modern assembly plant in town.

The Hometown Heroes Celebration, in Toledo's Promenade Park downtown, was part of the weekend RiverFest '97 celebration, and was conceived to pay public tribute to the many people who played a part in keeping Jeep in Toledo. Taking part in the celebration were Mayor Finkbeiner, members of the City Council, representatives of the United Auto Workers union and the late Eddie Boggs, a popular local folksinger and songwriter.

Also part of the program were several high school bands, a Marine Corps color guard and a short historical perspective of Jeep and its vital relationship with Toledo.

In Sandusky, the cable company—both under its founders and after being acquired by the Blocks—also showed local-programming enterprise by teaming at various times with the local radio station, WLEC, and the local daily paper.

Early on, a news reporter from WLEC would go to the cablevision office at 232 Fulton Street and read the news on camera daily from a makeshift studio. After several months, station management decided the acoustics weren't conducive to good cablecast quality and dropped the plan.

Later, the *Sandusky Register* began cablecasting news from its newsroom on Erie County Cablevision's Channel 7, and a local man, Tom Whaley, had a daily trivia show. In January 2014, BCSN, the 24-hour local sports channel started by Allan Block in 2004, developed a production trailer and placed a crew in Sandusky to produce local sporting events in the Erie County area.

In Monroe, local programming included such features as a talk show, *All Points Bulletin*, hosted by a Michigan State Police trooper, whose focus was people with some type of broad influence on residents, and *Keen Kids* and *Teen Kids*, in which students from a self-esteem class taught by a local woman and sponsored by the *Monroe Evening News* discussed such topics as pet care, recycling, crime and more. (See Chapter 5.)

BUCKEYE BITS

What Happened in the Stripper's Dressing Room?

Running any business entails a number of captivating moments, but Leo Hoarty experienced one of his most intriguing as general manager of Buckeye Cablevision when he found himself held prisoner in a stripper's dressing room in a Toledo burlesque house.

In March 1968, the notorious Town Hall Theatre, at St. Clair and Orange Streets downtown, was being torn down (though not one brick at a time, as some wags joked) to make way for a new building to house United Way.

"When it was announced that it was going to close, my production manager suggested we do a documentary on it," Hoarty said. He called the proprietor, Rose LaRose, who agreed that a crew could tape there, including parts of the final show on Tuesday, March 26.

"The whole programming department went down there, and there were lots of volunteers," Hoarty said. "When we were done, Ms. LaRose came up to me and said she wanted to see me in her dressing room."

He followed her there, whereupon she promptly locked the door and put the key in her pocket.

"She said, 'I want my check.' I said, 'What check?'"

LaRose told him she wanted $25,000 to cover expenses—"like electricity"—related to the Buckeye production. "I told her that wasn't my intent, and said I had to go to the bathroom and asked where it was.

"She told me I wasn't going anyplace until she got her check. So I asked to use her phone, and called John Willey"—associate publisher of *The Blade* and one of two executives to whom Hoarty reported.

"It was about 11 or 11:30 at night by that time. I told him I was locked in Rose LaRose's dressing room. He said, 'Is she there?', and I said yes. He said, 'Well, enjoy yourself.'"

"Wait, don't hang up!" I said. "She wants $25,000." He explained LaRose's demand. "Oh, my God," Willey replied. He told Hoarty to stall LaRose while he contacted her attorney.

When Willey called back, he talked to LaRose for several minutes. "John made her some sort of offer, and then I got back on the phone and he told me to give her the film we shot," Hoarty said.

Hoarty, set free, told the crew what happened, and gathered up the film. "I found out later that one of the guys kept one roll that I didn't know about," he said. "But we never showed it. As far as I know, no money changed hands."

LaRose apparently got only the (film) strips.

Burglars Steal Cops and Robbers

The Channel 100 studio on Angola Road was the target of burglars in 1975—thieves who apparently had a sense of humor.

Martin Kaplan, general manager of Channel 100, reported that among some $12,000 worth of video and audio equipment stolen in the overnight burglary was a copy of the film *Cops and Robbers,* which was slated for telecast.

Chapter Ten

"We Can Give Viewers Something They Won't See Elsewhere"

No Tower, No Transmitter:
TV5 Debuts as a Different Kind of Broadcast Operation

When Allan Block first broached the subject, I was against it.

"What could we possibly show on it that customers couldn't find on one of the 38 channels we carry?" was my reaction.

It was early 1989, and what Block was proposing was a local-origination station—but with a difference. "Local origination" refers to a channel that the cable company or an outside group programs with local content: notices of upcoming events, tapes of government meetings, church services, school-board meetings, video "blogs" and more.

Block was envisioning a local channel—an independent TV station but limited to cable—that would be programmed with syndicated material that was not shown locally. He realized that over the last couple of years programming was being produced to such an extent beyond the capacity of the broadcast stations to carry; independent TV stations were springing up to take advantage of the many hours of such programs. Even though WUPW had begun operating on Channel 36, he realized there still was much programming not being shown in the Toledo market.

He had recently returned from a meeting of the National Association of Television Programming Executives (NATPE) and determined that there existed a plethora of studio- and network-produced programming that was not "cleared" in Toledo—that is, it wasn't being shown on one of the four local network or independent broadcast outlets.

"I think we can create something of value to our customers by giving them something additional, something they won't see elsewhere," he said.

My pessimism failed to persuade him. "If we do it right," he said to me, "there'll be lots there for the customer." He then said he wanted me to plan and launch the channel. He had already chosen Channel 5 for it, as that was the channel Buckeye used in the early days to show public-domain movies and locally originated programs such as *From the Zoo* and *Sixth Grade Report.*

With some trepidation, I agreed to do it, not even knowing where to begin.

He sent me to Boise, Idaho, where the Blocks own KTRV, a TV station affiliated at the time with the Fox network. There I spent several days with Diane Frisch, its program director. She was extremely helpful, giving me a crash course in dealing with programmers, negotiating contracts for syndicated material, programming various portions of the day to attract the widest audience and hundreds of other tips she had picked up over the years.

When I returned, Block introduced me to Joseph F. Kiselica, who represented Viacom, one of the larger syndicators—companies that broker to local outlets syndicated programming produced by studios and networks—with whom he had dealt for the broadcast stations Block Communications owned.

Over the next few months, I met frequently with Kiselica as we went over which programs were available in the Toledo market, what terms might be arranged and the myriad other details of programming a station. He, too, provided valuable insight to the novice sitting across the table from him. I was always in awe when he could spout, from memory, the ratings of different programs at various times of day in other cities.

Having such information was significant. After all, what we were doing was akin to programming a new TV station about to go on the air. In a sense, this would be a television station in all aspects but one: It would not have a tower or transmitter for over-the-air broadcasting; it would be shown only on Buckeye.

I soon learned one of the major obstacles we faced: To that point, syndicators had dealt only with local broadcasters or national cable channels such as A&E, and were wary of us because we were neither fish nor fowl. Other than Kiselica, they didn't entirely trust our motives, knew we would be competing with their existing broadcast and cable customers and didn't want to antagonize any of those relationships.

Another problem was that a lot of the more popular syndicated material was already spoken for by one of the Toledo broadcasters, which had exclusive rights to show such fare in the Toledo market.

In the end, we had to settle for what's known in the trade as "evergreen"—older programs that maintain audience interest despite their age. *I*

Love Lucy, Gunsmoke, Bonanza, Rawhide, Gilligan's Island, The Andy Grif-fith Show, those sorts of programs.

With the programming settled and a vague launch date of late summer established, I next turned my attention to the technical and marketing details, about which I also knew nothing. Up until a few years earlier, I had spent virtually my whole career as a newspaper reporter and editor, completely ignorant of any technical or marketing tasks and certainly uneducated in television operations.

Chris Kasner, Buckeye's system engineer/master control at the time, was assigned the additional responsibility of day-to-day operations and supervision of the technical directors and film editor for the channel. He worked with me on all of the technical aspects of getting TedoVision5 up and running.

ToledoVision5 was chosen, Block said, to give the channel the panache then associated with radio station identities, such as MAGIC 105 or Wolf FM. "I wanted to do with video what radio was doing as far as an identity and recognition," he said.

Kasner proved just as valuable on the technical side as Frisch had been in teaching me about programming—although to this day my technical knowledge consists of telling an engineer, "I want to do such-and-such. How can you accomplish that for me?"

In addition, Kasner was involved in an amateur theater group and had a flair for entertainment production. For example, we had a contract for a number of old movies, and he came up with something he called *The Big Show.* For each movie, he taped an introduction, a chatty intermission segment and closing comments. That moved the program one step above merely showing a movie and upped our professionalism a bit.

That later became too time-consuming for him, though, so he arranged for an amateur actress to tape the advance commentary for each movie. The name *The Big Show* and its logo were even registered with the U.S. Patent and Trademark Office.

Kasner helped me make arrangements for getting the programming delivered to Buckeye's head end for transmission to customers' sets. We received some of it via satellite on one of the large dishes Buckeye had at the Angola Road property, and some was "bicycled," which referred to tapes sent by mail or other commercial delivery. When we received a tape, it came with instructions regarding how long we were to keep it and to whom and how we were to ship it to the next program outlet.

Kasner capably handled all the little details: scheduling reception of the programming via satellite dish; making sure everything was recorded and shown at the proper time; ensuring that certain commercials or public-service announcements (PSAs) were shown at the predetermined breaks (set by the producer of the program); and a thousand other things.

For marketing advice, I turned to John Fedderke, who owned a local public-relations and advertising firm and who had worked with the Blocks, specifically Allan, on a number of other projects. He, too, was most helpful.

He helped settle on the name ToledoVision5, later shortened to TV5, and worked to create a logo and associated marketing elements, laid out an advertising program and contracted for print space and time on local broadcast outlets. He also directed the creation of video spots, both as 30-second promotions for the channel and for the numerous station-break "bumps," the short (usually five-second) video and audio transitions played between programs at the top and bottom of the hour.

Fedderke also took the lead in planning the launch. A local civic group was arranging an event in August that included the visit of several "tall ships," replicas of old sailing vessels. These were to be docked for a few days along Toledo's recently developed riverfront. That development had seen old warehouses, bars and a burlesque theater torn down and replaced by a modern, gleaming 30-story headquarters for Owens-Illinois, a festive marketplace of shops and attractions and a riverfront green space named Promenade Park.

The development had come to fruition largely through a joint effort by Toledo Mayor Harry Kessler and Paul Block Jr., via *The Blade,* so it seemed only natural to celebrate the launch of Buckeye's newest feature in conjunction with the visit of the tall ships, which would be docked by the O-I building.

Fedderke worked his promotional magic to cut though the red tape of obtaining permission and getting the dock area reserved for Buckeye's announcement.

Nancy Duwve was appointed production/continuity coordinator, with responsibility for continuity and scripts. She also served as liaison for program suppliers and advertising sales, and coordinated cross-promotions of programming services, TV5 and image spots.

Duwve had been with Buckeye since 1980, when she was hired as administrative assistant to the late Gary Brubaker, Buckeye's marketing director. In that role, she scheduled the public-domain movies and public-service announcements on the original iteration of Channel 5, and bicycled tapes back and forth.

Later, she was named special projects director and was responsible for contracting with apartments, hotels and the like for cable service and working with the construction division to make certain the plant was ready to serve those locations. Following that, she was in charge of converter-box deployment when Buckeye introduced the converters as a precursor to the system rebuild, replacing the old dual-cable coaxial system with a single-cable fiber-optic/coaxial system.

I therefore knew she had the administrative skills and the old Channel 5 experience that would be necessary for the new TV5, and she performed admirably. Each year she managed to obtain newer programming, enabling us to eliminate some of the original "evergreen" material and update our overall look.

The launch on Monday, August 7, 1989, was successful, giving subscribers seven hours (5 p.m. to midnight) of early fringe, prime access, prime time and late fringe programming, as Block had promised, not otherwise being shown in Toledo.

In an interview following the launch, he said he'd stick with the concept for a year, and if it was well-received, it would become a permanent fixture. Now, some 25 years later, it remains a viable product—though under different ownership, as I'll get to later.

In addition to the syndicated programming scheduled for TV5, the channel showed baseball games. A few Mud Hens games were produced and shown live from Ned Skeldon Stadium in Maumee, but the bulk were either Detroit Tigers or Cleveland Indians games Buckeye obtained through arrangements with PASS, a Detroit regional sports channel, or through WUAB, a broadcast station in Cleveland that had rights to Indians games.

Buckeye carried them on a separate channel, but when there was a scheduling conflict, one of the games was shown on TV5. Finally, the company decided to slot one or the other team on TV5 regularly during the entire season and to brand the games "Buckeye Baseball"; it then sought to trademark the name.

The sports-licensing department at The Ohio State University in Columbus noticed the application with the U.S. Patent and Trademark Office and filed an objection, apparently fearing that someone was trying to infringe on the term "Buckeye," as the University's sports teams are known. Even though OSU did not have a valid registration for the term "Buckeye Baseball," I made an appointment to go to Columbus to meet with OSU officials to negotiate a resolution.

After the usual pleasantries at the start of the meeting, the intellectual-property attorney who handled licensing surprised me with her first question—and her provincialism.

"What gives you the right to use the term 'Buckeye'?" she asked, apparently thinking the world revolved around OSU's campus. I gave her a brief history of Buckeye Cablevision and mentioned additional companies with the same name: Buckeye Pipeline, Buckeye Brewery, Buckeye Fence and a few others.

"Furthermore, there is a tree called a 'buckeye,'" I said, somewhat sarcastically. "In fact, there are about two pages of listings for 'Buckeye *something*' in the Toledo Yellow Pages"—and the same was probably true in the Yellow Pages throughout Ohio.

I explained our proposed use of the term and described the somewhat limited, clearly defined, area in which the programming would be shown. We finally struck a deal whereby I would drop our trademark application and the university would grant Buckeye CableSystem a somewhat meaningless license to use the word "Buckeye" in conjunction with the TV5 baseball cablecasts.

To gauge the popularity of TV5 we had commissioned Stan Odesky, a local market-research guru, to see what kind of audience TV5 was garnering. He found it to be broadly popular among Buckeye customers, though it never showed up in audience rating reports by Arbitron, which at the time measured viewership of TV programs (a category now dominated by Nielsen). TV5's lack of "official" ratings made advertising difficult to sell.

Arbitron compiled ratings by sending diaries to families in the Toledo Designated Market Area (DMA), an area encompassing 13 counties in Northwest Ohio. We realized that not all viewers in the DMA could subscribe to Buckeye's cable service, dampening the possibility that audience numbers would be reported.

Allan Block solved the problem in his own unique way. He set up a meeting with an Arbitron vice president who dealt with the Blocks' various broadcast stations, all of which paid substantial amounts each year for the rating service. Present at the meeting, which took place at a NATPE gathering in New Orleans, were the general managers of the Blocks' stations, Allan Block, the Arbitron VP and me.

Block explained the situation: We had found through independent research that TV5 was popular with Buckeye's customers, yet because the rating system covered so many counties, it did not draw sufficient audience numbers to show up in the Arbitron report.

He then hinted—no, said outright—that if TV5 did not show up in the next Arbitron report, the other Block stations would no longer be Arbitron clients. Interestingly, Arbitron found that TV5 did, indeed, have enough viewers to be included in the next rating report.

In 2003, the channel's name was changed to WT05 to help with the rating system, under the assumption that viewers, when completing diaries, didn't identify TV5 the same way they recognized the four-letter call signs of broadcast stations.

In April 1991, I was asked to take a four-month special assignment in Columbus, and Cathy Smith took over running TV5 in the interim. She had been with Buckeye since 1978 in various accounting and customer-service positions and at the time was overseeing master control operations for TV5, supervising the crews that recorded and showed purchased programming, public-service announcements and commercials.

It was at this time— once I got out of it—that TV5 really took off. Smith and Duwve attended NATPE sessions and were able to obtain increasingly better programming. TV5 began to cablecast from noon to 8 p.m., then to midnight, and finally to 20 hours a day as programming improved.

TV5 obtained more than 200 episodes of *Murphy Brown*, CBS's popular sitcom starring Candice Bergen. The program debuted in 1988 and had gone into syndication, so reruns were available to independent operators.

Because of the *Murphy Brown* acquisition, which permitted several showings of each episode over several years, it became cumbersome to continue to "bicycle" tapes. Instead, Buckeye began to record the programming on three-quarter-inch tapes as it came in, send the syndicator's tape to the next venue, then store the tape. To make room for the burgeoning number of tapes, Smith's office was converted to a storage room with floor-to-ceiling shelves on rollers.

As TV5 operations grew, more staff was needed, and with more staff, more space was needed. Smith had been operating out of a small office in the cement-block head-end building on Angola Road, and Duwve worked from a desk crowded into one corner of the building, which also housed Buckeye's design department and all the electronic equipment needed to receive and transmit TV signals.

Because all parts of Buckeye were growing, no additional office space was available, so the company rented a converted trailer and anchored it adjacent to the warehouse in the Angola Road parking lot. That remained headquarters for TV5 for six years, and Block relished the idea of negotiating with syndicators in the trailer, the implication being that TV5 could not afford the syndicators' prices.

A big breakthrough came in 1995, however, when TV5 was named an affiliate of the WB Network just as it was being launched. Buckeye became the first such cable affiliation in the country. The network, founded by Warner Bros., was envisioned as being available only to broadcast TV stations.

The affiliation agreement came about in part as a result of negotiations at a NATPE conference in San Francisco in January 1995.

"Allan wanted to be the first cable channel to be an affiliate," Duwve said. She, Block and Smith met with a WB representative several times during the meeting, and finally struck an agreement midweek, but with one stipulation: TV5 had to begin cablecasting the network the following Monday.

That day marked the beginning of "sweeps," the period twice a year when audience ratings are measured. Since advertising sales and rates are heavily dependent on those results, both WB and Buckeye wanted to get exposure during the February ratings period, Duwve said.

Duwve and Smith hurried back to Toledo to put in place the marketing, scheduling and technical details to get the network to the customers. "It was done on a handshake, and we didn't finalize the contract until after we had been showing the WB programming for some time," Duwve said.

Initially, WB programming ran only from 8 to 10 p.m. weeknights. Later, Sunday prime-time programming was added, as were Saturday morning cartoons, Ms. Duwve recalls.

After some time, WB, seeing its ratings dropping, merged with CBS to form the CW Network, and TV5 is a CW affiliate to this day.

WTVG, the ABC affiliate in Toledo, expressed interest in affiliation with the CW to provide programming on one of its digital sub channels. Buckeye had the network under agreement until 2016, but in August 2014, after months of negotiations, Buckeye agreed to a deal by which it sold TV5 and its programming rights to WTVG in return for some cash and certain retransmission considerations in the future.

BUCKEYE BITS

When It Rains, It Pours—Into the Electrical Equipment Room

It was a dark and stormy night, as *Peanuts'* Snoopy was wont to write.

Well, it was actually a dark and stormy *morning* during late autumn in the mid-1990s. The day started cold and overcast with a steady drizzle, and got progressively worse.

By midday, a steady rain was pelting the windows of Buckeye's headquarters on Southwyck Boulevard, and the wind kept getting stronger.

Late in the afternoon, a potential disaster occurred.

Whoever designed the Southwyck building for some reason put the roof drain in the center of the building, with a drainpipe from the second-story roof down to an underground storm sewer.

The roof drain descended through the room designated for electrical equipment, which included the power for the building, the telephone equipment and the power for the data center—the computers that are the very lifeblood of Buckeye CableSystem.

Just as business activities in the executive offices were winding down and everyone was looking forward to going home, the call came from the first floor: The drainpipe in the electrical room had sprung a leak; water was covering the floor.

Buckeye president Dave Huey and I rushed down to examine things. A seam on the drainpipe had separated, and water was leaking rapidly from the break.

I went to look for something to use for a patch, while Huey stayed in the room to deal as best he could with the rapidly worsening situation.

I found a sheet of flexible plastic that I thought (or hoped) might work, and rushed back.

We wrapped the plastic and some nearby rags around the pipe break. Huey removed his necktie, wrapping it around the plastic, and we tried to tighten this makeshift tourniquet around the "bandage" we had fashioned.

As we worked, we frequently and nervously—very nervously—glanced at the water on the floor, which crept ever higher and closer to the electrical equipment.

We feverishly continued to position the plastic sheet and rags over the pipe while keeping Huey's necktie wrapped tightly around them.

Finally, enough pressure in the right place from the plastic, rags and necktie stopped the flow of water into the electrical room and reverted it harmlessly back into the storm sewer.

As we slogged through the water on the floor and headed for the door, Huey glanced at me. "I guess this is what that last line on our job descriptions covers—'and other duties as necessary,'" he said.

C-SPAN Fosters Creativity

Buckeye not only was an early player in the 1970s in the production of local programming, but through the years it also has provided the conduit by which outsiders could develop original programs of their own.

In 2004, a Perrysburg High School sophomore, Barrett Dorner, produced a video documentary, *Concealed Carry Concerns,* that garnered him an honorable mention in Campaign Cam, a national contest open to students throughout the United States. Dorner was the first local winner.

The contest, sponsored by C-SPAN and C-SPAN in the Classroom, was designed to engage students in the kinds of policy debates regularly discussed on the public-affairs network. Some 700 entries were submitted nationwide.

Dorner's effort was part of a class at Perrysburg High taught by Kathryn Housepian, who has since retired, called "The Cellar"—a course that encourages students to use technology for artistic expression. Through writing, drawing, photography and videography, students create productions that are shown on a closed-circuit TV station in the school. All projects were also shown on Buckeye's Community Channel.

Dorner, the son of Jeff Dorner and Barbara Jackson, examined Ohio's Concealed Carry Law, which had recently been enacted. He interviewed a Perrysburg teacher who was a member of the National Rifle Association, and two Toledo police patrolmen who offered opposing viewpoints. Dorner made the documentary with the school's video graphic and editing equipment; his award included a $500 cash prize.

That same year, Dorner parlayed his interest in videography into an unpaid internship at WUPW, the Fox affiliate in Toledo. He later earned a full-time paying job "doing just about everything," he said in 2014. That included serving as a general assignment reporter, videographer, producer and even meteorologist (he minored in meteorology in college). He was on the air nonstop for several hours on June 5, 2010, when a tornado devastated much of Lake Township in Wood County, including wiping out the Lake High School Building.

Following the sale of WUPW and the formation of a shared-services agreement with WTOL, the CBS affiliate in Toledo, Dorner joined WTOL's staff in 2011 as a producer. Among his other duties, he was instrumental in developing *Leading Edge,* a weekly public-affairs program hosted by Jerry Anderson, a prominent local newscaster.

Housepian also garnered national honors for her work with students when Buckeye nominated her in 2008 for a national Leaders in Learning award, given by Cable in the Classroom to teachers with a demonstrated commitment to improving education. Housepian was one of 44 finalists and received a $3,000 prize and an all-expenses-paid trip to Washington, D.C., for an awards ceremony at the Library of Congress.

C-SPAN and C-SPAN in the Classroom were created by the cable industry and offered as a public service. C-SPAN and C-SPAN 2 are carried on Buckeye CableSystem. Cable in the Classroom, of which Buckeye has been a sponsor, is the education foundation sponsored by the cable industry; it seeks to enhance and expand education for the nation's youth.

Chapter Eleven

"Everybody Wanted to Be Part of the Excitement"

BCSN Becomes a Local-sports Sensation

On a cold, blustery Friday evening in January 2003, Block Communications president Dave Huey had come home from a trying workday at the end of a trying workweek, and was relaxing with his family when the phone rang.

"Are you sitting down?" were the first words he said he heard from Allan Block. After-hours calls from him were nothing unusual.

"Sure. What's up?" Huey asked.

"I want to start a 24-hour sports network that concentrates on local sports."

As Block envisioned it, the network would focus on all local contests – high school, college, amateur, semi-professional and possibly some minor-league and major-league professional sports from Cleveland and Detroit. In his vision, it would produce 16 to 20 events each week, showing as many games live as schedules permitted, with the rest taped for telecasting later. All events would be shown several times throughout the following week.

He had seen a trade journal article about a proposed cable network which would cover only college sports. "I was thinking, why can't you take that one step farther and do all *local* sports," he said later. "Equipment costs were coming down rapidly and the technology was changing rapidly," he said of the new generations of digital controlled analog cameras.

There were two levels of video equipment, commercial and industrial, with the commercial suitable for television broadcasts and the industrial grade, still of excellent quality, but without all the bells and whistles needed

for the constant use that broadcasters demand. "The industrial-digital cameras were better that the best that TV stations had 10 years earlier," he said.

And so began a yearlong adventure: Block wanted the network up and
running by January 2004.

Huey explained the concept to Buckeye president Chip Carstensen, and
they mulled it over with other executives. After much analysis of costs and
other considerations, they tried to talk Block out of the idea. It would be
expensive, it would add large numbers to the payroll, there was little prospect
of sufficient revenue and there were other, more pressing, issues facing the
businesses under the Block Communications umbrella. Could the companies
afford to tie up executive talent on such a money-losing venture?

Block was not dissuaded. If losses could be held within the range that the
company paid to program other channels—not the stratospheric heights of
the hugely popular ESPN, certainly, but the charges of some of the lesser
channels—then it could proceed. "After all, we'd have to pay carriage fees to
offer a commercial channel, and this will give us a competitive edge," he
said. "We'll have something no other provider in our area will have."

A huge amount of planning was needed, and it had to begin quickly.
However, as chairman of Buckeye CableSystem and managing director of
Block Communications, Block had other concerns to occupy his time. The
two newspapers were losing advertising at a dismaying clip; the TV stations
recently had made large outlays for conversion to high-definition broadcasting; and then there was Buckeye TeleSystem. The phone business was less
than a decade old, and while it was growing satisfactorily, it was still was in
its infancy and needed constant executive oversight.

Thus no firm decision came from the BCI board meeting in the first
quarter of 2003. Huey kept pressing Block for a decision. "If we're going to
start this in January, we need to get rolling," he said.

No decision came from the second-quarter board meeting. Now it was
really getting to be crunch time, as Buckeye executives, particularly Huey
and Carstensen, knew from past experience that once his mind was made up,
Block's course of action would not be deterred. He was convinced that the
project was viable, but the other family members weren't as confident.

The January 2004 launch date remained firmly in his mind. Some rudi-
mentary planning was going on, mostly the kind that consisted of what-if
questions that executives tossed around. Without a firm directive to proceed
and no budget set, planning couldn't be much more extensive than that. In
late 2003, Nancy Duwve was brought in and asked to assess the situation
based on her experiences launching TV5. (See Chapter 10)

"Cool, I thought," Duwve said. "I loved launching TV5 and really looked
forward to starting BCSN," or Buckeye CableSystem Sports Network—assuming it really was going to happen, that is.

In late summer 2003, the board gave its approval—with January 2004, mere months away, as the confirmed start date. It was all hands on deck for the rest of the year.

Duwve began putting specifics in place where only concepts had existed. How many videographers and production people were needed? How many production trucks would it take, and what equipment should they carry? The budget dictated only one production vehicle. Where in a market Toledo's size could the on-air talent—the announcers and color commentators—be found? How would schools react? All these issues, Duwve recalled, caused her many sleepless nights.

Meanwhile, Huey and Carstensen were directly, and from a time standpoint, heavily involved in the entire project virtually full-time, in addition to their regular duties. Glen Cook, director of engineering for the broadcast television group of Block Communications and chief engineer at WDRB, Block's TV station in Louisville, was brought in to oversee the technical aspects. He wrote specifications for the myriad cameras, tape decks, character generators, and other equipment that would be needed to photograph athletic events and bring them to the viewers' television screens. Larry Jacquemotte, production programming manager, began ordering the video equipment.

Block felt that at least three production trucks would be needed to produce the number of events he wanted initially. With an eye toward keeping costs down, Cook recommended foregoing the expensive production trucks so prevalent with commercial television stations and cable channels such as ESPN. Instead he pushed the idea of production trailers.

They would be exactly like production trucks, but without an engine or drive gear, which add operational and maintenance expense; they would be pulled from location to location by truck. After all, Buckeye had some 30-plus trucks in its construction and technical fleets, and scores of drivers. (This concept would later prove impractical, however, so Buckeye ended up contracting with a local towing firm to deliver the trailers to venues and return them after the games.)

Bids were sought, and on November 5, 2003, the first trailer was ordered. It had been designed and created by Duncan Video in Carmel, Indiana. Because of the pressing kickoff date, crews from Carmel were in town putting the finishing touches on it over Christmas.

Equipment orders were placed and vendors pressured to provide the equipment much more quickly than their standard delivery schedules. The thorny problem of getting on-air talent remained. Maybe students could fill that need?

Veronica Pinciotti, who had been instrumental in reorganizing the warehouse and hiring and training subcontractors during the 1997–2002 fiber rebuild, was brought on board under Duwve's direction for her organizational skills and was tasked with staffing up.

The call went out to Bowling Green State University and the University of Toledo, both of which offered majors in radio, TV and film. If enough capable students could be found, they could work the varied and irregular hours required to cover a variety of high-school athletic events. In addition to the money that cash-starved college students always needed, they could garner a lot of valuable experience to put on their résumés, Duwve reasoned.

Pinciotti started with 35 students, whose experience and training varied greatly. "There was a lot of broken equipment at first as students learned on the fly to assemble and disassemble the variety of equipment needed for video production," she said. Andy Sanzotta, a Cleveland-area graduate of the University of Toledo but who stayed in Toledo and who had some video experience, was brought on board as lead talent. He also scheduled talent for all the BCSN events.

He would do the play-by-play announcing for the first two games when the channel launched. "It was a fun time," he reminisced. "It was quite a unique experience, going around doing games and getting paid. It was a great start."

Sanzotta, who went on to positions with the Dayton Bombers, the East Coast Hockey League team in the southern Ohio city, is an account executive with WEOL radio in the Elyria-Lorain market in the Cleveland area, where he also does some play-by-play announcing as well as a weekly football program in season.

Because of the tight schedule—a launch date of January 7 was now firm—the novice production team embarked on an intensive 10-day trial period, producing and taping five live games. The group then gathered to critique such things as equipment setup, camera angles, commercial breaks and announcer and color-commentator style, and to look for potential trouble spots and areas in need of improvement.

"I was really surprised at the quality of the youth we used for production—for the field crews, for master control and for the on-air talent," Pinciotti said. Initially hired as independent contractors, the students proved up to the task. "They were all professional and had excellent technical skills," she said. (A few years later the company decided, for the sake of efficiency, to make all BCSN field and technical staff full- and part-time employees rather than independent contractors.)

Tom Cole, an outgoing, personable salesman with a background in sports and who managed the Cumulus sports radio station WLQR, known as *The Ticket*, had a daily hour-long sports talk show called *Front Row*. Shortly after BCSN launched he began simulcasting the show on radio and BCSN.

In June, 2005, he joined Buckeye's ad-sales department full time, but kept on broadcasting sporting contests and sport shows on BCSN in his spare time. As the local sports channel grew, the duties mounted, and in mid-2007, Cole left the ad sales department and devoted full time to BCSN.

Cole, who had been a high-school teacher and coach for 22 years as a plus had about five years' experience doing color commentary on the Game of the Week, a precursor to BCSN. That venture, started in the late 1990s, entailed Buckeye covering one high-school game each week and showing it tape-delayed on TV5. A smattering of other sporting events, such as Mud Hens games, were also tape-delay cablecast on TV5.

Fred Beier, at the time the head football coach at St. John's Jesuit High School, was asked if he would like to do color on the Buckeye Cable Game of the Week in football. Beier thought about it and was grateful for the offer but decided he would pass on it. He then contacted his former offensive coordinator at the South Toledo Catholic school, Tom Cole, who had done a lot of sports TV at St. John's. He thought that Cole would do a good job for them.

Cole was thrilled for the opportunity to work for Buckeye in that capacity doing sports TV. Cole took the job and realized how much he enjoyed it and did the game of the week for four years. He gladly agreed to continue that role when, and if, the latest Block brain child were finally born.

What to call the new venture? John Fedderke, who had done a sterling job with the TV5 launch and still had a private PR and marketing firm, but who was working virtually full-time with Buckeye's marketing department, was pressed into service.

After seeking input from others at Buckeye and among his professional acquaintances, Fedderke came up with BCSN. It was descriptive and bore a close, alliterative relationship to the popular ESPN. Block was enthusiastic about it, and Fedderke began developing a logo and other marketing appurtenances.

The pace of planning, development and execution picked up rapidly. Contracts were signed with the student talent, space was secured to work on, and later house, the production trailer, and Buckeye allocated office and technical space for BCSN in the recently expanded Network Operations Center on Angola Road.

The company also began consulting with school athletic directors. Several were less than enthusiastic, some even antagonistic. The initial reaction from the school systems themselves was also decidedly lukewarm. Brad Rieger, superintendent of Sylvania Schools, remembered being concerned: "I had images of nothing but problems—students having to sign releases, calls from parents, inappropriateness of students on camera, incidents in the stands that would not be a great reflection on the school, that sort of thing."

School athletic directors, he added, were concerned about BCSN's possible impact on attendance. Other than the physical facilities and the salaries of the employees involved, all expenses of high-school athletics are covered by gate receipts and booster clubs. The athletic directors worried that if games were televised, even via tape delay, the stands wouldn't be full. They also fretted about the problems of integrating a TV production into everything else they had to do to host a game. But Duwve and Pinciotti plowed ahead with their planning. January 7 was getting dangerously closer with each passing minute.

Though Block's original concept was to have one live game and several others shown via tape delay, he determined that one live game a day would not suffice if BCSN were to catch on—more live games, more production trailers and more talent would be needed. This notion came to occupy his immediate thinking, and he began to envision several live games a week as early as, yes, January.

However, in order to carry live games, high-school gymnasiums would need a fiber-optic feed to get the signal back to the Angola Road head end to be fed to Buckeye's 150,000-plus subscribers. Buckeye TeleSystem had fiber optic lines into Toledo Public Schools buildings to provide voice and data services to all the schools in the system, but those lines obviously were in offices, not the gymnasiums. That meant construction crews would have to build new fiber, as no gymnasiums had been on the original fiber-build plans—there had never been any reason for such expenditures.

There was one big problem: It was Christmastime, and schools were closed for the holidays. Buckeye staffers tried to figure out how to surmount this latest roadblock. One employee was a friend of someone high up on the maintenance staff of Toledo Public Schools; he was able to persuade the man to open the schools over the holidays to allow Buckeye in to run the necessary lines. Similar pleas were issued to suburban school districts within Buckeye's footprint. Within days, a number of them had the needed fiber-optic equipment to allow for live telecasts.

Dave Huey and I spent the first days of January mending fences—apologizing to school superintendents for Buckeye's transgressions over the holidays and attempting to convince them that BCSN would benefit their schools. Not all were swayed, but most were at least receptive—and forgiving. Today, some 60 schools in the Toledo and Sandusky area have fiber connections, many at both football and basketball sites, permitting live telecasts.

The venue for the first live cablecast on January 7 was Owens Community College. Owens' women's basketball team thrashed Columbus State Community College, 97–51. BCSN also taped a girl's basketball game at Notre Dame Academy that night against Scott High School and showed it the next day. Notre Dame won, 56–40.

At Owens, Cole, Greg Franke, who is now manager of on-air talent for BCSN; Tom Duncan, a football player from Bowsher High School and the University of Toledo followed by pro experience with the New York Jets and the New England Patriots, and Mindy Woodrow, the daughter of a Buckeye employee, put on a two-hour live pregame show.

The show explained the concept of BCSN, outlining planned coverage, introducing BCSN's crews, interviewing students, coaches and other school personnel and community notables, and generally telling viewers what great things they could expect.

"When you really believe in it, it's pretty easy to talk about it and promote it," Cole said later. There were still bugs to be worked out, but overall the first BCSN cablecast was considered a success—a solid foundation on which to build the great things Block envisioned.

Two live games became the norm in the first half of 2004, with a limited number of other games shown tape-delayed. After all, BCSN had just the one production trailer, and schools played many basketball games on the same nights. The company later authorized a second trailer, which was put into service the second half of 2004, and Cole moved from ad sales and joined BCSN full-time.

In addition to dozens of students working as paid, part-time crew members, Duwve drew on other Buckeye staff to flesh out the ranks. In addition to Pinciotti, Renee Iott (now Ruetz), who had been with Buckeye for about 15 years, was assigned the task of scheduling on-air events on BCSN while continuing to schedule programming for TV5. Dennis Robedeau, an editor and producer with TV5, was named engineer in charge—the technical and mechanical wizard of the operation, essentially, the one who keeps the trailer and production equipment in working order and ready for each assignment.

BCSN's audience grew as it began to cover more games. High-school students involved in lacrosse, swimming, tennis, volleyball and even broomball now found themselves playing on television. They became minor celebrities to their friends. Parents, grandparents, friends and neighbors of the students began watching in ever-increasing numbers.

Betty Schulz, who had served many years on Toledo City Council, once commented that she and her husband frequently watched BCSN even though they no longer had children in high school and their friends' children were beyond that stage as well. It was just good wholesome entertainment, she said.

As schools began to see the good the coverage brought them, working relationships improved. "BCSN learned how not to interfere," said Rieger, the Sylvania superintendent. "Early on, BCSN would show up and the (athletic directors) didn't even know they were coming. Gradually we began to see the benefits, and by 2005 all of us—administration, teachers, athletic directors—were onboard. Now, having BCSN there elevates the event—kids are more motivated when BCSN covers a game. Kids are involved in social media, so the cameras don't really bother them. BCSN is really reality TV, but on a local level."

Next on the programming agenda was professional sports.

The Toledo Mud Hens, the AAA affiliate of the Detroit Tigers, had moved downtown in 2002 from the antiquated Ned Skeldon Stadium, a converted fairgrounds/harness horse-racing track in Maumee, to Fifth Third Field, a gleaming new structure which was named by *Newsweek* magazine that year as the best park in Minor League Baseball.

In late 2003, Allan Block and Dave Huey approached Joe Napoli, the Hens' president and general manager, with the idea of televising games live, then showing the game again tape-delayed. Napoli had some trepidation. What would fans' reaction be—would they stay away from the park if they could watch the same game on TV? Would the team's revenue suffer, or would the tape-delayed telecast increase interest?

"We said, 'Why don't we tiptoe into this?'" Napoli remembers. "The gate was doing well, the move to downtown was going great and while we could see a lot of upside in having the games televised, we wanted to temper it, and we asked (for) a couple of years to measure the impact on our attendance.

"So the original commitment was to televise the games we knew we would sell out—Friday and Saturday games. We did 20 to 25 that year. What we found over the next two years was that we truly believe that putting the Mud Hens on TV and promoting downtown, promoting Mud Hens baseball and promoting all the activities and events, actually grew our fan base and encouraged people to come to our games."

The team had to invest in some new technical gear; the only equipment it had at the time was what ran the video boards. Under its arrangement with BCSN, the Mud Hens do the entire production internally; BCSN provides the conduit to subscribers' homes.

The first game was cablecast April 8, 2004. "The beauty part was that with changes in technology, the price of equipment was coming down, and the community has a wealth of young talent," Napoli said. "We reached out to UT, and Don Reiber sent some very talented students our way. We really saw this as an incubator to enable these young people to get into the TV and entertainment business behind the camera. We saw that as a way to showcase the talent in the community, especially the young talent."

In 2005, BCSN cablecast every Mud Hens home game, including playoff games. "What we discovered was that televising all the home games really helped our home attendance during the playoffs," Napoli said. "We drew more fans at our home playoff games than all of the other three (playoff) teams combined."

"It became a no-brainer," Napoli said. "It's a free three-hour commercial for the Mud Hens."

Block decided to cablecast the road playoff games as well. On September 7, 2005, it began doing just that, televising a playoff game in Norfolk, VA, against the Norfolk Tides, the AAA affiliate of the Baltimore Orioles. "We had not been in the playoffs for something like 20 or 25 years, so we called the Tides and said we wanted to televise the upcoming game," Napoli said. "Dave Rosenfield (a Tides executive at the time) said, 'Boy, you guys are really excited about making the playoffs, aren't you?'

"So BCSN took their equipment and televised the game, and the folks in Norfolk were going, 'What in the world is going on in Toledo?'" Napoli said, laughing at the memory.

Ever since BCSN and the Mud Hens helped point the way toward televising minor-league baseball, four other teams in the International league—Lehigh Valley, Indianapolis, Rochester and Pawtucket—have copied the approach. None had done it before seeing how it worked with the Hens and BCSN, Napoli said.

Televising games has been helpful to the Hens' attendance. The team draws around 550,000 fans a season, so some 6 million spectators have gone through the turnstiles since the park opened in 2002. In the old stadium, Napoli said, "the crowds in April would be so small we'd run hot chocolate out to them and say 'Thanks for being here.' If the crowd were really small, we'd invite everyone up to the Diamond Club."

Toledo had had minor-league hockey, too, for more than half a century, operating under such names as the Mercurys, Hornets, Toledo Blades (no connection to the Blocks' newspaper), and the Goaldiggers. The most recent incarnation, the Toledo Storm, had been out of the area for several years as it awaited a new home after its former venue, the Sports Arena on the shore of the Maumee River in East Toledo, had been demolished.

In 2009, however, the Toledo Walleye, the East Coast Hockey League affiliate of the Chicago Blackhawks and Detroit Red Wings, moved into the Huntington Center, a sparkling new $105 million arena a block from Fifth Third Field. (The dual affiliation ended after the 2013-14 season, with the Blackhawks dropping out of the mix). Napoli assumed the duties of president and general manager of that franchise as well, and BCSN became a part of the Walleye operation. "And again," Napoli said, "we were thrilled to be able to put all the hockey games on TV."

BCSN telecasts had always been done digitally, then converted electronically in an effort to approach the quality of high-definition TV, but the results were always a bit lacking. About six months before the Hens' 2011 season was set to open, Allan Block approached Napoli and told him, "We have to convert to high-definition equipment by opening day."

Such conversion would be expensive for the Mud Hens, though—as in half-a-million-dollars expensive—and time was short. The team would have to buy and test equipment and train its staff.

The Mud Hens board of directors considered the request and for a number of reasons—not least the Block family's longtime support of the team and the community in general—decided to spend the money. "We had it in the long-range budget anyway, so we just moved the expense forward a few years," Napoli said. The timetable was tight, but everything was in place by Opening Day. "It was stressful, but it was happy stress."

While the Mud Hens were upgrading their equipment, BCSN was revamping its own equipment to HD as well, spending more than $1.6 million in 2011 alone.

The first high-definition Mud Hens cablecast occurred on April 14, 2011, for the team's doubleheader home opener against the Columbus Clippers. Unfortunately for the local fans, Toledo lost both games, 1–0 and 7–3.

Naturally, the Walleye season that fall was cablecast in high-definition as well. "Televising the games has been great for hockey," Napoli said, noting that HD makes a hockey game much easier to follow on TV. "When we first opened, the fan base was mainly the hardcore avid hockey fans, but now after seeing the televised games, people are really falling in love with hockey, and the crowds are bigger." The team's fan base has grown by some 40 percent since its first year.

No other minor-league hockey team has followed the BCSN/Walleye lead—yet.

The benefits of the partnership became especially clear in 2013, when the trade publication *Sports Business Journal* named Toledo the Top Minor League Market, making its determination based in part on game attendance as a ratio of the entire population and the number of seats filled as a percentage of the total seats available over the course of a season. "I believe BCSN played a major role in that honor," Napoli said, citing the growth of both teams' fan bases as a result of so many televised games.

As BCSN continued to add those kinds of live events to its programming schedule and increased the number of hours of both live and taped programming each day, its popularity continued to grow—with the audience, at least, if not some school athletic officials. Their aversion to live telecasts as a supposed threat to much-needed gate receipt remained. While permitting tape-delayed productions, some athletic directors, mainly in Toledo Public Schools and the Northern Lakes League, simply banned all live coverage of any games for which tickets were sold. They generally condoned live coverage of non-revenue sports.

Add to that a ban by the Michigan High School Athletic Association of live TV coverage of *all* high-school sports and a ban by the Ohio High School Athletic Association (OHSAA) of live coverage of Friday football games (Saturday football games, basketball and other sports did not fall under the same restrictions), and BCSN's emphasis on live programming was becoming a bit of a problem.

Any Ohio high school that flouted the OHSAA's ban on live TV games would be ineligible for postseason play. Enter the Toledo Area Athletic Conference, a group of smaller, mostly parochial and private schools, which usually didn't field talent that could be expected to look forward to the postseason. A few TAAC schools were willing to allow their Friday football games to be carried live. Those schools welcomed the exposure BCSN could give them, especially when it came to recruiting new students.

BCSN games became a real event for the schools. Amy Newman, whose son, Dan, was quarterback for TAAC member Toledo Christian School's Eagles in 2003 and 2004, fondly recalled the atmosphere. "We got bigger crowds at the BCSN games than we did at the non-televised games, as everybody wanted to be part of the excitement," she said. "And maybe they'd somehow be on television."

In addition, many players later bought tapes of games in which they had outstanding performances to send to colleges when they were pursuing athletic scholarships.

In lieu of rights fees to carry the games, Buckeye offered schools free time on the Community Channel for them to promote events, campaign for levies or provide whatever other programming they could envision. A specific time block was set aside for the home team of each live game cablecast. Schools began to recognize this as an attractive asset, and little by little they started scheduling more live games.

Eventually many even scheduled Thursday and Saturday football games to work around the OHSAA's restrictions.

BCSN's staying power and growing popularity, however, soon became impossible to ignore. Part of that popularity is attributable to the network's community-oriented philosophy. In 2006, in order to show schools that BCSN was more than just a showcase for student athletes, Steve Piller, at the time director of advertising sales and now vice president of advertising sales and local stations, hatched a plan to honor a student of the month and student of the year.

Schools would nominate outstanding students, with one chosen each month from every school in Buckeye's coverage area. Selected students would be promoted in spots on various Buckeye channels in addition to getting coverage on BCSN. At the end of the school year, one would be chosen as student of the year and would receive a $16,000 college scholarship.

The program was underwritten by an advertising package Piller and his staff developed. In order to avoid criticism or conflicts, Piller arranged to have the Toledo Community Foundation—a public charitable organization, founded in 1973, which was intended to enrich the quality of life for individuals and families in the area—screen the nominees, choose the honorees and handle the money.

The scholarship was a major prize, but just being recognized was a cherished honor. The family of one such student from Clay High School, Cole recalled, had their house destroyed by fire. The student asked if BCSN would replace the glass student-of-the-month plaque she received. "That's all she cared about," Mr. Cole said.

Overall, the program had a major impact on students' lives. Cole recalled that one recipient of the $16,000 scholarship had been living in a car, her parents were so poor. "This meant that she could go to college, which otherwise she probably would not have been able to," he said.

The program subsequently grew in 2008 to honor a teacher of the month and year and, in 2010, a coach of the month and year. Those honorees each received a cash award of $1,000, as did their schools—one more arrow in the quiver with which to hunt audience and educators' acceptance of BCSN, and advertisers' dollars.

"The teacher of the month and year is a real morale booster for our teachers," said Sylvania's Rieger, who retired in 2015. "The scholarships for students are great, and we really appreciate the halftime interviews with students. They give kids communication skills that are really needed."

Not all went smoothly at first, however. A few incidents—inappropriate chants during one basketball game and a fight between players during a hockey game—caused Rieger some concern. "But BCSN showed the first push and immediately went to commercial, showing none of the fight," he noted.

"BCSN has been great about playing up positives and downplaying negatives," he added. "Tom Cole's personality really helps—he accentuates the positive and always puts a positive spin on negative plays. Tom is a big reason it's taken off; he captures the good aspects of high-school athletics. It's a great partnership."

Pinciotti asserted that the purpose of BCSN is to enhance the schools, students, parents and teachers alike: "That's our mantra." She had to terminate one announcer who criticized referees and belittled players when they made a mistake. "That's not the BCSN way to do a broadcast, and he couldn't understand it," she said. "We're not untruthful, but we don't put a kid down."

It's all in the way you describe an incident, Cole said. "Say a kid drops a very catchable pass. You don't criticize him, you say he took his eyes off it but he's an excellent receiver and he'll catch the next one. You treat every kid as if he were your own. How would you like it if your kid was criticized on TV?"

"If there's a fight in the stands, we immediately pull off from it," Pinciotti added, pointing out that on a few occasions police have requested BCSN tapes to aid their investigations of disturbances at games. "There's nothing in there to help them, because we don't photograph the problems."

School administrators slowly welcomed the chance to get their message out to parents via halftime interviews and a weekly show that focuses on non-athletic school topics. Buckeye regularly gets compliments and thank-you letters from customers whose children or friends' children have been on BCSN, and the positive buzz in the community has been continuous. (For reasons both athletic and political: During the November 2005 elections, for all schools that had been covered by BCSN, voters passed every funding initiative on the ballot; those near Toledo but outside Buckeye's footprint and not covered by BCSN passed none.)

Producing the events is not cheap. In addition to the $640,000 production trailer, of which there are five, each event requires an announcer and color commentator, a director, an audio technician, a production assistant, a graphics-generator operator and three camera operators, with a fourth camera operator and a production assistant added for college games. Crew costs, which were $275 an event when BCSN started, now stand at $775, Pinciotti said—and BCSN covers some 1,200 events a year. That's more than $900,000 of overhead a year.

As the stable of trailers grew from two to five, the company had to find space to house and maintain them. Engineer in charge Dennis Robedeau was being stretched thin, so an additional engineer had to be added in Toledo, as well as one in Sandusky when that channel was added to the Erie County system.

Customer retention has been impressive. Professional market research done in March 2005 by an outside firm revealed that 44.3 per cent of viewers answered "very important" or "somewhat important" to the question "How important is the BCSN channel to your keeping cable service?"

The network continued to attract positive attention. Occasionally subscribers would include handwritten thank-you notes with their cable bill payments, praising BCSN for giving their students previously unattainable recognition.

As noted in Chapter 8, in 2004, the Ohio House of Representatives passed a resolution lauding Allan Block for developing BCSN. The resolution, introduced by the Honorable Jeanine Perry, then the 49th-district representative from Toledo, said in part, "You are deserving of high praise, for you have combined civic concern and commitment with selfless initiative to become a dynamic leader in the Toledo area.

"Your exceptional record of personal and professional achievement stands as a hallmark worthy of emulation, and you have inspired countless individuals to excel in numerous areas of endeavor. The respect and admiration you have earned throughout your life are clearly evident, and your accomplishments are a justifiable source of pride and an excellent reflection not only on you but on your family and your community.

"Thus, with sincere pleasure, we commend you on your outstanding service and salute you as a fine Ohioan."

Perry said she got the idea to introduce the resolution while attending a luncheon in Columbus with some Toledoans at which BCSN came up in conversation. "My husband and I both love to watch the channel even though we don't have kids that age," she said at the time. "I've heard nothing but good comments about it, and thought it appropriate that Mr. Block get some recognition for his foresight in doing something positive for the community."

In addition, *Multichannel News*, a national trade publication, presented BCSN with the 2004 Innovator Award in Programming.

In September 2008, Duwve arranged to add live Internet streaming of most BCSN programming. "This made it possible for Grandma in California to watch her grandson play sports in Toledo," she said.

BCSN steadily covered more games and engaged more crew members, necessitating a third production trailer in early 2005. The network was airing 900 to 1,000 events a year by this point, including leftfield fare such as a Cub Scout Pinewood Derby, bungee-ball games and cheerleading competitions.

Its coverage hasn't been limited to the local area and local viewers. Pinciotti recalled covering the finals of the 10th Annual National Football League Global Junior Championship football games, held at the former Pontiac Silverdome on January 25, 2006. The domed Michigan stadium, now known simply as the Silverdome, was home to the NFL's Detroit Lions for many years.

The Global Junior Championship is considered the Super Bowl of high-school football; teams from the United States, Canada, Germany, Mexico and Japan compete. BCSN beamed the production to a satellite and the games were shown live in Germany, Japan and China, Pinciotti said.

Unfortunately, the USA team, under the direction of Dick Cromwell—at the time head coach of Toledo's St. Francis High School team—lost 10–0 to Canada in the championship game.

Another offbeat event occurred on January 13, 2013: a Quidditch match between students at Bowling Green State University and the University of Toledo. Quidditch is the sport played in the Harry Potter novels; for this game, players dressed as wizards and witches riding broomsticks attempted to get one of three balls—the Quaffle, Bludgers and Golden Snitch—into one of six elevated ring-shaped goals. BCSN got calls ahead of time from viewers in Great Britain trying to find out how they could watch it via streaming video on the Internet.

In addition to sporting events, BCSN has aired local sports talk and interview shows, both live and taped.

Sports Wrap, a half-hour weekly show hosted by Cole, was inaugurated March 15, 2004, barely two months after BCSN launched. Each show featured five interviews with students, teachers and coaches, and was produced at the University of Toledo's media center using UT students as talent and production help. *Sports Wrap* was directed by John Eidemiller, media producer and director in UT's Department of Communication, and it ran until May 31, 2010.

"We gave Tom the summer off," Pinciotti said of Cole, "then on September 27, 2010, we started *The Score*"—a one-hour show in which Cole continued his interviews with students, teachers and coaches, with Ken Watlington, BCSN sports director and an anchor, replaying and discussing highlights of the previous week's games. It also was produced at UT, and ran through May 6, 2013.

BCSN entered into an arrangement with WTOL, Channel 11, in which the two entities combined forces, using some talent and the studios of the CBS affiliate plus BCSN personnel to produce *T-Sports,* a Friday-night show that started on Channel 11 during the 11 p.m. news and, when the station rejoined network programming at 11:30 p.m., continued on BCSN. *T-Sports* was produced for four years, but only from September to March to cover the football and basketball seasons, Cole said.

After the arrangement with WTOL ended in December 2012, Pinciotti wanted to continue the Friday-night show, but "people here said we couldn't do it with limited resources." Still, she pressed on.

"Really, the credit goes to Veronica," Cole said, "because nobody thought we could do it. Quite honestly, it was such a big endeavor to try to replicate what we did with Channel 11. But she built a case for it, and finally the powers that be said, 'If you think you can do it, then do it.'"

The new show, called *Overtime,* premiered February 8, 2013. It ran for five Friday-night shows through the end of basketball season, and was produced at UT. It started again that August. At the time, Buckeye was negotiating with WTVG, Toledo's ABC affiliate, to form an alliance in part to showcase BCSN. On December 13, 2013, BCSN staffers began doing *Overtime* Friday nights on Channel 13. That ran until January 10, 2014, and three days later, BCSN began cablecasting *Sports Nightly,* a half-hour show Monday through Thursday, and an hour-long production on Fridays.

"The salient point here," Cole said, "is that *Sports Nightly* would never have happened If Veronica hadn't pushed so hard for *Overtime.*"

A weekly live call-in show, *Rant and Rage,* featuring Cole and *Blade* sports editor Frank Corsoe, was the creation of Duwve and premiered April 5, 2007. Before it was ended on June 20, 2013, after 274 shows, it attracted (in addition to local sports personalities) such national figures as Danica Patrick, the race-car driver; Len Dawson and Paul Hornung, pro-football Hall of Famers; and Sam Rutigliano and Rob Chudzinski, former Cleveland Browns head coaches.

A program called *Light Side* provided a venue for such events as dog Frisbee matches and dogs jumping into pools in distance competitions—fare that isn't necessarily worthy of a whole production, but that can make for breezy entertainment when combined into one show, Pinciotti said.

Games of the Toledo Cherokee, one of nine Tier II Junior League teams in the North American 3 Hockey League, or NA3HL—considered a top training ground for players between 17 and 21—were covered early on, and other coverage was ramped up, as various Bowling Green State University, University of Toledo and Owens Community College games became regular fare. Lourdes College, a non-residential Catholic liberal-arts school in Toledo, was expanding its course offerings and adding dormitory facilities around the same time; it became Lourdes University, and added intercollegiate sports. BSCN began covering its games as well.

On January 7, 2013, BCSN's ninth anniversary, BCSN 2 was unveiled, providing twice the capacity for programming—and advertising. A year later, Buckeye placed an additional trailer and crew in Sandusky to produce local sports in the Erie County area. Those programs are shown on Channel 7 in the Sandusky area; when locally produced events aren't airing, BCSN's regular programming, developed in Toledo, is shown. All scheduling is done from Toledo.

Cole, in addition to his on-air duties, actively promotes BCSN in the community, talking to school classes and civic groups. He has addressed well over 30,000 grade-schoolers, encouraging them to do their homework and listen to their parents, prodding them to become better students and good citizens. "All of them want to be on BCSN someday," he said.

His community outreach has paid off. "Literally thousands of people over the years have personally thanked us for the job we've done," he said. The entire staff's philosophy has always been to get things done and treat everybody with the utmost respect, he added.

In 2010, Buckeye took BCSN to area youngsters and others to give them the chance to be TV-sports announcers by funding a permanent exhibit, *LIVE Report!* in Imagination Station, a hands-on science museum on Toledo's riverfront.

Opened February 24, 2010, *LIVE Report!* features a mock BCSN TV studio in which visitors can pretend to be a sports reporter reading a prepared script from a teleprompter, while actual footage from an area game plays behind them.

Simulating a live cablecast, a prerecorded anchor "throws" the show to the reporter, who comments just as if it were a live telecast. The set contains permanent seats resembling a grandstand, from which family members and friends can watch the reporter's performance, and the production is recorded so the reporter can watch it afterward on a TV set outside the exhibit.

LIVE Report! was the result of a promise Allan Block had made to Imagination Station, which in 2008 was trying to pass a levy and reopen the former Center of Science and Industry (COSI), which had closed a year earlier for budgetary reasons. Block assured the community that if the levy passed and the center reopened, the Buckeye companies would provide funds for a permanent exhibit.

He turned to several executives to come up with a meaningful plan for one. In addition to *LIVE Report!,* Buckeye's sponsorship also includes the Interactive Distance Learning facilities that Imagination Station uses to deliver classroom instruction to schools in Toledo and around the world. This portion of the sponsorship, including the transport of the classroom material, is provided by Buckeye TeleSystem.

Interactive Distance Learning is an educational-outreach program designed to give students all over the world the opportunity to explore scientific concepts, experience current technology and view exciting demonstrations free from the limits imposed by geography. At Imagination Station, kids can view IDL programs being delivered from inside *LIVE Report!* through a glass wall that separates the two.

"I thought, Buckeye Cable is involved in science and industry," Block told *The Blade* after the exhibit opened. "We're involved in electricity, we're involved with electromagnetic radiation, we're involved with transmitting communications of wire, fiber optics; there's no reason why we can't do something for the science museum."

David Waterman, a Toledo attorney who was chairman of the board of Imagination Station, lavishly praised the partnership. "You just can't imagine the impact that show of support had," he told *The Blade* in an article published the day following the exhibit opening. "This is going to be just a fantastic experience for kids."

In February 2014, BCSN took another step to widen its appeal by teaming with *The Blade.* Now the BCSN Web site, bcsn.tv, provides all sports coverage from the newspaper's site, ToledoBlade.com, plus video highlights from BCSN and in-depth sports schedules and statistics from high schools in the coverage area and nearby colleges.

All *Blade* sportswriters' blogs are accessible via bcsn.tv, which also includes news of all professional sports, including NASCAR, the NHL, NFL, NBA, Major League Baseball and others. The site contains links to scores of related sites as well.

The goal of the site, Piller said, "is to grow our coverage of high-school and college sports by providing real-time scores, user-generated photo galleries and player statistics. We will provide software for team statisticians to upload scores and even provide online action from games in real time."

Momentum continues to build as growth in both programming and audience picked up speed. "I don't think that there is a local cable company in the United States that produces as many sporting events as BCSN," Cole said." We do on average 1,000 events a year (covering) 57 different sports."

The channel covers high school boys and girls sports equally and regularly covers UT, BGSU, Owens, Lourdes University, and such small colleges as Defiance and Bluffton Colleges and Findlay and Ohio Wesleyan Universities in Ohio and Adrian College and Siena Heights University in Michigan.

Add to that the local Mud Hens and Walleye and the myriad of amateur sports and its own local daily and weekly shows and "no other local cable company has been able to do that," Cole enthused.

ESPN signed exclusive carriage deals with the Mid-American Conference, of which UT and BGSU are members, for a time cutting BCSN off. However, BCSN was able to work out an arrangement under which BCSN produces about three football and three basketball games at each school each year, shows them live, then feeds them to ESPN for carriage on ESPN 3, he said.

Advertisers noticed. In 2010, BCSN ad revenue exceeded local ad revenue sold for ESPN for the first time, and since then ad revenue for the local outlet topped ESPN's local numbers 10 months in 2011, 8 months in 2012, and 11 months in both 2013 and 2014, Piller said.

BCSN's popularity became so widespread that when AT&T introduced U-verse, its cable-TV offering, in the Toledo area, door-to-door sales representatives touting it were met with objections from customers who didn't want to lose BCSN programming and so wouldn't drop Buckeye CableSystem. Buckeye got word that some U-verse salespeople were telling residents that U-verse would soon offer BCSN; Buckeye had to contact AT&T legal counsel to halt that practice.

Time Warner Cable, which offered service in some of Buckeye's coverage areas, approached the company about obtaining BCSN programming for its system. Block's foundational concept for BCSN—that Buckeye would "have something no other competitor will have"—resulted in a swift rejection.

A lot of hard work by a lot of people built BCSN. "Nancy (Duwve) deserves a lot of credit," Cole said. "When people said it couldn't be done, Nancy said, 'Let's do it.' After Nancy retired, Veronica and Steve took it to another level—and there is no other BCSN in the country because nobody else will commit the resources Allan Block was willing to commit."

BUCKEYE BITS

All the Sports, All the Time

Allan Block envisioned a channel that would cover local sports when he hatched the idea for BCSN in 2003, but it's doubtful that even he ever envisioned the plethora of programming it would come to deliver.

In its first decade, the staff produced more than 6,000 high-school events, more than 2,000 sports talk shows, 1,155 college sporting events, 635 Mud Hens games and 175 Walleye games. It covered more than 50 different sports.

In addition to offering the BCSN scholarships and honoring the student, teacher and coach of the month and year, the staff also picks an All-Around All Star team every year, choosing outstanding scholar-athletes in football, basketball, baseball, ice hockey, field hockey, gymnastics, track and field, soccer, tennis, lacrosse, softball, golf, volleyball, swimming and diving, cross country, wrestling, cheerleading and dance team from schools in Buckeye's coverage area.

Mishap on the Way to Building the Information Superhighway

To break the tedium that's sometimes a feature of the technical, informational sessions at the annual meeting of the Ohio Cable Telecommunications Association (OCTA), conference organizers occasionally would plan a relaxing or unusual session.

During the mid-1990s, most systems were undergoing massive building projects, either converting to fiber optics or extending fiber optics deeper into their plants to offer Internet service—at the time commonly referred to as the "Information Superhighway." At one of the annual meetings during that hectic expansion phase, Maryann Kafer, OCTA's public relations director, devised a team-building quiz.

Employees from different cable systems in the state were organized into teams, each of which was asked to solve hypothetical problems that cable employees might face.

The audience of experienced cable staffers then would judge the best answer, and the winning team would receive a prize.

One question was how best to handle a situation in which a technician, finishing a service call at a home and backing out of the driveway, ran over and killed the customer's pet dog.

The teams naturally suggested apologizing profusely and sympathizing with the customer; some advised offering to replace the dog, to send the customer a large flower arrangement or to make a substantial cash payment for the loss.

The winning team had a more tongue-in-cheek solution, however.

Led by Bob Gessner, president of Massillon Cable TV (now MCTV), the team suggested that there really wasn't much that would placate the customer in such a situation. So the technician should merely admit what he had done and explain, "When we're building the Information Superhighway, there's bound to be some road kill."

Chapter Twelve

"Their Demands Are Outrageous on Their Face"

*Negotiating with Satellite Programmers
and Large Broadcasters:
Not for the Faint of Heart*

Cable operators, in the industry's earliest days, had basically one source of programming: broadcast television signals received over the air and then sent to customers' homes via the coaxial-cable plant they had built.

Of course, some operators supplemented this with alphanumeric bulletin boards, cameras focused on teletype machines and old movies—the latter generally a limited option given Hollywood studios' reluctance to release films for fear of hurting ticket sales at theaters. Some operators, including Buckeye, produced local programming.

The original concept for cable television was to bring improved broadcast signals to towns and villages too distant from broadcast towers in big cities to get a clear signal. Importing distant signals was something broadcasters liked at first, because it helps them broaden their audience. However, once cable operators started to string cable in close proximity to Designated Market Area (DMA) of broadcasters, the latter saw it as a threat and headed for the courts.

The first such suit was filed in 1958 by KXLF-TV in Butte, Montana, alleging that a cable operator in Helena, some 65 miles away, was "pirating" its signal, according to Matt Stump and Harry Jessell in "Cable, The First Forty Years," published in the November 21, 1988, issue of *Broadcasting* magazine (which was subsequently renamed *Broadcasting & Cable*). A district court dismissed the suit, claiming that broadcasters did not have common-law rights to their programs.

The Federal Communications Commission seized upon the opportunity offered by the various disputes and claimed jurisdiction over cable, a move that would drastically inhibit cable's growth, at least for several years. The agency denied a western cable firm's request to expand its physical plant, a ruling upheld in a 1963 appeals-court decision. The FCC said it was using its licensing powers over common carrier relays to safeguard broadcasters from this incursion by cable.

In 1966, the agency, emboldened by its earlier actions, ordered cable operators to carry local signals but denied them permission to import distant (out-of-market) signals—and in 1969 required cable operators with more than 3,500 customers to originate local programming. (A court later overturned that ruling.)

Not to be deterred, however, the FCC charged ahead and in 1970 expanded the earlier restrictions on distant signals and set limits on importing sports programming. The FCC found itself under mounting pressure from the cable industry, which was being fought by broadcast interests. Finally, the two warring parties were able to reach a cease-fire, and in 1972, the FCC permitted cable operators in the top 100 markets to pursue limited expansion. (Toledo falls under that category; this ruling is what enabled Buckeye to expand into remaining unserved areas in Toledo and continue building plant in Perrysburg. (See Chapter 1)

Also in its 1972 ruling, the FCC required cable operators to carry 20 channels, some of which were to be earmarked for educational purposes, and relaxed the distant-signal rules somewhat. At the same time, broadcasters were taking cable operators to court, claiming cable was violating copyright law by retransmitting broadcasters' signals. The issue became mired in the courts and the federal legislature, and nothing was settled until Congress passed the 1976 Copyright Act.

This law established an arcane formula for copyright fees, and called for cable operators to pay the sums yearly to the newly established Copyright Royalty Tribunal. This tribunal in turn would adjust copyright royalty rates for cable retransmission of broadcast signals, rates for recording new versions of previously recorded songs and rates for noncommercial educational stations that broadcast musical, pictorial, graphic and sculptural works.

The tribunal would then distribute to the proper copyright holders the royalty fees deposited by cable operators with the Copyright Office after considering what harm had been incurred by the copyright owners and what benefit the cable customer received, based on the marketplace value of the work, the time the work was aired and the quality of the cablecast.

At the same time, entrepreneurs were beginning to develop pay, or subscription, television. The first such example cropped up on the West Coast, where a company wired homes in Los Angeles and San Francisco for delivery of movies and baseball games. Opposition arose, the issue was put on the ballot and subscription television was voted out. The company owner sued, but his firm went out of business before the court ruled that such operations could in fact continue.

In 1972, Time Inc., publisher of the eponymous newsmagazine, created Home Box Office. Initially, it too delivered sports and movies to cable subscribers who paid an additional monthly fee. On September 30, 1975, HBO delivered via satellite the "Thrilla in Manila," the legendary 14-round boxing match between Muhammad Ali and Smokin' Joe Frazier in the Philippines, in which Ali knocked out the former champ. The biggest winner might have been HBO, which used the fight and its attendant publicity to roll out a plethora of uncut movies and live sports delivered via satellite. The race was on.

HBO quickly moved from a regional to a national network and showed other programmers that they, too, could remake themselves into national brands via satellite. Among them were broadcasters WTBS in Atlanta and WGN in Chicago, and non-broadcasters such as ESPN, Discovery Channel and hundreds more since.

Two basic revenue plans evolved. Some channels, such as ESPN, get part of their revenue directly from the cable firm as a per-subscriber fee (commonly called a carriage fee), and sell advertising, touting their national subscriber numbers. They also offer cable operators a certain number of commercial spots, called local avails, into which they can sell local advertising, allowing the operator to recoup some of the carriage fee.

Others, such as HBO and Showtime, have become known as premium channels and have no commercials. The channel owners charge the cable operator a larger fee, and obviously offer no local avails. The operator in turn sells these premium channels to subscribers on a per-channel/per-month or even per-day basis, usually separate from other program tiers.

Each time programmers come to Buckeye to negotiate carriage fees for the next year (or whatever terms they ultimately agree upon), their demands seem to increase—not only in monetary terms but in something known in the industry as "tying and bundling." This is a practice wherein a programmer essentially says, "If you want to carry my popular channel"—such as ESPN—"here is the price, and you must also carry these three other channels we have, and at this additional price."

Sometimes programmers demand that the operators agree to carry, at a price not yet determined, a channel or channels the programmer *plans* to launch at some point. Talk about buying a pig in a poke!

Buckeye, like most cable operators, faces bandwidth constraints and cannot just add new channels willy-nilly without some negative impact, either in equipment and bandwidth costs and carriage fees, or in having to take something off the air in order to make room for new channels.

Those are the issues Buckeye management must weigh in each negotiating session with each programmer: What is the channel worth to customers, and can the company devote the channel capacity to the tying and bundling terms? Once those parameters are set, negotiations begin. When talks reach an impasse, Buckeye management faces the possibility of being forced to take satellite-fed programming off the system until favorable terms are agreed upon, or possibly not returning it at all if positive terms can't be reached.

When Buckeye takes a channel off, it usually results in upset customers who deluge the company with angry phone calls. In most cases, when customers hear what the numbers are and recognize what they would mean to their monthly cable bill, they're able to see Buckeye's side, however upset they are that the channel has gone dark.

In several instances, Buckeye has taken popular programs off the air when no agreement could be reached. One notable instance occurred in 1997 and involved Fox Sports Network.

Buckeye had been carrying Pro-Am Sports System, a regional sports network commonly known as PASS. It was founded in 1982 by a Detroit broadcaster and in 1992 became the property of Post-Newsweek Stations, which owns WDIV, the NBC affiliate in Detroit.

In 1996, Rupert Murdoch, the Australian media baron, announced plans to form a regional sports network and won a surprise bid to carry the games of the NBA's Detroit Pistons, which had formerly been on PASS. In 1997, it outbid PASS for the rights to carry Detroit Red Wings hockey games as well. Post-Newsweek executives determined that the area could not support two regional sports networks, so they signed over to Fox their remaining rights to carry Detroit Tigers baseball, the last of the three major sports it held, and ceased operations on October 31, 1997.

Fox came to Buckeye to negotiate a new contract, and demanded a 700 percent increase over the fees PASS had been receiving. The Red Wings, always popular in the Toledo market, were being touted as championship material, but Buckeye couldn't stomach the large increase that would have to be passed on to subscribers if it acceded to Fox's demands. Off the channel went—and while it was dark, the Red Wings won the Stanley Cup.

Over the years, Buckeye also stood up to what management considered exorbitant price increases sought by Court TV, Univision, Fox Sports Ohio and the Tennis Channel, and removed each of them at various times rather than yield. Subsequent negotiations brought agreed-upon prices with Court TV, the Tennis Channel and Fox Sports Ohio, which were returned to the system; Univision has not been returned.

The Univision negotiations turned especially contentious. Univision, a Spanish-language channel, had provided its service to Buckeye at no charge for 10 years when, in 2001, it said it now wanted a substantial fee to continue. Hispanics at the time made up about 5 percent of the population in Buckeye's service area, and while Buckeye executives recognized the importance of the Hispanic market, they objected to two primary things: the fee demand, of course, but also the fact that Univision did not charge for carriage in 32 other U.S. cities, including New York, Los Angeles and Miami.

Buckeye also felt the requested price was too high, and offered to put Univision on a tier so that anyone interested in its programming could purchase it separately. Univision demanded to be on the entire system and to be paid a service fee based on Buckeye's entire subscriber base. Buckeye deemed this too high a price to ask 95 percent of customers to pay for programming they were unlikely to watch.

Politicians were drawn into the fray by various local Hispanic groups, who appealed to Louis Escobar, the lone Hispanic on Toledo's City Council. He introduced a resolution "urging Buckeye CableSystem and Univision to work together to continue quality Spanish-language television in Toledo." Hispanic groups demonstrated before City Council, which passed the resolution unanimously. Univision also sent representatives to Toledo to encourage both the dissenters and politicians to pressure Buckeye.

Toledo's mayor at the time, Carleton F. "Carty" Finkbeiner, publicly urged Buckeye to keep the programming on, and suggested that if Univision were removed Hispanics should abandon Buckeye and go to satellite dishes for programming. He was either not realizing, or ignoring, the fact that Toledo itself would lose money in that case: Cable firms pay local franchise fees, but satellite firms do not.

Another problem with the mayor's suggestion that Hispanics take money out of city coffers is the fact under the 1992 Cable Act, it is illegal for local franchise authorities (i.e., politicians) to wield any influence over cable programming, but Buckeye chose not to pursue legal action against the mayor or City Council.

Buckeye didn't bend—and today has a programming tier with 12 Spanish-language channels, Univision not among them.

Another dust-up over rising programming costs and Buckeye's efforts trying to hold customers bills down came in 2004, when NBC, which had the rights to telecast the 2004 Summer Olympics in Athens, Greece, came in with an outlandish plan.

The network was going to have around-the-clock Olympic coverage on CNBC, MSNBC and Bravo!—a total of 17 days of non-stop Olympic activity starting with the opening ceremony on Aug. 13.

The catch – NBC wanted Buckeye CableSystem to pay $250,000 a month to air the complete Olympics on all the NBC cable channels. "We felt this was an unfair price to pay and a cost too high to ask our customers to pay," Dave Huey, Buckeye president, said at the time. The average cost per subscriber would have been $1.92 per month, and that was for the entire year, not just the month the Olympics were being shown.

There was no option for a special tier or program package to enable those customers who were avid fans to pay a premium and receive the programming while those with little or no interest could avoid the extra cost—NBC wanted its Olympic coverage on the three cable-only channels to be available to everybody. (Buckeye did not carry MSNBC at the time, and would have had to add that channel.) NBC was offering some 226 hours of Olympic coverage on its affiliate broadcast stations, so WNWO would have that available. In addition, Canada's CBET in Windsor had scheduled more than 300 hours of coverage, Telemundo planned 169 hours, and USA Network had slated 47 hours— a total of 742 hours of coverage over the 17 days on channels already on the Buckeye system at the then-existing rates—customers could see most of the Olympic action at no extra charge. Customers who complained about the lack of the NBC coverage were told the costs that would have been involved and the CBET option, and Buckeye suffered little, if any, subscriber defection.

In an attempt to show what the true driver of cable price increases was, Buckeye executives compared the programming and overhead costs from 1979 to 2015.

Back in 1979, when virtually all channels carried broadcast television stations with only a handful of satellite channels available, the rate for the basic cable service was about $8.00. Of that, programming, or content, costs were roughly 12 cents per subscriber or 1.5 per cent of the monthly charge. The remaining $7.78 was the cost of running the system—amortizing the capital costs of constructing the plant and electronics, personnel, general overhead, and of course, profit margin

In 2015, the average standard service fee for video only is $74.99, which includes the video service fee but does not include any additional equipment such as DVRs and DTAs needed for video only. Of that nearly $47 goes for programming and the rest to operating the system.

In short, the content cost rose from 12 cents per month per subscriber to nearly $47, or a whopping increase of more than 39,000 per cent! The cost of running the system rose from $7.78 per month per subscriber to $28, or an increase of 260 per cent.

During the same period, the Consumer Price Index rose 326 per cent, according to the U.S. Department of Labor's Bureau of Labor Statistics.

In addition to the expenses of satellite-fed networks, the 1992 Cable Act introduced another obstacle for cable operators to overcome. Whereas the FCC years earlier had mandated that cable operators must carry local broadcast signals, the 1992 act provided for two scenarios:

The broadcaster could request must-carry, and the cable operator had no choice but to put it on the system in the channel slot designated by the broadcaster, with no money changing hands.

Or the broadcaster could choose "retransmission consent," in which the two parties would be obligated to negotiate some business (that is, monetary) arrangement in order for the cable operator to carry the broadcast signal.

In short, the deck is heavily stacked in favor of the broadcaster. In those scenarios, the cable operator has absolutely no say; it is all up to the broadcaster. In the first, he says, in effect, "You *will* carry me, and on X channel." Only in the second case can the cable operator even negotiate. If negotiations fail, the broadcaster can order the signal taken off the cable system; the operator then has no option but to remove it.

The law stipulates that the first retransmission-consent agreements were to be three years, but after those expired, some agreements have been negotiated for longer terms.

In the early years of retransmission negotiations, Buckeye dealt with the local heads of the broadcast stations in Toledo, and "we tried to do what was best for the community," Dave Huey, Buckeye's president at the time, said. For example, Buckeye put fiber optics from each broadcast studio to its head end on Angola Road to provide clearer pictures to customers and improve system reliability. Buckeye and the broadcasters agreed on advertising swaps by which each could promote itself on the other's medium, as well as some other non-monetary exchanges.

Gradually a change in the business model of broadcasters throughout the country led those broadcasters to demand money from the cable companies for the rights to carry their broadcast signals, just as satellite-fed programmers such as ESPN had been doing almost since their inception.

Initially, the local stations kept the fees (usually negotiated as so many cents per subscriber per month) that they received from the cable operators.

However, programming costs continue to drive cable subscription prices upward, in part as a result of the 1992 Cable Act. That law, enacted ostensibly to protect consumers from rising cable prices, imposed certain price controls on the cable industry but exempted programming costs, which could be passed along dollar for dollar.

After only a few agreement renewals following implementation of the 1992 Cable Act involving such terms both local and national broadcasters saw the same dollar signs in their eyes that the cable-only programmers had seen much earlier, thanks to the 1992 law. They began requesting monetary payments in the manner of channels like ESPN. The cable industry was being held hostage, as demands got increasingly onerous with each contract renewal.

"They (the broadcasters) compared ESPN and its smaller audiences with their wider audiences and wanted the same kinds of fees," Allan Block would say later. "They didn't recognize that ESPN is available *ONLY* via multi-channel video providers, while their (broadcasters') signals reach about 30 per cent of the audience, free, over the air. That has to diminish the value."

Again, as with the PASS/Fox Sports Detroit situation, a Rupert Murdoch company was a central player. In 1984, Murdoch had bought 20th Century Fox, a major Hollywood film studio, and later formed a fourth broadcast network, known simply as Fox. Some of the programming on his new affiliated stations consisted of movies from 20th Century Fox's rich library, but to speed its way to higher ratings, and the resultant advertising dollars, Fox began paying premium prices for sports rights fees and original programming of high quality (at least in viewers' perceptions).

To offset the higher costs it was paying to sports organizations and program producers, it turned to its affiliates and demanded money from them—a reversal of the original broadcast business model, whereby networks paid local affiliates to carry network programming.

Other networks followed suit, demanding payment from local affiliates for network fare – sort of a reverse compensation plan. When any local broadcaster anywhere complained, the networks simply told them to charge the cable companies higher carriage fees. After all, the reasoning was, the 1992 Cable Act said programming costs could be passed through to subscribers dollar-for-dollar and were not subject to the early-term price controls on the cable operators.

Adding to the increased costs, local station heads were no longer able to negotiate with Buckeye; instead, the head of the out-of-town owners took over negotiations—and, predictably, failed to display the same sense of community well-being for a city hundreds or thousands of miles away that the local executives had shown.

"The affiliates looked at retransmission money as an unlimited pot of gold – there's more where that came from," Block said.

Their huge demands for carriage fees represent a "suicide-bomber mentality. In the long term, it's going to hurt them," he said, pointing to the many options in addition to cable that are available for viewers to receive programming.

Nationally, the FCC reports, the sum cable operators paid local broadcasters for the right to carry the broadcaster's free, off-air signal skyrocketed from $28 million in 2005 to $2.4 *billion* in 2012. Remember, too, that the broadcasters hold the upper hand—they can refuse to allow the cable operator to carry the signal unless its financial demands are met. In other words, the broadcast signal is blacked out to the cable subscriber at the same time it's provided free to the non-subscriber.

Nationwide, broadcaster blackouts increased from 12 in 2010, 51 in 2011, 91 in 2012, 127 in 2013, and 107 in 2014 according to the American Cable Association.

Locally, negotiations between Buckeye and broadcasters have been a mix of contention and amicability. WUPW withheld its signal on December 12, 2012, as a result of an ongoing legal dispute involving American Spirit Media LLC, a Charlotte, North Carolina–based owner of WUPW; Raycom Media, based in Montgomery, Alabama, the owner of WTOL, and Buckeye.

American Spirit Media and Raycom demanded that Buckeye pay more to rebroadcast WUPW, a Fox station, because WUPW shares facilities, staff and news broadcasts with WTOL, a CBS affiliate. WTOL is one of the top stations in Toledo's DMA; WUPW is one of the lowest. Buckeye executives did not feel the extra charge was worth it, as the payment would have been more than top stations in Toledo, Detroit and Cleveland were being paid.

The retransmission agreement between Buckeye and LIN Media Group of Austin, TX, owner of WUPW, had expired May 21, 2012, and Buckeye had been transmitting WUPW programs under a temporary agreement ever since. However, WUPW had been bought by American Spirit Media from LIN Media that March, with American Spirit Media entering into a shared-services agreement with Raycom. That agreement called for the two local broadcast stations to share news staff using WTOL's staff and facilities to produce WUPW's local news programs—from 7 to 9 a.m., 6:30 to 7 p.m. and 10 to 11 p.m. Monday through Friday, and from 10 to 10:30 p.m. Saturday and Sunday.

The agreement also opened up shared access to studios, technical facilities, maintenance and promotional efforts, which was a critical piece of a lawsuit and part of the reason Raycom and American Spirit wanted to increase the retransmission fee that Buckeye paid to WUPW.

That June, Buckeye filed suit in Lucas County Common Pleas Court to resolve the issue of whether WUPW was covered by the WTOL retransmission-consent agreement, asking the court to declare the two stations separate entities and force American Spirit Media to negotiate directly with Buckeye concerning WUPW.

The suit was later transferred to federal court, and in December 2012, WUPW notified Buckeye that retransmitting the news programs might violate copyright laws while a court decision was pending, and ordered the signal withheld from Buckeye's customers. Buckeye offered customers a free antenna so they could receive the WUPW signal off-air.

"The amount we agreed to pay WTOL for retransmission consent is based on the high audience ratings of that station," Brad Mefferd, Buckeye's president and general manager at the time, said. "WUPW's ratings are nowhere near that high, and the value to our customers is less, so we don't feel those customers should be asked to pay a high price for the WUPW programming. We have a longstanding reputation in which we repeatedly have stood up for our customers and negotiated hard to keep programming costs as low as possible so we can keep our rates low.

"Programming is our largest single operating expense, even larger than our personnel expense, and programmers such as WUPW must understand the impact their unreasonable demands have on viewers." Programming costs had come to amount to about 60 percent of Buckeye's total operating budget each year, and had been increasing more than 10 percent annually in recent years.

WUPW remained off the Buckeye system until January 20, 2013, when the two sides reached agreement and the station was restored; the federal-court suit was dismissed.

Deals such as the American Spirit/Raycom relationship sometimes are called 'sidecar' arrangements and are drawing the attention of the FCC, said Jason Rademacher, a Washington attorney with Cooley LLP, who represented Buckeye. By law, a firm cannot own two broadcast stations in the same market unless there are at least eight full-power broadcasters in the market or unless one station is failing financially. Neither case existed in the WUPW situation.

But Raycom's deal with American Spirit allows Raycom to operate WUPW as a sister station to Raycom's own station WTOL. This allowed Raycom to garner revenue virtually as soon as American Spirit took possession of WUPW.

American Spirit formerly was known as Ottumwa Media Holdings LLC and changed its name to American Spirit Media LLC in August 2006. In 2003, Thomas B. Henson purchased a television station, along with a shared services agreement with Raycom, in Ottumwa, a city of some 25,000 persons along the Des Moines River in south central Iowa. Since 2003, Mr. Henson, who would become president and CEO of American Spirit, has bought television stations and entered into a number of shared services arrangements with Raycom in markets across the country.

Under current rules total financing arrangements are not required to be filed in certain circumstance, and the financial arrangement between the two parties is not publicly known, Mr. Rademacher said.

Later in 2013, Buckeye became involved in another dispute with a local broadcaster that had been purchased by a large, out-of-town media company. Sinclair Broadcasting Group, based in the Baltimore area, ordered WNWO, the NBC affiliate, be taken off Buckeye on December 15, 2013. Sinclair had acquired that station on November 25—just 20 days earlier—from Barrington Media Group, which had offices in Chicago and Shelton, Connecticut.

The retransmission contract with Barrington expired August 31, 2013, and the two sides began negotiations in July. Barrington, however, announced that it was being sold to Sinclair and that any agreement would have to be approved by Sinclair, which rejected the early terms upon which Barrington and Buckeye had tentatively agreed.

Realizing that they could not sign any agreement that would bind Sinclair after the sale, Barrington officials decided to terminate negotiations and grant an extension of the then-current agreement until December 15.

However, after Sinclair took over, the firm ordered the station off the Buckeye system effective December 15, invoking network non-duplication to prohibit Buckeye from carrying WDIV, the NBC affiliate out of Detroit, in the Ohio portion of the Buckeye system. Because Detroit is in a separate DMA, Sinclair could not halt it from being shown in the Michigan portion of Buckeye's system. (Network non-duplication, also part of the 1992 Cable Act, permits a broadcaster to forbid a cable operator from carrying programming from an imported signal of the same network.)

The two sides continued to negotiate until February 7, when Sinclair publicly announced it was ending the talks. In response, Buckeye filed a complaint with the FCC claiming the broadcaster was not negotiating in good faith.

The parties ultimately came to an agreement, and WNWO was back on the Ohio portion of the Buckeye system as of July 14, 2014. However, WDIV remains on the Michigan portion but not the Ohio portion of Buckeye's system.

Because of the system configuration, a hub in Toledo near the state line supplies Buckeye's signal to the Monroe County, Michigan, area. In changing electronics to eliminate WDIV from the Ohio area served by that hub while keeping it on in Michigan, the signal erroneously remained available to a small portion of Ohio, Brad Mefferd, now Buckeye's chief administrative officer, said.

As soon as it was brought to the company's attention after a few days, the problem was fixed and the WDIV signal was no longer available in Ohio. Sinclair nevertheless filed a complaint with the FCC claiming that Buckeye had violated the network non-duplication order. When the dispute was settled, both Buckeye and Sinclair withdrew the FCC complaints they had filed against one another.

During the blackout, NBC had the contract to televise the 2014 Winter Olympics from Sochi, Russia, and that naturally gave Sinclair some advantage because viewers would want to be able to watch the Olympic games.

Nevertheless, Buckeye, always cognizant of programming costs and their impact on customers' bills, stood firm. Leading up to and during the Olympics, Buckeye ran frequent full-page advertisements in *The Blade,* on cable channels and on local broadcast stations pointing out other sources for Olympic coverage, and continued the practice after the Games ended, telling readers where else they could get NBC programming.

As with the WUPW blackout at the end of 2012 and in early 2013, Buckeye offered customers a free antenna so they could receive the signal off-air, as well as a 24-cent-per-month credit, which is what the company was saving by not paying the WNWO retransmission fee, which had been negotiated earlier. When customers called to complain about WNWO being off the air, Buckeye representatives explained how big increases in retransmission fees would impact customer bills and most sided with Buckeye, though the company did lose some customers as a result of the blackout.

The previous September, the American Cable Association (ACA), of which Buckeye is a member, filed a petition with the FCC, asking the agency to block the sale or attach conditions to Sinclair's acquisition of TV stations in Harrisburg, Pennsylvania, and Charleston, South Carolina, claiming that approval would give Sinclair dual monopolies as a result of its ownership of the ABC and CBS stations in Harrisburg and the ABC and Fox stations in Charleston.

The petition was not a direct result of the WNWO situation, Ted Hearn, the ACA's vice president of communications, later said, but it did show support for it. The petition was in fact part of a national effort the organization had mounted several years earlier to urge Congress to take up the retransmission-consent issue and make needed changes.

The ACA, which represents smaller cable operators throughout the country, had been spearheading a drive to get retransmission restrictions changed to make the relationship between cable operators and broadcasters more equal. Buckeye, as other ACA members had, set aside space on its Web site where customers could send a letter to their Representatives and Senators expressing displeasure with the skyrocketing costs brought about by broadcasters' fees and asking for changes to the relevant portion of the 1992 Cable Act.

Following the Sinclair decision to take WNWO off Buckeye's system, Allan Block penned an article that was published in a daily newspaper in Washington, D.C., published by Capitol Hill Publishing Corp., a subsidiary of News Communications, Inc., that covers Congress.

Block, in the article which first appeared in *The Hill Newspaper* March 11, 2014, laid out the issues in part thusly:

> This week, a House committee is taking up possible changes to more than 20-year-old rules that govern 'retransmission consent'—the fees paid by cable and satellite providers to local over-the-air television broadcasters to carry their stations.
>
> According to the Federal Communications Commission, those fees have skyrocketed, going from $28 million in 2005 to $2.4 billion in 2012. While it may seem on the surface like a business dispute, consumers are feeling the impact by paying the price in higher rates. Even worse, many viewers are enduring broadcaster 'blackouts,' as local stations pull their programming off of cable and satellite systems as a negotiating tactic to extort higher fees.
>
> Broadcaster blackouts are also on the rise—there were 12 blackouts in 2010 but 114 last year, an 850 percent increase. My community, Toledo, Ohio,

is the latest victim. More than 106,000 cable subscribers have gone without the local NBC station since mid-December.

I view this issue with a unique perspective. Our family-owned business, founded by my grandfather in 1900, owns Buckeye CableSystem, the Toledo cable provider that's been hit with the broadcaster blackout. Our business also owns a number of television stations in other cities. I have seen this battle from both sides. I can accept a system that requires a payment to the television stations because it helps support local broadcasting, but the system today is dysfunctional and is not working for the average viewer at home.

The owners of television stations have been given valuable licenses to use the public airways for free, and that means they have an obligation to serve the public. What needs to change is the current law, which gives the broadcasters all the advantages, ties the hands of the cable and satellite operators and, most importantly, does not serve the public interest. The Toledo situation is a case in point.

If this were a free-market situation, the local Toledo NBC station would not have been able to use federal regulations to prevent us from offering NBC programming from the neighboring Detroit NBC affiliate. The two cities are just 60 miles apart, and Toledo viewers have traditionally watched the Detroit stations since the dawn of television. We would have happily negotiated with the Detroit station to continue to carry that NBC programming. But our hands are tied—the law allows the local station to block us from bringing in an NBC-affiliated station from another market.

Block's article also explained how the retransmission consent law tied the hands of consumers by preventing them from freely choosing what stations they wanted and were willing to pay for:

When you go to a supermarket or restaurant, you can purchase or order whatever items you want. But that's not the case with local broadcasters and cable. Believe it or not, the law actually requires that we include all the broadcast stations on our basic tier, even those that demand payment for carriage, and requires our customers to buy that tier before gaining access to any other programming we offer.

These are just two of the ways that the current law hamstrings cable operators and hurts consumers.

The law [1992 Cable Act] was passed before the Internet had taken off; before you could watch TV on your computer or smartphone; before TiVo and DVRs; and before video on demand. The world of technology has changed dramatically, and Congress needs to revisit this archaic law and make changes that restore some semblance of a free market to serve the public, not special interests.

In May 2014, Block Communications filed a petition for rulemaking with the FCC, seeking to level the playing field by getting the FCC to adopt rules to make sure that pay-tv operators and broadcasters negotiate in good faith.

When Buckeye and Sinclair reached agreement in July 2014, and WNWO was put back on the system, both companies withdrew the petitions they had filed with the FCC as a result of the dispute.

The 2014 dustup was not the first encounter involving the two parties. WNWO and Buckeye went toe-to-toe in negotiations in 2010 and were close to a deadline when agreement was reached and Barrington did not withhold the signal.

BUCKEYE BITS

Programming Deals Were Forged in Smoke-Filled Rooms

In days past, programming negotiations took on a more insalubrious atmosphere in the early days as both sides were jockeying to stake out their positions. Who had the best bargaining power; who needed whom the most? Were the programmers more important to the success of cable operators than were the cable operators to the profitability of the programmers?

Representatives of programmers who came to the Byrne Road office of Buckeye in the John Karl regime during the 1970s and early 1980s found themselves at a definite disadvantage.

Smoking in offices was acceptable and fairly widespread in those days, and Karl was a heavy smoker – the epitome of a chain smoker. Co-workers recall seeing him frequently use a finished cigarette to light another before snubbing out the first in an ash tray.

When a sales representative would show up, he'd be escorted into Karl's office and the door closed. The obligatory small talk soon gave way to discussing the details of the contract, all the time Karl puffing merrily away. The longer the talks went, the heavier the smoke got. "You wouldn't just smell it," Allan Block said later. "You could actually see the thick atmosphere when you walked into the office" even when Karl wasn't present and no cigarettes were burning.

No one today knows whether Karl had that objective in mind, but the door wouldn't open until a contract was signed, usually favorable to Buckeye. "It wasn't malicious," Block recalls, "but he wasn't about to change his ways just because a sales representative was in his office."

Al Jazeera English

One of the more controversial channels Buckeye CableSystem offered to viewers was Al Jazeera English, the world's first English-language news network headquartered in the Middle East.

Buckeye announced the addition of the programming in early March 2007, and it became available March 19, less than six years after the destruction of the World Trade Center in the September 11 attacks. Feelings still ran hot, and Buckeye's addition of the channel drew immediate criticism from some viewers.

The channel, located in Doha, Qatar, with broadcast centers in Kuala Lampur, Malaysia; London; and Washington, D.C. (it also has several news bureaus scattered around the globe) was seen by some as a tool of terrorists—though Qatar is a U.S. ally in the Middle East.

Buckeye executives had viewed the channel for some time and found it to be balanced and interesting; nevertheless, the company recognized why some viewers might not wish to view it.

However, Allan Block, a frequent world traveler, believed it was important to make a wide array of political, social and news viewpoints available to customers. Al Jazeera English joined channels on Buckeye whose content was provided by Russia and China, to name two countries antagonistic to the United States. "It offers a better chance for world understanding," he said later.

"The channel is committed to impartial, independent and objective reporting, and we feel this is an additional and important information source to provide our viewers," the company said at the time.

Buckeye also took care to inform customers that the new network was vastly different from its older cousin, the controversial Arabic-language Al Jazeera, which was seen largely in the Middle East. The English-language network's coverage was much broader, and it had hired journalists from the BBC and CNN, Buckeye stressed.

In addition to a heavy schedule of news, the channel at the time carried such programming as *Witness,* in-depth documentaries on everyday people in world news; *Frost Over the World,* in which the late Sir David Frost, a legendary TV host, interviewed some of the world's most fascinating and powerful people; *The Fabulous Picture Show,* whose host gave viewers an inside look at the global film industry; and *Sportsworld,* a look at all manner of sports worldwide.

Buckeye continued to draw criticism from viewers, however, who called the company to protest and wrote letters to the editor of *The Blade.* A few customers dropped their subscriptions. "Most of the objections came from out of the area," he said. He received "standardized postcards from other areas of the country," obviously produced at a central source then distributed for different signatures and mailing. The source of the objections is unknown, but he pointed out only a hundred or so postcards were received.

Block stuck to his convictions. After all, customers had the freedom *not* to watch the channel, which Buckeye made available at no additional charge, and parents were given instructions about how to use the parental-control feature on their remotes if they didn't want their children to see it.

At the time, Buckeye was among a very few American cable firms to carry the channel, though it has since drawn wider interest among cable operators around the country. In this case, it seems, the Block family wasn't merely ahead of the curve—instead, it traced the arc of the curve for others to follow.

Local furor over Al Jazeera English soon died down, and the channel continues to draw an audience, albeit a small one.

WorldGate

One concept that showed considerable promise after the implementation of fiber optics into Buckeye's system was WorldGate, a unique technology that provided Internet and e-mail that customers could view on their television sets, no computer necessary.

Introduced in late 1999, when computers in the home were not as universal as they are today, WorldGate was promoted as a way to surf the Web or send e-mail to grandchildren while being able to switch back and forth from a favorite TV program.

Channel HyperLink, a feature unique to Buckeye WorldGate, enabled viewers instantly to access the Internet and other information related to the current show or channel.

For instance, a viewer with particular interest in a show on the Arts & Entertainment network could push a button and be taken directly to the A&E Web site for more information about the cable channel, the program, and other A&E content. The viewer could also see a product advertised on TV and go directly to the vendor's Web site.

In addition to the Internet, Buckeye WorldGate offered local weather and information about the community, entertainment, restaurants and a number of other local topics.

To use it, viewers typed on a keyboard that sent an infrared signal to the CableSystem CableServer, as the standard set-top converter was called following the conversion to fiber.

The service allowed unlimited Internet access and provided speeds more than four times faster than the typical 28.8 Kbps telephone modems in common use at the time.

The rapid adoption of personal computers into the home soon made the WorldGate technology obsolete, and Buckeye dropped the service a few years later.

IV

The Future

Chapter Thirteen

"Broadband Is the Business"

*For Cable, Telecom, and Media in General,
the Times They Are A-changin'*

That sentiment, the times they are a-changin,' the title of a famous 1964 Bob Dylan album and song, is true everywhere these days—maybe nowhere more so than in telecommunications.

Gallons of ink have been spilled on the topic; gallons more will follow, as the scene changes almost by the hour. A common industry joke: If you go out for a coffee break, you'll need to be retrained when you get back, as everything will be different.

What lies ahead for the industry could fill a lengthy separate book all by itself. Here, though, is a brief look at some of the upheaval of recent years and an examination of what Buckeye executives believe the future holds for smaller operators.

Cord-cutting is an increasingly common phenomenon as more and more people eliminate their cable video service in favor of other sources of programming—what those in the industry call "over-the-top-TV."

Viewers' habits, it hardly needs to be said, are a-changin.' They want to watch video when it fits their schedule, not on the rigid programming schedules prevalent since television's early days. In addition to the ability to watch *when* they want, they want control over *where* they watch—on a traditional TV or a mobile device such as a smartphone, tablet or laptop computer, in a coffee shop at 2 p.m. or their den at 2 a.m.

Plus, they want to be able to pay for only what they want to watch— they're rebelling against channel tying and bundling, which has been the content producers' business model for years (see Chapter 12) The frequent refrain: Why should I pay for hundreds of channels when I watch only 10 or 12?

The advent of broadband at faster and faster speeds fostered innovations such as Netflix, Apple TV, Hulu, YouTube and Roku, to name just a few of the "over-the-top TV" choices viewers now have from which to get their video, a source other than a cable operator.

Some operators have dropped programming as vendors try to impose ever-higher prices, programmers are inking deals to deliver content directly to consumers via the Internet, and several large cable operators have begun discussing possible mergers, which would give them more clout in negotiations with programmers.

Comcast, the largest cable operator in the country with almost 20 million customers, offered $45.2 billion to buy Time Warner Cable, with 15 million customers; ATT, with some 5.7 million video customers on its U-verse service, has sought to acquire satellite service DirecTV and its 20 million video customers in a $50 billion deal.

While the ATT/DirecTV is undergoing regulatory scrutiny as of publication time, in late April, 2015, Comcast dropped its Time Warner merger proposal after encountering stiff resistance from the FCC and the Justice Department.

At that point, the national and trade media were rife with speculation that Charter, Liberty Media, Cablevision Systems, Cox Communications, Time Warner, and Bright House Networks all figured in some form of amalgamation, joint venture, merger, or buyout, affording further evidence that the industry is in a state of flux.

"The threat to small and mid-size cable operators exists with the continuing consolidation of the industry," Allan Block said of the industry turmoil. "Barring Washington determining (that) they want smaller players, you could wake up with the whole industry consolidated."

In addition, by 2018, one in five Americans, according to research group Forrester, simply no longer will be watching traditional TV. So how does Buckeye, with 130,000 customers, see its place in this changing landscape?

Experiencing the same trend as the rest of the industry, Buckeye found itself in March 2014 with more broadband customers than video customers.

"Broadband is the business," Block said. Currently, broadband can deliver all three of Buckeye's services: video, voice and data. "All three separate services work together and cross-subsidize each other, but if it all becomes broadband delivery, obviously that has implications for what the price of broadband will be. It'll have to cost more. The key to the future will be to differentiate the broadband in a positive way. You can't allow the broadband service to suddenly just become a commodity service" on which price is the only factor by which the customer makes decisions about the broadband provider.

"You have to define broadband as value-added—more bandwidth and better service," he said. "That means keeping the speeds as fast as possible, the technology the latest and providing the best customer service."

As part of its positioning for the future, the company developed both Buckeye Smart Home and Buckeye Brainiacs (see Chapter 7).

Brainiacs, offered only to customers of Buckeye Express, is "extremely important," Block said. "The idea is that average people do not have the ability to do everything they have to do with their computers. We're going to support the average people and keep the charges reasonable. We want to recover our costs, but we don't view it as a profit center."

Just as the Internet fostered such innovations as Netflix and others, which began poaching video customers from cable operators, so will the Internet nurture additional new services for consumers, Block reasoned.

The Web will be a "total communications wire that's going to provide everything that anybody could possibly want or need," he said. "It will be possible to call up any video that's ever been produced—any TV show or movie—as easily as you can call a phone number. Whatever content that exists will be retrievable. The idea of channels is going away. The idea of programming having to be scheduled" is passé.

What is now a competitive business, he said, he sees getting even more competitive—and "the winner is going to be the one who provides better technology, better customer service, added features, and value."

He's sanguine, too, about the possibility of further consolidation. "Is there a chance that the government is going to allow everybody to be swallowed by a few big companies? I suppose there is, but that's not the future I choose to predict and see. I don't really believe that's going to happen."

The government is going to allow a place for small operators like Buckeye, "and there will be more than one competitor."

While Block views the industry in the context of a larger media and communications universe, it is up to Buckeye management, he said, to run the business on a daily basis and keep it profitable.

Jeff Abbas, who was named the company's president and general manager in May 2013, sees the future in terms of "boutiques and Walmarts. There will always be massive players who have a lower cost structure and (a greater) ability to market nationally than we will ever have," he said.

Abbas, who has a wealth of experience in cable-television management and programming, envisions Buckeye as one of the boutiques, with its strength a direct result of its localness and nimbleness. "We're big enough to get economies of scale and small enough to be responsive to our local customers, and there's a niche there," he said. "There's no chance we can be the low-cost provider of things like video, but we have the local data pipe, and there, we are the low-cost provider—we have a cost edge" for that transport.

"So as the world migrates more and more toward data-centric information, we have a real good spot there."

Among ways to service that customer who deals more and more with data-centric information, Buckeye plans to introduce in late 2015 or early 2016 a cloud service whereby Buckeye Express customers have automatic back up for anything done on their home computer.

Buckeye operates two world-class data centers, one local and one in another state to offer redundancy, said Sean Brushett, chief revenue officer who is in charge of developing and marketing new products.

"It is a secure place to store anything – passports, pictures, videos, financial records – away from the customer home where they could be more easily destroyed" as by a fire, for example.

The customer can sync any number of devices to be backed up automatically and the data can be accessed from anywhere in the world, he noted.

All Buckeye Express customers will get a basic level of storage space, and can purchase additional space if the demands warrant it.

The interface has been designed with simplicity in mind, for the average customer in the home. There's no complicated procedure to save information to the cloud and to retrieve it in the event it is needed.

"If the customer's hard drive fails, a simple operation will retrieve and restore everything that was lost," he said.

That's just one of many new features and services Buckeye plans to roll out to keep ahead of the competitive curve. Brushett and his staff have adopted an ambitious set of goals, with a new service, product, or operational change scheduled each month going forward. The initial plan adopted in early 2015 covered only that year, but the one-improvement-a-month plan "will go on forever," he said.

Goals include such items as improving the already above-average customer service, building a better retail presence and using that presence to target market specific ethnic and other demographic groups. The latter includes some bi-lingual training for some staff members.

A number of other projects are on the drawing board, but for competitive reasons Brushett chooses not to outline them for publication. In short, the company has embarked on a program of adding features often and regularly, notably to Buckeye Express. "It's not just an Internet connection," Brushett said, "it's a whole product line."

Abbas, before joining Buckeye, was president and CEO of the National Cable Television Cooperative (NCTC), an industry organization that negotiates equipment and programming contracts, among other functions, for smaller cable firms representing some 850 small and medium-sized independent operators who provide voice, video, and data services to some 7 million customers nationwide. Buckeye is a member of NCTC, which is allied with the American Cable Association.

Abbas sees a time in which margins from video "become so compressed" that at some point smaller cable operators, like Buckeye, will be forced to quit providing it—"but we'll do it for a long time as a convenience for customers who want their services from one provider.

"But there will come a time when it becomes uneconomical for us to provide video, so what we need to do is find ways to deliver video that's connected to our data pipe," he said. "There's nothing wrong with selling somebody a 50-meg (Mbps) connection and Netflix. Even if I don't get anything for the Netflix part of that, that customer's going to love me for the 50-meg connection."

Prior to his stint at NCTC, Abbas was vice president of programming for the former Adelphia Communications Corp. of Coudersport, Pennsylvania, which at the time was the fifth-largest cable operator in the country. That experience helps him look at the bigger picture.

"If the video-content producers decide their business needs to be a direct-to-the-consumer relationship, there's really no one left to take a customer-service call," Abbas said. "That goes back to local. If you're local and you know how to respond to that customer complaint, there's a value on that that can be greater than what you lose on margins because of your inability to negotiate on economies of scale" the way the mammoth nationwide cable providers do.

When will this all occur? Abbas, a lawyer by training, sees it coming in stages, "and there's a broadcast piece to that"—a regulatory and legal framework that must be put in place to ensure that broadcasters will be part of distribution networks, whatever form they take.

Cognizant of the continued and accelerating demand for spectrum, the Federal Communications Commission plans an auction in 2016 in which broadcasters could release some of their spectrum in return, they hope, for huge payments.

Some broadcasters are mulling over the possibility of selling *all* the spectrum now assigned to them and striking deals with cable companies or other Internet service providers to feed their programming directly to the distribution networks.

Although that's still just a topic of discussion, should some form of it come to pass, Abbas sees a sort of "content bifurcation" taking place, in which "the more valuable stuff will go to a cable channel, while the less valuable stuff"—such as shopping networks and news—"would be left on the broadcast-distribution platform."

He anticipates that a number of customers will want to receive their video from one source rather than having to deal with Netflix, Apple TV, Hulu, Roku and other similar services yet to come.

"There'll always be an aggregator for that," he said, "and that could be us. It probably *will* be us, and it probably will be a lot of other people as well.

We can say, 'Here's your collection of your most popular Web sites, and we bring all those links to you on your homepage' on the computer that we power," and on the computer that Buckeye maintains via the Brainiacs.

The advantage is that customers have someone to call if the service goes down, he noted.

Winston Churchill once observed that "it is always wise to look ahead, but difficult to look further than you can see." Prognostication is never easy, but one thing seems like a safe bet: The same strengths that led to the conception and incubation of Buckeye 50 years ago and that have engendered its success ever since will continue to serve it well in the new competitive landscape.

The localness, quality customer service, nimbleness and inventiveness Buckeye has exhibited so strongly for half a century are certain to be just as important in the next five decades as they have been in the last five.

And don't forget the Block family's gene for strategic thinking.

Appendix

BUCKEYE CABLESYSTEM PRESIDENTS

Wayne Current: 1965–1975

Paul Block, Jr.: December 10, 1975–December 13, 1977

John Karl: General Manager, January, 1975–May 18, 1990
Executive Vice President, April 11, 1975–December 13, 1977
President, Buckeye Cablevision, Inc., December 13, 1977–May 18, 1990
Vice Chairman, May 18, 1990–Retired Oct. 1, 1990

David G. Huey, Executive Vice President, March 6, 1985–May 18, 1980
President/General Manager, Buckeye Cablevision, Inc., May 18, 1990–January 1, 2002
President of Block Communications, Inc., January 1, 2002–Retired September 30, 2007

W.H. "Chip" Carstensen, Field Operations Manager, April 4, 1990–September 1, 1992
Senior Manager, Technical Operations. September 1, 1992–November 2, 1998
Vice President Rebuild/Technical Operations, November 2, 1998–June 11, 2002
President, Metro Fiber and Cable Construction Co. (Buckeye subsidiary), November 13, 1999–October 27, 2010
President, Buckeye Cablevision, Inc., June 11, 2002–August 1, 2010

President, Block Communications, Inc., August 1, 2010–Planned retirement in 2015

Brad Mefferd, Treasurer, July 1, 1990–January 1, 1991
Secretary/Treasurer, Jan. 1, 1991–January 1, 2000
Executive Vice President, January 1, 2000–January 1, 2003
Executive Vice President/Chief Operating Officer, Jan. 1, 2003–August 15, 2010
President, Buckeye Cablevision, Inc., August 15, 2010–January 21, 2013
Chief Administrative Officer, January 21, 2013–Present

Jeff Abbas, President, Buckeye Cablevision, Inc., May 13, 2013–Present

Index